"Moll Pitcher at Monmouth"
by Joel T. Headley, 1859 (see No. 2N)

A MOLLY PITCHER SOURCEBOOK

MOLLY PITCHER AT THE BATTLE OF MONMOUTH

DAVID G. MARTIN

LONGSTREET HOUSE
HIGHTSTOWN, NJ
NEW BOOK NO. 150
2003

CONTENTS

ILLUSTRATIONS

PREFACE

Was Molly Pitcher fact, fiction or something in-between? Was she a real woman named Mary Hays who brought water to the thirsty troops and then helped fire a cannon after her husband fell casualty at the battle of Monmouth, or was she a remembered image of all the female warriors who fought in the War of the Revolution? Was she a German girl, born with the name Mary Ludwig, or was she Mary Hanna, an Irish lass?

The answers to these and countless other questions concerning Molly Pitcher are difficult to answer today, despite all that has been written about her in the 225 years since the battle of Monmouth was fought in 1778. Original primary source material concerning the heroine of Monmouth is scarce and difficult to interpret, and secondary sources are all too often biased, inaccurate or repetitive.

The purpose of this book is to present the source material concerning Molly Pitcher and let the readers decide for themselves what to believe or not believe concerning her background and history. The text of each source is given in full, followed by a commentary as to its contents and relationship to earlier and later sources, and a conclusion about what is notable or significant. The sources are arranged chronologically in Chapters 1-8 and topically in Chapters 9-13. The concluding chapter consists of two essays, one summarizing the evidence for the existence of Molly Pitcher and one summarizing the evidence against her existence. Thoughtful readers are invited to review the sources and draw their own conclusions concerning the most famous female warrior of the Revolution.

ACKNOWLEDGEMENTS

This book has its genesis in a talk presented to the Battleground Historical Society in Englishtown in November 2000. Revised versions of the talk were given later to the Friends of Monmouth Battlefield in Freehold, to a senior history seminar at Seton Hall University, and to the Allentown-Upper Freehold Historical Society in Allentown. I wish to thank these groups and their audiences for their input and criticism.

I am greatly indebted to a number of good friends who have generously shared their scholarship, advice and resources in the preparation of this book. I owe great thanks to: John Fabiano, President of the Allentown-Upper Freehold Historical Society; Stacy Roth, alias "Molly Pitcher;" Dr. Garry Wheeler Stone, Historian at Monmouth Battlefield State Park; Jim Raleigh, Vice President of the Friends of Monmouth Battlefield; and Richard Walling, President of the Friends of Monmouth Battlefield. Also to: Eric and Kathy Doherty of the Friends of Monmouth Battlefield; Marc Mappen, Executive Director, New Jersey Historical Commission; Gary Saretsky, Director, Monmouth County Archives; and Carla Tobias, Librarian, Monmouth County Historical Association Library.

Research assistance was provided by the staffs at: The American Antiquarian Society, Worcester, Mass.; Firestone Library, Princeton University; Hamilton Library, Cumberland County Historical Association, Carlisle, Pa.; Monmouth County Historical Association Library, Freehold, NJ; Speer Library, Princeton Theological Seminary; United States Army Military History Institute, Carlisle, Pa.; and Deborah Petite of Warrenton, Va.

Thanks are owed to the following for permission to quite from copyrighted sources: to Little, Brown and Company, for the excerpt from *Private Yankee Doodle* by Joseph Plumb Martin; to James T. Raleigh, for the text of *A Molly Pitcher Chronology* by Samuel S. Smith; and to the New Jersey Historical Commission for the excerpt from *New Jersey Women* by Carmela A. Karnoutsas.

David G. Martin
Hightstown, NJ
June 2003

A MOLLY PITCHER SOURCEBOOK

1. PRIMARY SOURCES

FIRST-HAND CONTEMPORARY SOURCES FROM THE TIME OF THE REVOLUTION

There are no first hand contemporary sources from the time of the Revolution that mention Molly Pitcher at the battle of Monmouth.

FIRST-HAND CONTEMPORARY SOURCES FROM AFTER THE TIME OF THE REVOLUTION

1A. Narrative of Private Joseph Plumb Martin of the 8th Connecticut, 1830.

One little incident happened during the heat of the cannonade, which I was eye-witness to, and which I think would be unpardonable not to mention. A woman whose husband belonged to the artillery and who was then attached to a piece in the engagement, attended with her husband at the piece the whole time. While in the act of reaching a cartridge and having one of her feet as far before the other as she could step, a cannon shot from the enemy passed directly between her legs without doing any other damage than carrying away all the lower part of her petticoat. Looking at it with apparent unconcern, she observed that it was lucky it did not pass a little higher, for in that case it might have carried away something else, and continued her occupation.[1]

COMMENTARY

Martin was born in Becket, Massachusetts on November 21, 1760, and first enlisted in 1776 at the age of 15. At the battle of Monmouth he was a 17-year-old private in the 8th Connecticut regiment of Varnum's brigade. He wrote his recollection about his war experiences around 1828 and published it anonymously in a short run printed in Hallowell, Maine in 1830. We do not know if he used notes or a diary, or wrote his account entirely from memory. He died at Fort Point, Maine on May 2, 1850.[2]

Martin's account is significant for describing a woman helping to fire a cannon at the battle. It states that the woman was with her husband and his unit "the whole time" and that she helped by bringing up cartridges (powder packed in bags) from the powder chest to the front of the cannon (this was the job of the assistant bombardier). There is no mention of the woman's name, her husband's name, or the name of his unit. Note that the woman's husband is not described as being killed or wounded, and that there is no mention of the woman bringing up water for the men or the cannon. The story of the cannon ball passing between her legs may be a common camp story, perhaps sexual in intent.

CONCLUSION

Martin's account is our only first hand account of someone who saw a woman working an artillery piece at the battle of Monmouth. The incident occurred in the early afternoon "during the heat of the cannonade," when Martin was posted in a detachment formed as a covering party directly in front of the main American artillery line on Perrine Hill.[3]

SECOND-HAND CONTEMPORARY SOURCES FROM THE TIME OF THE REVOLUTION

1B. Journal of Dr. Albigence Waldo, dated in camp opposite New Brunswick, July 3, 1778.

One of the camp women I must give a little praise to. Her gallant, whom she attended in battle, being shot down, she immediately took up his gun and cartridges and like a Spartan heroine fought with astonishing bravery, discharging the piece with as much regularity as any soldier present. This a wounded officer, whom I dressed, told me he did see himself, she being in his platoon, and assured me I might depend on its truth.[4]

COMMENTARY

Dr. Albigence Waldo was born in Pomfret, Connecticut on February 27, 1750. After being apprenticed to a surgeon in Canterbury, he served as a surgeon in the Connecticut militia in 1775. He was then surgeon in a Connecticut Continental regiment from January 1777 to October 1779, when he had to resign because of bad health. After the war he settled in Windham County, Connecticut, where he died on January 29, 1794.[5]

Dr. Waldo does not give a name to the woman he describes in this passage. Nor does he give a name for her husband or his unit. The story tells how she took up his "gun" and fired it. This makes it sound like the woman's husband was in the infantry. Some sources interpret that "gun" could mean "cannon" as well as "musket," [6] since both used "cartridges." However, this is unlikely because the term "platoon" used by Waldo refers only to infantry units, not artillery units. Note that this account does not specify whether the woman's husband was killed or wounded. Lastly, Waldo does not tell who his source was for the story. There were only a few American officer casualties at the battle, but enough that we cannot narrow down the source of Waldo's story.

Dr. Waldo kept a well known diary during the winter at Valley Forge (November 1777 to January 1778). Unfortunately, the passage cited above does not come from this diary. In fact, the present day location of the journal cited by Stryker as the source of this passage is not presently known.

CONCLUSION

Waldo's account describes how a woman took up the musket of her fallen husband at the battle of Monmouth. This account cannot be used to support the story of Molly Pitcher at the battle, though it is still good evidence that at least one woman was present on the battle field and took part in the infantry fighting.

SECOND HAND CONTEMPORARY ACCOUNTS FROM AFTER THE TIME OF THE REVOLUTION

1C. Pension application by Rebecca Clendenin, May 12, 1840.

On this twelfth day of May in the year of our Lord one thousand eight hundred and forty, personally appeared before the Court of Common Pleas of the County of Lycoming in the State of Pennsylvania, in open court, Rebecca Clendenin, a resident of the Township of Hepburn in the County of Lycoming aforesaid, aged about seventy-two years, who having first been duly sworn according to law, doth on her oath make the following declaration, in order to obtain the benefits of the provision made by Congress, passed July 7th,

1838, entitled "An act granting half pay and pensions to certain widows;" That she is the widow of John Clendenin, who was a Sergeant in the army of the Revolutionary War. That to the best of her knowledge her husband belonged to the Pennsylvania line, that he frequently told her the name of the Colonel under whom he served was Craig and that to the best of her recollection his Captain was named Powers; he stated to the deponent that he at first enlisted for three years or during the war, & that he served altogether seven years as a soldier of the revolution, that he lived at the time of his enlistment in York County, Penna. near Codorus [?] Creek, that he was for some time a recruiting sergeant, that he often mentioned to this deponent the toils and fatigues which he underwent, and related particularly that he was at the Battle of Monmouth, and suffered greatly with the heat and thirst, that a woman who was called by the troops Captain Molly was busily engaged in carrying canteens of water to the famishing [sic] soldiers... Sworn and subscribed in open court the day & year first shown written, Rebecca Clendenin, her mark.[7]

COMMENTARY

Rebecca Clendenin (also spelled "Clendenen" in some sources) was born around 1768 and so was around 72 years old when she made this pension application in 1840, some 62 years after the battle of Monmouth. Her husband, Sergeant John Clendenin, served in Captain Powers' company of Colonel Thomas Craig's 3rd Pennsylvania Continental Regiment of Conway's 3rd Pennsylvania Brigade at the battle. Rebecca and John Clendenin were married in Northumberland County, Pennsylvania, in October 1788, and had a total of twelve children, nine of whom were still living in 1840. John Clendenin died in January 1813.[8]

This is the second earliest source to refer to a "Captain Molly" at the battle of Monmouth; the earliest is an 1837 article in the *New-Jersey State Gazette* (No. 2B). Note that she is not called "Molly Pitcher" and that her real name is not mentioned. Nor is there any mention of her firing an artillery piece or having a husband at the battle. It is especially interesting that she is described as carrying water to the troops in canteens, not a pitcher or bucket. The 3rd

Pennsylvania brigade was posted for much of the afternoon on the right wing of Washington's line on Perrine Ridge. Around 4 P.M. it advanced along with Malcolm's and Spencer's regiments under the command of General Wayne to strike the 1st Battalion of British Grenadiers at the Hedge Row, but was pushed back to the Parsonage.[9]

CONCLUSION

This account is significant for mentioning a "Captain Molly" who brought water to the American troops at the battle. For the use of the term "Captain Molly" in relation to Margaret Corbin, see the Commentary to No. 2I.

"The Battle of Monmouth." Benson Lossing's sketch of painting by G.W.P. Custis, ca. 1840-1850 (see Nos. 2F, 2J and 2K).

2. SECONDARY SOURCES, 1832-1871

2A. John Greenleaf Whittier, Poem, "Moll Pitcher," 1832.

She stood upon a bare, tall crag,
Which overlooked her ragged cot –
A wasted, gray and meager hag,
In features evil as her lot.
She had the crooked nose of a witch,
And a crooked back and chin,
And in her gait she had a hitch,
And in her hand she carried a switch,
To aid her work of sin,
A twig of wizened hazel, which
Had grown beside a haunted ditch,
Where a mother her nameless child had thrown
To the running water and merciless stone.[1]

COMMENTARY

John Greenleaf Whittier was born in Haverhill, Massachusetts on December 17, 1807 and died in Hampton Falls, New Hampshire on September 7, 1892. Whittier published this poem in 1832 and republished it in 1840 with a second poem called "The Minstrel Girl."[2] It had about 900 lines and was divided into three parts. However, he did not care for the poem at all and did not include it in any later collections of his works. In 1886 he wrote to a friend, "I am ashamed to own it as mine."[3] One critic noted that the poem "as a whole does not deserve to be perpetuated."[4]

Part of the poem "Moll Pitcher" included lines from his 1830 work " Extract from a New England Legend." Other parts of the poem were reused in various of his later poems; one section was re-used as the first stanza of his poem "Memories."[5]

Moll Pitcher was a well known fortune teller from Lynn, Massachusetts. She was also the subject of a play by Joseph S. Jones (No. 2C below).

CONCLUSION

This poem does not mention the Battle of Monmouth, nor does it describe the woman traditionally known as "Molly Pitcher."

All it shows is that the name "Moll Pitcher" was in common parlance at that time.

2B. Newspaper article from the *New-Jersey State Gazette*, 1837.

MOLLY PITCHER. – For the benefit of that class of full grown children and embryo patriots, who talk much more of New Jersey chivalry *about election times* than they ever learned, or likely to learn from history, it may be proper here to add – what every New Jersey *boy* should know – that at the commencement of the battle of Monmouth this intrepid woman contributed her aid by constantly carrying water from a spring to the battery, where her husband was employed, as a cannonier, in loading and firing a gun. At length he was shot dead in her presence, just as she was leaving the spring; whereupon she flew to the spot – found her husband lifeless, and, at the moment, heard an officer, who rode up, order off the gun "for want of a man sufficiently dauntless to supply his place." Indignant at this order, and stung by the remark, she promptly opposed it – demanded the post of her slain husband to avenge his death – flew to the gun, and, to the admiration and astonishment of all who saw her, assumed and ably discharged the duties of the thus vacated post of cannonier, to the end of the battle! For this sterling demonstration of genuine WHIG spirit, Washington gave her a lieutenant's commission upon the spot, which congress afterwards ratified. And granted her a sword, and an epaulette, and half pay, as a lieutenant, for life! She wore the epaulette, received the pay, and was called "Captain Molly!" ever afterwards. --- *N.B. Times.*[6]

COMMENTARY

The author of this article is known. It is evidently copied from an undated article in the *New Brunswick Times*.

This account has Molly bringing water to her husband's battery until he is killed, whereupon she takes his place on the gun crew rather than see the piece withdrawn from the field; for this she was given a lieutenant's commission by General Washington, as well as a sword, an epaulette, and half pay for life.

This is the first documented appearance of the Molly Pitcher story in print, and it already contains the essential elements of the fully developed myth: she brought water; her husband was in the artillery and was killed; she helped serve the cannon; she met General Washington on the battlefield; and she was rewarded with a commission and a pension. These elements appear in many later versions of the story (for example, Nos. 2D, 2G, 2I, and 2K below). However, Molly's receiving of a sword from Washington does not figure in any later accounts.

Note that the account does not give her husband's name, his unit, or Molly's full name. She is called "Captain Molly" and not "Molly Pitcher." The reference to her as "Captain Molly," a woman who serves a gun after her husband is killed, and then gets a military pension, may be a confusion with the story of Margaret Corbin, who was wounded at the battle of Fort Washington, New York, on November 16, 1776 while serving a gun after her husband was killed (see Commentary to No. 2I below).

CONCLUSION

This is the earliest printed version of the Molly Pitcher story, and it already contains most of the essential elements of the developed myth. The source for this account appears to be the *New Brunswick Times,* but the source beyond that is not known. It may well be a local New Jersey story. The story may contain some elements from the story of Margaret Corbin. This account is significant for having Molly draw water from a spring not a well.

2C. Joseph S. Jones, Play, "Moll Pitcher, or the Fortune Teller of Lynn," 1839.

Joseph Stevens Jones was born in Boston on September 28, 1809 and died on December 29, 1877. He is an otherwise obscure playwright who wrote about 200 plays, a mixture of histories, melodramas, comedies and farces. Only a few were published in his day, and none have survived to the present.[7] His play, "Moll Pitcher," was set in 1790 and was first performed in Boston in 1839. It was later seen also in New York and Philadelphia. Its heroine was a historical figure named Moll Dimond Pitcher, a fortune teller from Lynn, Massachusetts who was consulted by sailors and sea captains before putting out to sea. She was born Mary Dimond in 1738 and moved to Lynn in 1760 after marrying a local shoemaker, Robert Pitcher, by whom she had one son and three daughters. She took up fortune telling to help support her family, and became more successful than she ever anticipated. Lynn's town historian wrote that "There was no port on either continent, where floated the flag of an American ship, that had not heard of the fame of Moll Pitcher."[8] She died on April 9, 1813 and was buried in the West Lynn Burial Ground.

Moll Pitcher was also the subject of an 1832 poem by John Greenleaf Whittier (No. 2A above). Whittier considered her a "wasted hag," but Alonzo Lewis, Lynn's town historian, idealized her as "one of the most wonderful women of any age."

CONCLUSION

This play does not mention the Battle of Monmouth, nor does it describe the woman known traditionally as "Molly Pitcher." All it shows is that the name "Moll Pitcher" was in common parlance at the time.

2D. George Washington Parke Custis, "The Battle of Monmouth," 1840.

Nor must we omit, among our incidents of the Battle of Monmouth to mention the achievement of the famous Captain Molly, a *nom de guerre* given to the wife of a matross in Proctor's Artillery. At one of the guns of Proctor's Battery, six men had been killed or wounded. It was deemed an unlucky gun, and murmurs arose that it should be drawn back and abandoned. At this juncture, while Captain Molly was serving some water for the refreshment of the men, her husband received a shot in the head, and fell lifeless under the wheels of the piece. The heroine threw down the pail of water and, crying to her dead consort, "Lie there my darling while I avenge ye," grasped the ramrod the lifeless hand of the poor fellow had just relinquished, sent home the charge, and called to the matrosses to prime the gun and fire. It was done. Then entering the sponge into the smoking muzzle of the cannon, the heroine performed to admiration the duties of the most expert artilleryman while loud shouts from the soldiers rang along the line, the doomed gun was no longer deemed unlucky, and the fire of the Battery became more vivid than ever. The Amazonian fair one kept to her post till night closed the action, when she was introduced to General Greene, who, complimenting her upon her courage and conduct, the next morning presented her to the Commander-in-Chief. Washington received her graciously, gave her a piece of gold, and assured her that her services should not be forgotten.

This remarkable and intrepid woman survived the Revolution, never for an instant laying aside the appellation she had so nobly won, and levying contributions upon both civil and military, whenever she recounted the tale of the doomed gun and the famed Captain Molly at the Battle of Monmouth.[9]

COMMENTARY

George Washington Parke Custis was born in Mt. Airy, Maryland, on April 30, 1781, son of John Parke Custis, the stepson of General George Washington. When his father died, he grew up at Mount Vernon as Washington's adopted son. After George Washington died in 1799 and Martha followed in 1802, he set up his own estate at Arlington, where he would live the life of a country gentleman. He was for a time a colonel in the army, and also dabbled in writing and painting (see No. 2F below). In 1804 he married Mary Lee Fitzhugh; their daughter Mary Anne married future Confederate General Robert E. Lee in 1831. Custis died at Arlington on October 10, 1857.[10]

Custis helped to welcome the Marquis de Lafayette when the Frenchman returned to visit America in 1824, and gave him a ring containing a snippet of the General's hair when they visited Washington's tomb at Mount Vernon. He wrote an account of the visit in a series of thirty articles called "Conversations with Lafayette," which were published in the *Alexandria Gazette*. These proved so popular that he was asked in September 1825 to write a series of articles "to develop, as if by moral painting, the individual character of General and Mrs. Washington, as they appeared in domestic and every day life."[11] His first article of the new series, entitled "Recollections of Washington," appeared in the Washington, D.C. *United States Gazette* in 1826. Additional articles were written "at intervals of many months, sometimes of a year" during the next thirty years, and most appeared initially in the Washington, D.C. *National Intelligencer*.[12] After Custis died in 1857, his daughter, Mrs. Robert E. Lee, gathered the Washington articles together and published them in book form in 1859. The book went under a variety of titles including *Recollections and Private Memoirs of Washington* and *Memoirs of Washington, by his Adopted Son*, the latter being edited with notes by Benson J. Lossing.[13]

The selection given here, from an essay on "The Battle of Monmouth," was published in the *National Intelligencer* (Washington, D.C.) on February 22, 1840, with the note, "From the Custis Recollections and Private Memoirs of the Life and Character of Washington." It was reprinted word for word the same in Chapter 5 of his 1859 book of collected essays, *Recollections and Private Memoirs of Washington, by his Adopted Son, G.W. Parke Custis*.

This account has "Captain Molly," wife of a matross in Proctor's artillery, bringing water to the men, and then taking the place of her husband after he was killed. Additional details add that six men had already been killed or wounded in the battery, and that her husband was felled by a wound in the head. After the fight, she was introduced to General Greene, who in turn introduced her to General Washington the next morning. Washington gave her a piece of gold and a promise "that her services would not be forgotten."

Custis' account includes all the essential elements of the version cited above from the 1837 *New-Jersey State Gazette*: that Molly brought water to the troops; her husband was in the artillery; her husband was killed; Molly manned the cannon after he was killed; and she was afterwards introduced to General Washington, who gave her a reward. A significant difference is that the only reward that Custis mentions is a gold piece, whereas the 1837 newspaper specifically mentions a lieutenant's commission, a sword, an epaulette, and a pension.

Molly's speech at the death of her husband is clearly contrived by Custis. His claim that six men had already been killed or wounded in the battery is unlikely, since the American artillery is only known to have lost a dozen or so men total in the entire battle.[14] In addition, the claim that Molly's husband was felled by a wound to the head may have been added by Custis to increase the drama of the incident.

We are not able today to tell where Custis got his additional information.[15] It is possible that he heard the story from General Washington himself, or from the Marquis de Lafayette in 1824, but it is more likely that he added some of the embellishments himself. The information about Molly being introduced to Washington by General Greene may have been obtained from Mrs. Alexander Hamilton when she was living in Washington, D.C., not far from Custis' home at Arlington (see Commentary to No. 2I below).

CONCLUSION

Custis' essay is significant for being the first full printed account of the "Molly Pitcher Story" outside of New Jersey. He included all the major elements of the story except for calling her "Molly Pitcher." This account is also significant that this account places Molly with Proctor's Artillery.

2E. George Washington Parke Custis, "Washington's Headquarters," 1843.

Among the great variety of persons that were to be found from time to time at and about the headquarters, was the famed Captain Molly, already mentioned in the chapter on the Battle of Monmouth. After her heroic achievements at the battle of Monmouth, the heroine was always received with a cordial welcome at headquarters, where she was employed in the duties of the household. She always wore an artilleryman's coat. with the cocked hat and feather, the distinguishing costume of Proctor's artillery. One day the chief accosted this remarkable woman, while she was engaged in washing some clothes, pleasantly observing: "Well, Captain Molly, are you not almost tired of this quiet way of life, and longing to be once more on the field of battle?" "Troth, your Excellency," replied the heroine, "and ye may say that; for I care not how soon I have another clap at them red-coats, bad luck to them." "But what is to become of your petticoats in such an event, Captain Molly" "Oh, long life to your excellency and never do ye mind them at all at all," continued this intrepid female. "Sure and its is only in the artillery your excellency knows that I would sarve, and divil a fear that the smoke of the cannon will hide my petticoats."[16]

COMMENTARY

For the life and writings of George Washington Parke Custis, see the Commentary to No. 2D.

This excerpt is from an article first published in the Washington, D.C. *National Intelligencer* on February 23, 1843. It was reprinted word for word the same in Chapter 9, "Washington's Headquarters," of the 1859 book of collected essays published by his daughter, Mrs. Robert E. Lee.[17]

Custis' source for this story, if it is true, could only have been General Washington himself, or one of the General's staff or guards. It appears, though, to be apocryphal, since it is not repeated elsewhere.

CONCLUSION

This story appears to be apocryphal, and is not mentioned elsewhere. It is significant for having Molly be Irish and a member of Procter's Artillery.

2F. George Washington Parke Custis, Painting, "The Battle of Monmouth," ca.1840-1850.

COMMENTARY

For the life and writings of George Washington Parke Custis, see the Commentary to No. 2D.

This is an oil on canvass painting at the Custis Mansion, Arlington House, at Arlington, Virginia. It depicts a female figure, clearly meant to be Molly Pitcher, servicing the front of a cannon while male gunners prepare to fire the gun. A fallen figure waves encouragement as General Washington and his staff progress triumphantly towards the center of the scene. The painting is presently in damaged condition because it was once rolled upon around some boards when placed into storage. The painting cracked along the rolls, and it has never been fully restored.[18]

Benson Lossing, who saw this painting in 1850, included a sketch of it in his 1851 book *A Pictorial Field-Book of the American Revolution*, along with the following description:

This outline sketch is form a copy of the picture at Arlington House (the seat of Mr. Custis), which I made by permission, in November, 1850. As it exhibits none of the horrid scenes of slaughter which generally characterize battle-pieces, I have not hesitated to introduce it, for the purposes of giving a specimen of pictorial composition upon an interesting historical subject from the pencil of the adopted son, and the sole surviving executor of the will of the great Washington. The engraving was executed by Dr. Alexander Anderson, the pioneer wood-engraver in America, at the age of seventy-seven years. Both painter and engraver have passed several years beyond the age allotted to man. Since I made this copy, Mr. Custis has completed two other historical pictures – *Germantown* and *Trenton*; and it is his intention, if his life shall be spared, to thus perpetuate on canvas the memory of all the battles in which his illustrious foster father was engaged.

In the picture here given, the chief is seen most prominently on his white charger, with his general officers. Washington and Greene are in front; Knox on the right, upon the most prominent horse; and behind them are Hamilton, Cadwallader, etc. On the left is seen the group of artillery, with "Captain Molly" at the gun. In the distance is seen a portion of the British army, and Colonel Monckton falling from his horse. On the right, in the foreground, lying by a cannon, is Dickinson, of   Virginia; and, on the left, by a drum, Bonner, of Pennsylvania. In the center is a wounded rifleman.[19]

Custis' daughter, Mrs. Robert E. Lee, wrote the following about her father's avocation as a painter:

One of the principal amusements of Mr. Custis' later years, was painting revolutionary battle-scenes in which Washington participated. Upon these he worked with the greatest enthusiasm. Considering the circumstances under which they were produced – painted without being first composed or drawn in outline, by an entirely self taught hand more than threescore and ten years old, they are remarkable. In general conception and grouping, they are spirited and original. He was not disposed to devote the time and labor requisite to their careful execution. And therefore, as works of art merely, they have but little merit. Their chief value lies in their truthfulness to history in the delineation of events, incidents and costumes. They are all at Arlington, six in number, namely, battles of *Trenton, Princeton, Germantown,* and *Monmouth, Washington at Yorktown,* and the *Surrender at Yorktown.*[20]

Unfortunately the exact date of this painting is not known, which makes it difficult to relate the painting to Custis' writings on "Captain Molly" at Monmouth. Mrs. Lee says that these paintings were all done when her father was past seventy years old, which would put them after 1851, but this cannot be so because Benson Lossing saw the Monmouth painting in 1850. Perhaps Custis did the Monmouth painting to accompany one of his articles on Molly, or the articles were written to accompany the painting.

CONCLUSION

The existence of this painting reinforces Custis' key role in establishing (or transmitting) the earliest versions of the "Molly Pitcher Story" in the mid-1800s. However, we do not know how widely it was seen at the time. It may be more significant for its influence on Benson Lossing.

2G. John W. Barber and Henry Howe, Historical Collections of the State of New Jersey, 1844.

The story of a woman who rendered essential service to the Americans in the battle is founded on fact. She was a female of masculine mold, and dressed in a mongrel suit, with the petticoats of her own sex and an artilleryman's coat, cocked hat and feathers. The anecdote usually related is as follows: Before the armies engaged in general action, two of the advanced batteries commenced a severe fire against each other. As the heat was excessive, Molly, who was the wife of a cannonier, constantly ran to bring her husband water from a neighboring spring. While passing to his post she saw him fall, and on hastening to his assistance, found him dead. At the same moment she heard an officer order the cannon to be moved from its place, complaining he could not fill his post with as brave a man as had been killed. "No," said the intrepid Molly, fixing her eyes on the officer, "the cannon shall not be removed for the want of some one to serve it; since my brave husband is no more, I will use my utmost exertions to avenge his death." The activity and courage with which she performed the office of cannonier, during the action, attracted the attention of all who witnessed it, and finally of Washington himself who afterward gave her the rank of lieutenant, and granted her half-pay during life. She wore an epaulette, and was called ever after *Captain Molly.*[21]

COMMENTARY

John Warner Barber was born in East Windsor, Connecticut, on February 2, 1798 and died on June 22, 1885. He was known as a historian, traveler and engraver. He published a number of historical works, for which he did most of the engravings himself. He wrote *Connecticut Historical Collections* in 1837, and then published similar books on Massachusetts (1839) and New York (1841) before his volume *Historical Collections of the State of New Jersey* appeared in 1844. His junior partner on the New Jersey title, Henry Howe, was born in New Haven on October 11, 1816 and died on October 14, 1893. The two authors also collaborated on a mammoth book entitled *Our Whole Country,* which was five years in preparation before it appeared in 1861. It contained 1500 pages and over 600 engravings, two-thirds of them by Barber. Their engravings were better known for their quantity than their quality, and their writing has been called "superficial, but full of picturesque detail."[22]

This source includes all the basic elements of the developed story: Molly was the wife of a cannoneer who as killed at his post; she had been bringing up water but bravely took her husband's place at his gun; she was presented to General Washington, who gave her a commission as a lieutenant and also a pension. It contains all the elements of the 1837 *New-Jersey Gazette* account (No. 2B above), except for Washington presenting her a sword. Her quotation about serving the cannon is expanded for dramatic effect. It does not include the gold coin reward mentioned by Custis in No. 2D.

Note that Molly is referred to as "Captain Molly," not "Molly Pitcher," and that her husband's name and unit are not mentioned.

CONCLUSION

This account is clearly drawn from the 1837 *New-Jersey Gazette* article (No. 2B above). Molly's battlefield quote is clearly expanded for dramatic effect.

2H. Nathaniel Currier, Engraving, "Molly Pitcher, The Heroine of Monmouth," 1848.

COMMENTARY

Nathaniel Currier was born in Roxbury, Massachusetts on March 27, 1813 and died on November 20, 1888. He was an engraver of note before he took into partnership the artist J. Merritt Ives in 1850, so forming the team that is famous to history as Currier & Ives.[23]

This engraving first appeared in 1848 under the title, "The Women of '76. 'Molly Pitcher' at the battle of Monmouth." It was reissued later at an unknown date with the expanded title, "The Women of '76. 'Molly Pitcher' the Heroine of Monmouth." It depicts Molly serving a cannon at which her husband lies fallen.[24]

Later versions of Currier & Ives engravings of Molly Pitcher at Monmouth helped popularize her story on the national level. One engraving copyrighted in 1876 was titled "The Heroine of Monmouth," and bears the legend "Molly Pitcher, the wife of a gunner in the American army, who when her husband was killed took his place at the gun and served throughout the battle [June 28th, 1778]." It shows Molly swabbing a cannon barrel with a fallen figure, probably her husband, at her feet and an American flag in the background.[25]

CONCLUSION

This engraving is significant as the first appearance of the name "Molly Pitcher" outside of New Jersey to describe the heroine of Monmouth.[26] The first appearance of this name in New Jersey was in 1837 in the *New-Jersey State Gazette.* She was previously known more commonly as "Captain Molly" (see above Nos. 2D, 2E , and 2G).

2I. Interview by Benson J. Lossing with Elizabeth Schuyler Hamilton, widow of Alexander Hamilton, 1848.

For fifty years after her terrible bereavement Mrs. Hamilton lived to mourn his loss, the last thirty of which were spent at Washington in the home of her only daughter, Mrs. Holley. After her death a large pocketbook was found upon which her person; it contained the last letter written to her by her husband on that fatal day [July 11, 1804]. At the close of the year 1848, the celebrated historian, Benson J. Lossing, called upon Mrs. Hamilton. In his account of the interview, he says: "She was then in the ninety-second year of her age, and showing few symptoms in person or mind, of extreme longevity. The sunny cheerfulness of her temper and quiet humor, which shed their blessed influences around her all through life, still made her deportment genial and attractive. Her memory, faithful to the myriad impressions of her long and eventful experience was ever ready with its various reminiscences to give a peculiar charm to her conversations on subjects of the buried past. She was the last living belle of the Revolution, and possibly the last survivor of the notable women who gave a charm to the Republican Court at New York and Philadelphia during Washington's administration. When I revealed to Mrs. Hamilton the object of my visit, her dark eyes gleamed with pleasurable emotion. She seated herself in an easy chair near me and we talked without ceasing upon the interesting theme until invited by her daughter to the tea table at eight o'clock; where we were joined by a French lady, eight or ten years the junior of Madame Hamilton. 'I have lately visited Judge Ford of Morristown,' I remarked. 'Judge Ford, Judge Ford,' she repeated musingly. 'Oh, I remember now. He called upon me a few years ago and brought to my recollection many little events which occurred while I was at Morristown with my father and mother during the war and which I had forgotten. I remember him as a bright boy, much thought of by Mr. Hamilton, who was then Washington's secretary. He brought to mama and me from Mrs. Washington, an invitation to headquarters soon after our arrival at Morristown in 1780.' 'Had you ever seen Mrs. Washington before' I enquired.

'Never,' she said, 'never; she received us so kindly, kissing us both, for the general and papa were very warm friends. She was then nearly fifty years old, but was still handsome. She was quite short; a plump little woman with dark brown eyes, her hair a little frosty, and very plainly dressed for such a grand lady as I considered her. She wore a plain, brown gown of homespun stuff, a large white neckerchief, a neat cap and her plain gold wedding ring which she had worn for more than twenty years. Her graces and cheerful manner delighted us. She was always my ideal of a true woman. Her thoughts were then much on the poor soldiers who had suffered during the dreadful winter. And she expressed her joy at the approach of a milder springtime.' 'Were you much at headquarters afterward' I enquired. 'Only a short time the next winter and an occasional visit,' she replied. 'We went to New Windsor after we were married, and there a few weeks afterward Mr. Hamilton left the general's military family. I made my home with my parents in Albany, while my husband remained in the army until after the surrender of Cornwallis. I visited Mrs. Washington at headquarters at Newburgh, or her invitation, in the summer of 1782, where I remember she had a beautiful flower garden planted and cultivated by her own hands. It was a lovely spot. The residence was an old stone house standing on a high bank of the river and overlooking a beautiful bay and the lofty highlands beyond. We were taken from Newburgh in a barge to the headquarters of the French army, a little beyond Peekskill, where we were cordially received by the Viscount de Noailles, a kinsman of Madame Lafayette, who was Mr. Hamilton's warm friend. We remained there several days and were witnesses of the excellent discipline of the French troops. There we saw the brave Irish woman called "Captain Molly," whom I had seen two or three times before. She seemed to be a sort of pet of the French.' 'Who was Captain Molly, and for what was she famous?' I asked. 'Why don't you remember reading of her exploit at the battle of

Monmouth? She was the wife of a cannoneer – a stout, red-haired, freckle-faced young Irish woman named Mary. While her husband was managing one of the field pieces in the action she constantly brought water from the spring near by. A shot from the British killed him at his post, and the officers in command having no one competent to take his place, ordered the piece withdrawn. Molly (as she was called) saw her husband fall as she came from the spring, and so heard the order. She dropped her bucket, seized the rammer, and vowed that she would fill the place of her husband and avenge his death. She performed the duty with great skill, and won the admiration of all who saw her. My husband told me that she was brought in by General Greene the next morning, her dress soiled with blood and dirt, and presented to Washington as worthy of regard. The General admiring her courage, gave her the commission of a sergeant, and on his recommendation her name was placed on the list of half-pay officers for life. She was living near Fort Montgomery in the Highlands at the time of our visit and came to the camp two or three times when we were there. She was dressed in a sergeant's coat and waistcoat over her petticoats, and a cocked hat. The story of her exploit charmed the French officers and they made her many presents. She would sometimes pass along the French lines when on parade and get her hat nearly filled with crowns.'"[27]

COMMENTARY

Elizabeth Schuyler Hamilton was born in 1757 to the wealthy Schuyler family from Albany. In 1779 she met a handsome young staff officer, Alexander Hamilton, at the colonial camp at Morristown, and they were married just over a year later on December 14, 1780. When Hamilton was mortally wounded in a duel with Aaron Burr on July 11, 1804, she went to live with one of her daughters in Washington, D.C. As noted in this selection, she was 92 years when she gave this interview to Benson Lossing in late 1848 when the latter was doing research for his book *Pictorial Field-Book of the Revolution* (see Nos. 2J and 2K). Mrs. Hamilton died on November 9. 1854 at the age of 97.[28]

In her account Mrs. Hamilton states that she was visiting Newburg, New York in the summer of 1782 and there saw the brave woman known as "Captain Molly," whom she had seen several times before. She then goes on to tell that this Captain Molly had won fame at Monmouth when she was bringing water to the troops and then took her fallen husband's place at his cannon. She was next day presented by General Greene to General Washington, who gave her a commission as a sergeant as well as a pension. Captain Molly was dressed in s sergeant's coat, and was a favorite of the French officers, who often gave her a hat full of coins.

This account is interesting in several regards. It contains the basic elements of the developed Molly Pitcher myth, but with variants and some key additions. The basic elements are that Molly was bring water to the troops; her husband fell casualty; her vow to fight in his stead; the meeting with Washington; and the commission with a pension. Variants are that Molly was getting water from a spring; her husband was "fallen" without specifying if he was dead or wounded; she was presented to Washington by a Greene; and Washington gave her a commission as a sergeant (not lieutenant). Significant additions to the story are her description as Irish; the description of her uniform; that she was living near Fort Montgomery; and that she was a favorite of the French.

Her story is most like that told by Barber and Howe in their 1844 book *Historical Collections of New Jersey* (No. 2G above). Both state that Molly was getting water from a spring; that she was determined to taken her fallen husband's place; that Washington gave her a commission as a Lieutenant, with a pension; and that she was called Captain Molly. The only significant variation included by Barber and Howe is that her husband was killed. These points of similarity are significant, but it is difficult to interpret their significance. It is possible that Mrs. Hamilton had refreshed her memory by reading Barber and Howe's account shortly before she saw Lossing. Or, it is possible that Mrs. Hamilton had told her story earlier, and that a report of it had reached Barber in Howe when they were writing their book. What is most interesting to speculate is that Mrs. Hamilton might have met sometime with George Washington Parke Custis while she was living in Washington and Custis lived nearby at Arlington. In this way she might have been the source for Custis' 1840 account that Molly was presented to Washington by Greene, the first time that information appeared in print (No. 2D).

Mrs. Hamilton's account shows a confusion, however, between Captain Molly Corbin and the Captain Molly of Monmouth (Molly Pitcher).

Margaret Corbin was born in Franklin County, Pennsylvania on November 12, 1751. In 1772 she married John Corbin of Virginia, who enlisted in the 1st Company of Pennsylvania Artillery when the Revolutionary War broke out. Corbin's unit was heavily engaged on November 16, 1776 at the battle of Fort Washington, New York. When he was mortally wounded, Margaret took his place as a matross (assistant artillerist) and was severely wounded herself by a grapeshot that struck her in the arm and breast. After recovering she was assigned to the Corps of Invalids (wounded soldiers who could not serve on active campaigns but could still do garrison duty). On July 6, 1779 Congress voted her the following pension: "Resolved, That Margaret Corbin, who was wounded and disabled in the attack on Fort Washington, whilst she heroically filled the post of her husband who was killed by her side serving a piece of artillery, do receive, during her natural life, or the continuance of said disability, the one-half of the monthly pay drawn by a soldier in the service of these states; and that she now receive out of the public stores one complete set of cloaths, or, the value thereof in money." She was mustered out of the army in April 1783 and settled in Highland Falls (also known as Buttermilk Falls) near West Point, New York. There she died, broken down and poor, in 1800. In 1926 her body was reburied at West Point.[29]

Muster and pay records show that Margaret Corbin was stationed at West Point from 1781 until her muster out in April 1783.[30] In 1782 she took a second husband, but for some reason continued to be called "Mrs. Corbin." Despite being remarried, her condition remained poor, both physically and monetarily.[31]

These records make it clear that the woman whom Mrs. Hamilton saw at Newburg in the summer of 1782 was Margaret Corbin, not Molly Pitcher as she was told. The confusion is not surprising, since both women were known as "Captain Molly" and both were noted female combatants who served in the artillery. Nor was Mrs. Hamilton the only person to confuse the two Mollies. Benson Lossing also spoke to at least other elderly informants in the West Point area, Mr. Beverly Garrison and a Mrs. Rose, who also claimed that their Captain Molly was the same person as Molly Pitcher of Monmouth fame. Mrs. Rose also remembered Captain Molly as being called Dirty Kate, because of her lifestyle and the fact that she died from the effects of syphilis (see 2J below).[32]

It should also be noted that there is no evidence for Proctor's Pennsylvania artillery, with which Mary Hays was serving at Monmouth, being stationed along the Hudson after 1780.[33]

Consequently, Mrs. Hamilton's comments on the Captain Molly whom she saw at Newburg must be applied to Margaret Corbin, not Molly Pitcher. It was Margaret Corbin who was "a stout, red-haired, freckle-faced young Irish woman named Mary," and it was Margaret Corbin who was dressed in a sergeant's uniform and received monetary gifts from the French soldiers. This confusion between Molly Corbin and Molly Pitcher also brings up the possibility that some of Margaret Corbin's actions at Fort Washington may have been misattributed to Molly Pitcher at Monmouth, particularly the elements concerning the death of the husband and the heroine's determination to help fire the cannon.

There is no evidence that Margaret Corbin ever met General Washington on the battlefield or received a commission or any other reward from him. In addition, it appears that she was not known by her neighbors in the West Point area as "Captain Molly" until after 1783.[34]

We return now to Mrs. Hamilton's account of Molly Pitcher at Monmouth. Regardless of her confusion in 1782 over the person of Margaret Corbin, Mrs. Hamilton's account of Molly Pitcher is in tune with the general lines of the legend, as already noted. The most interesting element she adds is that she heard from her husband that it was General Greene who introduced Molly to General Washington on the morning after the battle. Alexander Hamilton was present at Monmouth as an officer on Washington's staff, but he was injured early in the afternoon when he was thrown from his horse.[35] For this reason he probably would not have taken part in the afternoon's artillery action during which Molly Pitcher earned her fame. Even so, he could have heard her story soon afterwards from his fellow staff officers.

This evidence is a key bit of information, since it would establish Molly's presence for certain at the battle, and would also establish that Molly met General Washington on the battlefield. However, this incident is suspicious on several accounts. Firstly, it is not included in any of the primary sources that mention Molly at the battle (Nos. 1A and 1C above). Secondly, this meeting in not mentioned in any of the numerous early biographies of Washington.

Thirdly, it can be questioned if a 92 year old woman could remember the details of such a long story as Lossing relates, particularly when Mrs. Hamilton was already confused as to the identity of Molly Corbin/Molly Pitcher. The account becomes all the more suspicious in view of the fact that Lossing recites it in such detail and length here and then uses virtually the same language in his account of Molly Pitcher in his 1851 *Field-Book* (No. 2K below). Lastly, it needs to be noted that the first written account of a meeting between Molly and Washington does not appear until 1837, 59 years after the battle (No. 2B above), when it may have been inserted for patriotic purposes.

It is always difficult to explain away what appears to be a clear first hand account of a key historical event. In this case, though, it seems preferable to ascribe Mrs. Hamilton's recollection to misinformation, faulty memory, or perhaps the over eager approach of Benson Lossing.

CONCLUSION

Mrs. Alexander Hamilton gives a detailed description of a woman she saw in Newburg, New York, in 1782 and thought was Captain Molly, the heroine of Monmouth. Instead she saw Captain Molly Corbin, the heroine of Fort Washington, who lived in the Newburg area from 1781 to her death in 1800. For this reason the description that Mrs. Hamilton gives of Captain Molly's appearance and dress applies to Margaret Corbin, not Molly Pitcher. This error was picked up by Benson Lossing in his 1851 *Pictorial Field-Book of the Revolution*, which transmitted the mistake to numerous other later authors.

The confusion of Margaret Corbin and Molly Pitcher may have brought two elements into the Molly Pitcher myth, the story of the half pension and the title "Captain Molly." It also may have introduced the death of Molly's husband (Margaret Corbin's husband was definitely killed at Fort Washington, while versions vary as to whether of not Molly Pitcher's husband was killed at Monmouth).

Mrs. Hamilton's statement that it was her husband, Alexander Hamilton, who told her that General Greene introduced Molly to General Washington on the Monmouth battlefield, is difficult to interpret. The preponderance of evidence suggests that she was mistaken or misinformed.

2J. Benson J. Lossing, Pictorial Field-Book of the Revolution, 1851.

Mr. Garrison remembered the famous Irish woman called *Captain Molly,* the wife of a cannonier, who worked a field piece at the battle of Monmouth, on the death of her husband. She generally dressed in the petticoats of her sex, with an artilleryman's cloak over. She was in Fort Clinton with her husband when it was attacked. When the Americans retreated from the fort as the enemy scaled the ramparts, her husband dropped his match and fled. Molly caught up, touched off the piece, and then scampered off. It was the last gun fired by the Americans at the fort. Mrs. Rose (just mentioned) remembered her as *Dirty Kate,* living between Fort Montgomery and Buttermilk Falls, at the close of the war, where she died a horrible death from the effects of a syphilitic disease. I shall have occasion to refer to this bold camp follower, whom Washington honored with a lieutenant's commission for her bravery in the field of Monmouth, nearly nine months afterward, when reviewing the events of that battle.[36]

COMMENTARY

Benson J. Lossing was born in Dutchess County, New York on February 12, 1813 and died near Dover Plains, New York on June 3, 1891. After working briefly as a watchmaker and newspaperman, he moved to New York City in 1838 to become an engraver on wood. Three earlier books featuring his own illustrations were followed in 1850 by his mammoth *Pictorial Field-Book of the Revolution,* for which he prepared over 1000 illustrations by himself; he traveled over 9000 miles to visit every major battlefield of the war and make his own sketches. Numerous later works included his popular *Pictorial History of the Civil War* (1866-1868).[37]

This is the only account to place Captain Molly at the battle of Fort Clinton, New York, which was fought on October 6, 1777. Molly is said to be Irish. Her husband flees the battle, so Molly fires his piece and then flees herself after firing the last gun of the fight. It does not mention Molly as carrying water.

The reference to Molly as "Dirty Kate" and living near Fort Montgomery is a confusion with Margaret Corbin, who was badly wounded while serving a cannon after her husband was killed at the battle of Fort Washington, New York, on November 16, 1776 (see Commentary to No. 2I above).

Lossing draws his evidence for Molly being at Fort Clinton solely from the testimony of Mr. Beverly Garrison, as cited in this passage. There is no other evidence that the Molly Pitcher of Monmouth was ever at Fort Clinton, since no earlier accounts mention this (nor do most later accounts). It is probable that Mr. Garrison confused Molly Pitcher with Molly Corbin, and also confused Molly Corbin's fight at Fort Washington with the fight at Fort Clinton.[38]

CONCLUSION

This account appears to be a garbled version of Margaret Corbin's fight at Fort Washington, New York on November 16, 1776. It contains little similarity to Molly Pitcher's role at Monmouth, beyond the fact that it features a woman firing a cannon in battle.

2K. Benson J. Lossing, Pictorial Field-Book of the Revolution, 1851.

It was during this part of the action that Molly, the wife of a cannonier, is said to have displayed great courage and presence of mind. We have already mentioned her bravery in firing the last gun at Fort Clinton. She was a sturdy young camp-follower, only twenty-two years old, and, in devotion to her husband, she illustrated the character of her countrywomen of the Emerald Isle. In the action in question, while her husband was managing one of the field pieces, she constantly brought him water from a spring near by. A shot from the enemy killed him at his post; and the officer in command, having no one competent to fill his place, ordered the piece to be withdrawn. Molly saw her husband fall as she came from the spring, and also heard the order. She dropped her bucket, seized the rammer, and vowed that she would fill the place of her husband, and avenge his death. She performed the duty with a skill and courage which attracted the attention of all who saw her. On the following morning, covered with dirty and blood, General Greene presented her to Washington, who, admiring her bravery, conferred upon her the commission of sergeant. By his recommendation her name was placed upon the list of half-pay officers for life. She left the army soon after the battle of Monmouth, and, as we have already observed, died near Fort Montgomery, among the Hudson Highlands. She usually went by the name of *Captain Molly*. The venerable widow of General Hamilton, yet living (1852), told me she had often seen Captain Molly. She described her as a stout, red-haired, freckle-faced young Irish woman, with a handsome, piercing eye. The French officers, charmed by the story of her bravery, made her many presents. She would sometimes pass along the French lines with her cocked hat, and get it almost filled with crowns.[39]

COMMENTARY

For the life and career of Benson J. Lossing, see Commentary to No. 2J above.

The nucleus of this account gives the same basic elements as the version told by the *New-Jersey State Gazette* in 1837 (No. 2B) and by Barber and Howe in 1844 (No. 2G). Molly was the wife an artilleryman killed in the battle; she brought water; she took her dead husband's place when the cannon was on the verge of being withdrawn; she was presented to General Washington and commissioned with a half pension. There is a slight difference in that the *Gazette* and Barber and Howe say that Washington gave her a commission as a lieutenant, but Lossing says she became a sergeant. Added details include her description as being Irish and the coins given by the French officers. These elements were added by Lossing's informant, the widow of General Hamilton. It is not known where Lossing got the information that Molly was 22 years old at the time of the battle.

This account also has close similarities to the version told by Custis in 1840 (No. 2D above). Here Molly was also the wife of an artilleryman killed in battle; she was bringing water to the troops; she helped fire the cannon; she was presented afterwards to General Greene and then to General Washington.

The thrust of the two accounts, however, is different. Custis' emphasizes Molly's determination to serve her husband's gun in order to avenge his death, whereas Lossing (and the *Gazette* and Barber and Howe) emphasize Molly's courage in serving her husband's gun in order to prevent it from being withdrawn from the field. In addition, Custis' account contains a number of details not followed by Lossing: her husband was a matross in Proctor's artillery; six gunners were felled in her husband's battery before he was killed; her husband was killed by a shot in the head; and Washington gave her a gold coin. Conversely, Lossing's account contains a number of details not found in Custis': Molly was Irish and 22 years old; Washington gave her a pension and a commission as a sergeant; and the gifts from the French officers; not to mention her fighting at Fort Clinton and her later life in the Hudson Highlands. The most significant detail mentioned by both Custis and Lossing is that Molly met both General Greene and General Washington after the battle.

This internal evidence suggests that Lossing used elements of Custis' and Barber and Howe's accounts in preparing his version of the "Molly Pitcher Story," but his account is closer to Barber and Howe's than to Custis'.[40]

Lossing's account also conflates the stories of Molly Pitcher and Captain Molly Corbin. This is due to the fact that several of his informants were confused on the issue, and he transmitted their error.

Lossing visited the Hudson Highlands in 1848, when he was told about the life and adventures of Margaret Corbin by a number of informants, including 87 year old Beverly Garrison and 80 year old Mrs. Rebecca Rose, who remembered her as both "Captain Molly" and "Dirty Kate." Late in 1848 Lossing also interviewed the widow of Alexander Hamilton, who mistakenly believed that the Captain Molly whom she had seen in Newburg in 1782 was the same person as the Captain Molly at Monmouth (see 2I above and its Commentary). It was only natural that Lossing would pick up and repeat the error (as Edward C. Boynton did later, see No. 2P below).[41]

CONCLUSION

Lossing's version of the story is essentially that of Barber and Howe (No. 2G), with some added elements from Custis (No. 2D). He adds details of her later life that are from the life of Margaret Corbin. Lossing picked up this erroneous information because of a postwar misidentification of Molly Corbin and Molly Pitcher by three of his informants, the widow of Alexander Hamilton, Mr. Beverly Garrison, and a Mrs. Rose.

The confusion of Molly Pitcher with Captain Molly Corbin appears to have brought these three elements into the Molly Pitcher story: the death of Molly's husband, the half pension, and the title "Captain Molly."

2L. Dennis Malone Carter, Painting, "Molly Pitcher at the Battle of Monmouth," 1854.

COMMENTARY

Dennis Malone Carter was born in 1827 and died in 1881. He was known as a painter of historical as well as religious works and portraits in the mid nineteenth century.

His painting of Molly Pitcher at the battle of Monmouth was done in 1854 and is now owned by Fraunces Tavern in New York City. It features Molly at the front of a cannon, facing the enemy and holding up a rammer defiantly. A fallen soldier, probably her husband, lies at the foot of the cannon, and behind her flies an American flag. In the left background General George Washington can be seen astride a white horse. Molly is shown wearing the same brown dress and blue military coat as Carter has her wearing in his 1856 painting of her being presented to General Washington after the battle (No. 2M below).

CONCLUSION

Carter's painting continues the visual tradition of Molly helping to fire a cannon at the battle of Monmouth, a tradition begun by Custis (No. 2F), and Currier (No. 2H) and carried on by numerous other artists in the 1850s and later.

2M. Dennis Malone Carter, Painting, "Molly Pitcher Presented to General Washington," 1856.

COMMENTARY

For the life of Dennis Malone Carter, see Commentary to No. 2L above.

This painting was completed in 1856. It depicts Molly being presented after the battle by General Greene to Generals Washington and von Steuben. General Greene and Molly are on foot, while Washington and Steuben and their staff are mounted. Molly is looking at the ground rather than at Washington, either through modesty or in sadness at the loss of her husband. She is wearing the same brown dress and blue military coat as Carter has her wearing in his 1854 painting of her at the battle (No. 2L above). This painting was presented by Mrs. J. Amory Haskell in the Monmouth County Historical Association in Freehold, New Jersey, in 1941.

CONCLUSION

Carter's depiction of Molly being presented to General Washington by General Greene follows an account first seen in the 1837 *New-Jersey State Gazette* (No. 2B above). For a discussion of the historicity of this incident, see the Commentary to No. 2I above.

2N. Joel Tyler Headley, The Illustrated Life of Washington, 1859.

It was during this part of the battle that an Irishman, while serving his gun, was shot down. His wife, named Molly, only twenty-two years of age, employed herself, while he loaded and fired his piece, in bringing water from a spring near by. While returning with a supply, she saw him fall, and heard the officer in command order the gun to be taken to the rear. She immediately ran forward, seized the rammer, declaring she would avenge his death. She fought her piece like a hero to the last. The next morning, Greene, who had been struck with her bravery, presented her to Washington, who immediately promoted her to a sergeant, and afterward had her name put on the half-pay for life. Previous to this she fired the last gun when the Americans were driven from Fort Montgomery.[42]

COMMENTARY

Joel Tyler Headley was born in Walton, New York, on December 30, 1813, and died in Lexington, Massachusetts on January 16, 1897. He wrote a number of history books in the popular style between 1846 and 1864 on subjects ranging from Napoleon to the American Civil War.[43]

Headley in this passage follows closely the account given by his friend Benson Lossing in his 1851 history *Pictorial Field-Book of the Revolution* (Nos. 2J and 2K above). That the two were closely connected is shown by the fact that Lossing authored a study of

Mount Vernon that was appended to Headley's biography of Washington cited above. Headley is confused when he says that Molly fired the last gun at the battle of Fort Montgomery. Headley's source, Lossing, relates that Molly fired the last gun at the battle of Fort Clinton, and that she lived near Fort Montgomery after the war. Headley obviously confused the names of the two forts.

Headley's account is accompanied by a picture of Molly firing a large barreled cannon with her fallen husband at her feet. She is depicted as heavy set and a bit coarse looking, contrary to the usual portrait of her as young and buxom.[44]

CONCLUSION

Headley's account is derivative from Lossing's and adds nothing to the myth. It even alters Lossing's story by confusing Fort Clinton with Fort Montgomery as noted above. Its most notable contribution is a sketch of Molly as a heavy set and somewhat coarse looking woman.

2O. Dr. James Thacher, *Military Journal,* 1862.

Molly Pitcher, wife of one of the officers, was engaged in bringing water from a spring for the men at the guns, when she saw her husband struck down, and instantly killed; and at the same time she heard the commandant order his piece to be withdrawn as he had no one to fill his place.

Maddened at her loss, Molly rushed forward, and with great activity and courage, continued to work the gun until it was withdrawn. This so strongly enlisted the feelings of the soldiers, that they obtained for her an interview with Washington, and her enrollment on the list of half-pay officers, for life. She was ever afterward called Capt. Molly.[45]

COMMENTARY

Dr. Thacher was born in 1754 and studied medicine under Dr. Abner Hersey in Barnstable, Massachusetts. At the opening of the Revolution he accepted a commission as surgeon in Colonel Gibson's regiment, and later transferred to Colonel Henry Jackson's Additional Continental Regiment. Jackson's regiment was present at the battle of Monmouth, but Thacher himself was on detached duty at a hospital in the Hudson Highlands at the time. He died in 1844.[46]

Thacher first published his wartime journal in 1823, and put out a second edition in 1827. A third edition appeared in 1854, ten years after his death. None of these three editions mentions Molly Pitcher at the battle of Monmouth. Curiously, the passage given above was inserted in the 1862 fourth edition of his work.[47] Exactly who added the passage and why is not known.

This account is a bare bones summary of the version published by the *New Jersey State Gazette* in 1837 (No. 2B above) and Barber and Howe in 1844 (No. 2G above). Its most significant variation is that it calls the heroine "Molly Pitcher" in the first line, which the *Gazette* article did but Barber and Howe did not do. Perhaps the term "Molly Pitcher" was reintroduced in order to straighten out the growing confusion between "Captain Molly" (Margaret Corbin) and "Captain Molly" (the heroine of Monmouth) (see Commentary to No. 2I above). This account also varies from the *Gazette* and Barber and Howe by saying that Molly's husband was an officer.

CONCLUSION

This account is significant for introducing the Molly Pitcher story in the 1862 edition, when it had not been mentioned in earlier editions.

2P. Edward C. Boynton, *History of West Point*, 1871.

Near Swimstown, now called Buttermilk Falls, upon the premises now owned by Mr. Alfred Pell, there lived and died the soldier's wife "Molly ---,better known as *Captain Molly.* She was in Fort Clinton at the time of its capture by the British, in October, 1777. When the enemy scaled the parapet, her husband, who was an artilleryman, dropped his port-fire and fled, but Molly caught it up, and discharged the last gun fired by the Americans. Nine months afterwards, at the memorable battle of Monmouth, although but twenty-two years of age, she illustrated her devotion to her husband, who was serving a gun, by bringing him water during the action from a neighboring spring. A shot from the enemy killed him at his post, and the officer in command, having no one competent to fill his place, ordered the piece to be withdrawn. Molly saw her husband fall as she came from the spring, and also heard the order. She dropped her bucket, seized the rammer, and vowed she would fill his place at the gun, and avenge his death. She performed the duty with a skill and courage, which attracted the attention of all who saw her. On the following morning, covered with dirt and blood, General Greene presented her to Washington, who, admiring her bravery, conferred upon her the appointment of Sergeant. By his recommendation her name was placed upon the half-pay list for life. She is described as a stout, red-haired, freckle-faced young Irish woman, with a handsome, piercing eye. She was a great favorite in the army, usually appearing with an artilleryman's coat over her dress, and wearing a cocked hat.

After taking up her residence near West Point, she received her subsistence through the commissary at the Post, and supplies of various kinds were sent to the family employed to take care of her, direct from the Secretary of War...

Molly, it is believed, died on the spot where she lived for so many years, in 1789, as at that date her name ceases to appear on the Commissary's books.[48]

COMMENTARY

Brevet Major Edward C. Boynton was a captain in the 11th United States Infantry before being receiving an appointment as Adjutant of the United States Military Academy at West Point on October 10, 1861. He published the first edition of his *History of West Point* in 1863, with the second edition appearing in 1871.[49]

This account of Molly's action at Monmouth is clearly drawn from Lossing (see Nos. 2J and 2K above), as one of Boynton's footnotes indicates.[50]

Boynton is confused about Molly's presence at Fort Clinton, as was Lossing, his source (No. 2K above). His account of her later life is confused with the later years of Margaret Corbin (see Commentary to No. 2I above). Boynton is incorrect in assuming that Molly died in 1789, since Margaret Corbin died in 1800.[51]

CONCLUSION

Boynton's account only repeats the version told by Lossing (Nos. 2J and 2K above), and continues the incorrect tradition that Molly was at Fort Clinton in 1777. It also confuses Molly's postwar life with that of Margaret Corbin.

"Molly Pitcher at the Battle of Monmouth"
Engraving of painting by Alonzo Chappel, ca. 1860.

3. SECONDARY SOURCES, 1876-1899

3A. Sarah Smith Stafford, 1876.

Molly Pitcher was a daughter of John Hanna of Allentown; he was an Irish Presbyterian, and had another daughter named Betty, who married Hugh Ager. Ager was a servant of Samuel Rogers, who was reputed to be of noble descent, and Betty was brought up by him. Molly lived as a servant with Mr. Bruere, father of Captain Bruere, of the Monmouth Militia. Her father (Hanna) and Ager were said to have been Irish redemptionists, that is, were sold for a time to pay for their passage. The name Pitcher was a nickname given by the soldiers because she often carried a huge pitcher around to water them. Some said she also followed the soldiers as the wife of John Maban.[1]

COMMENTARY

Sarah Smith Stafford was born in Allentown, New Jersey, on July 27, 1802 and died in Trenton on January 6, 1880. Her father, James Bayard Stafford, was a lieutenant in the navy during the Revolutionary War, and was wounded while serving with John Paul Jones during the famous fight between the *Bon Homme Richard* and the *Serapis* in 1776. Sarah became a school teacher in Trenton in 1828 and then moved to Washington, D.C. to open up a school there after her father died in 1838. She was a zealous advocate of the Union cause during the Civil War, and maintained a large collection of Revolutionary War relics, including what she claimed to be John Paul Jones' starry flag from the *Bon Homme Richard*.[2]

This account was reported in the March 16, 1876 issue of the *Monmouth Inquirer* (No. 3B). It is not known where Miss Stafford got her information. This is the first account to claim that Molly was a resident of New Jersey. Miss Stafford's claim that Molly was an Irish Presbyterian, daughter of John Hanna of Allentown, is not supported by any earlier sources or by any primary source material. The soldier mentioned as her possible husband, John Maban, cannot be otherwise identified. This account has been the source for a number of later accounts that followed her information (see Nos. 3B, 3C and 3F and 3K below).

Miss Stafford was apparently the conveyor of a number of oral traditions concerning the Revolutionary War and the history of the Allentown area. Some historians, however, question her accuracy, particularly her claim to possess a flag flown by John Paul Jones during the war. Reportedly one historian asked Polly McClaester, granddaughter of Mary Hays McCauley, the most likely candidate to be the historical Molly Pitcher, if she believed her grandmother was born under the name Mary Hanna, and Polly replied that she "never heard of Mary Hanna."[3]

CONCLUSION

This account is significant for its claim that Molly was an Irish Presbyterian and daughter of John Hanna of Allentown, possibly married to a soldier named John Maban. Its claims are not otherwise substantiated.

3B. Article from the *Monmouth Inquirer*, March 16, 1876.

Communications
Molly Pitcher—Who Was She?
Her History before and after the Battle of Monmouth

Does any reader of the *Inquirer* know of any tradition relating to the history of Molly Pitcher before or after the war?

Miss Sarah Smith Stafford, now of Trenton, but formerly of Allentown, says:

"Molly Pitcher was a daughter of John Hanna, of Allentown; he was an Irish Presbyterian. And had another daughter named Betty, who married Hugh Ager. Ager was a servant of Samuel Rogers, who was reputed to be of noble descent, and Betty was brought up by him. Molly lived as a servant with Mr. Bruere, father of Captain Bruere, of the Monmouth Militia. Her father (Hanna) and Ager were said to have been Irish Redemptionists, that is, were sold for a time to labor to pay for their passage. The name Pitcher was a nickname given by the soldiers because she often carried a huge pitcher around to water them. Some said that she followed the soldiers as the wife of John Maban."

Miss Stafford is now 75 years old, and is well known for general intelligence and a wonderfully retentive memory. She was acquainted with some of the parties above named, and knew Betty and her husband.

After the war Molly followed the soldiers off, and finally died in the vicinity of Fort Montgomery, near Buttermilk Falls, among the Hudson Highlands. Those who knew her there described her as a stout, red-haired, freckled face young Irish woman, with handsome piercing eyes. Her life as a camp follower, with "brevet" husbands, soon lowered her reputation, and she finally received the sobriquet of "Dirty Kate," and about the close of the war died a miserable death of syphilitic disease. The story of her receiving a sergeant's or lieutenant's commission is exceedingly mythical, unless some one gave it to her as a joke. PILOT.[4]

COMMENTARY

The identity of the author of this article, perhaps the "Pilot" mentioned at the end, is not known. For the biography of Sarah Smith Stafford, see Commentary to No. 3A. This article is the source for No. 3A. The background of Miss Stafford's statement is discussed in the Commentary there.

The author's summary of Molly's post war career is drawn directly from Benson Lossing's account in his *Field-Book of the American Revolution* and therefore contains Lossing's error attributing the later life of Margaret Corbin to that of Molly Pitcher (see text and Commentary to No. 2I). In his last sentence, the author expresses skepticism about Molly ever receiving a battlefield commission for her heroism.

CONCLUSION

This article is the actual source for Sarah Smith Stafford's statement given in No. 3A that Molly Pitcher was an Irish Presbyterian daughter of John Hanna of Allentown. The last paragraph confuses the later life of Margaret Corbin with that of Molly Pitcher.

3C. Reverend George Swain, Historical Discourse in Connection with the Presbyterian Church of Allentown and Vicinity, ca. 1876.

From among us it is said was the famous Molly Pitcher; she who, at the battle of Monmouth, acted the *role* of cannoneer in the place of her husband or some other brave who had fallen beside his gun. She is reputed to have been the daughter of one Jno. Hanna, of Allentown, was of North Ireland extraction, and had been for a time a servant in the family of the father of Captain James Bruere. She was, perhaps, the wife of a soldier named Jno. Maban.[5]

COMMENTARY

This passage is taken from a sermon preached by Reverend Swain at the Allentown Presbyterian Church on June 20, 1876. It was written in compliance with a request from the Presbyterian General Assembly in 1875 "that every pastor, in this the Centennial year (1876) of the nation's existence, preach a discourse on the history of his Church."[6] Reverend Swain was born in Glasgow, Scotland on June 20, 1841, and came to Brooklyn with his family in 1849. He graduated from Rutgers in 1863 and took up a pastorate in Brooklyn in 1873. He was installed as Pastor of the Allentown Presbyterian Church on November 10, 1874. He held this position until his resignation in 1911, though he stayed on until a replacement was found in 1912. He died on November 7, 1914.[7]

Reverend Swain states in a footnote that he drew his information on the authority of Miss Sarah Smith Stafford of Trenton.[8] He shows confusion as to whom Molly replaced at the cannon, her fallen husband or another man who was a casualty.

CONCLUSION

This account is derivative from that of Sarah Smith Stafford (No. 3A above) in claiming that Molly was the daughter of John Hanna of Allentown.

3D. John G. Raum, The History of New Jersey, 1877.

"One Molly Pitcher, or as she was called, Captain Molly, rendered essential service to the Americans in the battle. She was of masculine mould, and dressed in a mongrel suit, with the petticoats of her own sex, and an artilleryman's coat, cocked hat, and feathers. The anecdote usually related of her is as follows: Before the armies engaged in general action, two of the advanced batteries commenced a severe fire against each other. As the heat was excessive, Molly, who was the wife of a cannonier, constantly ran to bring her husband water from a neighboring spring. While passing to his post she saw him fall, and on hastening to his assistance, found him dead. At the same moment she heard an officer order the cannon to be removed from its place, complaining that he could not fill the post with as brave a man as had been killed. 'No,' said the intrepid Molly, fixing her eyes upon the officer, 'the cannon shall not be removed for the want of some one to serve it; since my brave husband is no more, I will use my utmost exertions to avenge his death.' The activity and courage with which she performed the office of cannonier during the action, attracted the attention of all who witnessed it, and finally of Washington himself. She wore an epaulette, and was ever afterward called *Captain Molly.*

Lossing, in his "Field-Book of the Revolution," thus mentions Molly Pitcher: "She was a sturdy young camp follower, only twenty-two years of age, and in devotion to her husband, who was a cannonier, she illustrated the character of her countrywomen of the Emerald Isle. In the action (battle of Monmouth) while her husband was managing one of the fieldpieces, she constantly brought him water from a spring near by. A shot from the enemy killed him at his post; and the officer in command, having no one competent to fill the place, ordered the piece to be withdrawn. Molly saw her husband fall as she came from the spring, and also heard the order. She dropped her bucket, seized the rammer and vowed that she would fill the place of her husband at the gun and avenge his death. She performed the duty with a skill and courage which attracted the attention of all who saw her. On the following morning, covered with dirt and blood, General Greene presented her to General Washington, who, admiring her bravery, conferred upon her the commission of Sergeant. By his recommendation her name was placed upon the list of half-pay officers for life. She left the army soon after the battle of Monmouth, and died near Fort Montgomery, among the Hudson Highlands. She usually went by the name of Captain Molly. The venerable widow of General Hamilton, who died in 1854, told me she had often seen Captain Molly. She described her as a stout, red-haired, freckle-faced young Irish woman, with a handsome piercing eye. The French officers, charmed by the story of her bravery. Made her many presents. She would sometimes pass along the French lines with her cocked hat and get it almost filled with crowns."

The same writer [Lossing] visited the locality of Forts Montgomery and Clinton on the Hudson, where Molly Pitcher ended her days, and there found old residents who "remembered the famous Irish woman called Captain Molly, the wife of a cannonier who worked a field-piece at the battle of Monmouth on the death of her husband. She generally dressed in the petticoats of her sex, with an artilleryman's coat cover. She was in Fort Clinton with her husband when it was attacked in 1777. When the Americans retreated form the fort, as the enemy scaled the parapets, her husband dropped his match and fled; Molly caught it up, touched off the piece and then scampered off. It was the last gun the Americans fired in the fort. Mrs. Rose remembered her as Dirty Kate, living between Fort Montgomery and Buttermilk Falls, at the close of the war, where she died a horrible death from syphilitic disease. Washington had honored her with a Lieutenant's commission for her bravery in the field of Monmouth, nearly nine months after the battle, when reviewing its events."[9]

COMMENTARY

John O. Raum was born ca. 1824 and died in 1893. His additional works include *A History of the City of Trenton,* which was published in 1871.[10] His description of Molly Pitcher is copied almost word for word from two earlier sources. The first paragraph given above is taken from Barber and Howe's *Historical Recollections of the State of New Jersey* (No. 2G above), with the significant addition of calling her "Molly Pitcher" in the first sentence. Raum's second paragraph given above is taken from Lossing's *Pictorial Field-Book of the American Revolution* (No. 2K above). Here again, Raum calls his heroine "Molly Pitcher," a term not used in his source. The long quotation used in Raum's third paragraph given above is also taken word for word from Lossing's *Pictorial Field-Book of the American Revolution* (No. 2J above).

CONCLUSION

Raum's account of Molly Pitcher at the battle of Monmouth is totally derivative, being copied almost word for word from earlier versions by Barber and Howe (No. 2G above) and Lossing's *Pictorial Field-Book of the American Revolution* (Nos. 2J and 2K above). In the process, he continues Lossing's error concerning Molly's presence at Fort Clinton in 1777, and also repeats Lossing's confusion about the last years of Margaret Corbin and Molly Pitcher (see Commentary on No. 2I above). The only new element that Raum adds is to call his heroine "Molly Pitcher," a sobriquet not used in either of his sources.

3E. Rev. C.P. Wing, Letter to The Pennsylvania Magazine of History and Biography, 1878.

Carlisle, June 15, 1878

Dear Sir: Your letter of the 13th Inst. Reached me yesterday P.M., and I immediately set about some inquiries for the purpose of verifying the received traditions regarding the subject of your inquiry. I visited the President of the Monument committee, and the granddaughter of Mrs. Hays, and took notice of some contemporary files of the newspapers. The amount of what I obtained, with what I had before, is the following:

The original name before marriage was Mary Ludwig (so recorded in the family Bible). She herself probably came from Germany. The first we discover of her was at Trenton, N.J., where she had quarters with Gen. Irvine. Her husband was John Hays, a barber, a sergeant in a company of artillery. He was an Irishman, or an Englishman. He was in the battle of Monmouth, and is said to have had, at least for a while, the direction of a cannon. When he was struck down she was coming on the ground with a pitcher of water for him and others. It was a very hot day, and the soldiers suffered much

from heat and thirst. Her husband had been borne from the
ground, and she instantly took his place by the gun, and some
say served several rounds, but others say only loaded and
fired once, and insisted on continuing at the post, and was
induced very reluctantly to retire. It is also said that she was
seen at this service by Gen. Washington, but we only know
that he was informed of her conduct, and gave her a
commission as sergeant by brevet. She was very active in
various ways, for she was excitable, being then about 30
years of age, and confident and prompt when she saw
anything to be done. She had a friend also in the battle, who
was rendered insensible, and was thrown with many others
into a pit for dead, and to be buried—but she went the
morning after the battle and found him alive, bore him in her
arms to the hospital, and took care of him until his recovery.
At some time late in life she received a box of presents from
this friend, with an invitation to come and make her home
with him, where he promised to keep her in luxury. Her
friend wrote that he had only just heard through the pension
office of her residence. After the battle she served with her
husband in the army. In all, she was in the army seven years
and nine months.

Soon after the disbanding of the army, she came to reside
in Carlisle, Pa., where her husband died and was buried. She
remained a widow for a while, and was employed as a nurse
in many families. She was very fond of children, and loved to
stop them and tell them stories. But when having the charge
of them, she was considered by those of whom she had
charge, to be very strict and severe. She was to all persons
very communicative and talkative, rather rough in manners,
sometimes, when excited, even profane, but well understood
to be at heart tender and kind. She never turned away any
who were in trouble, and enjoined it on her children never to
do so. Much against the remonstrance of her friends and
kindred she married Sergeant John McAuley [McCauley], a
worthless fellow, who made her subsequent life miserable by
drunkenness and personal abuse. He did nothing but live on
her earnings, how many years I never heard. She, however,
lived for some time after his death, and died January 1832, at

the age of eighty-nine. She was buried with military honors, several companies attended her remains to the grave, where she was buried under a deep snow, with her first husband. A military salute was fired at the interment. She seldom if ever attended any place of worship, though she always treated religion and religious people with great respect. She never received any pension except forty dollars a year, as the widow of Mr. Hays. It is said by her granddaughter, that on the last week of her life, a pension was granted to her in her own right.

She had a son John, who was born in Trenton, who also had children who reside now in Carlisle. One of the daughters of this John still lives, and unveiled the monument which the citizens of Carlisle erected over "Molly Pitcher's" grave, on the fourth of July in the centennial year (1876). The name of Pitcher was given her with reference to her services by her companions in the army in 1778. This monument is a very appropriate one in the old cemetery of Carlisle, where lie so many of the heroes of the American Revolution.

It may be that some purist of the Niebuhr school may yet demolish some of the romance of the story. By searching the records of the Pension Office at Washington, perhaps something might be learned. But the substantial facts are well established, and the whole story now constitutes a part of what is dear and true to the national heart.

Yours very truly, C.P. Wing[11]

COMMENTARY

Wing in this letter accepts that Mary Hays McCauley of Carlisle was the Molly Pitcher of Monmouth fame. This is the earliest written source to state that she was born in Trenton, New Jersey, under the name of Mary Ludwig. She was first married to John Hays, a sergeant in the artillery, and was bringing water to the troops at Monmouth when her husband was "struck down." She then helped service the cannon, for which she was rewarded by Washington the next day with a commission. The rest of the letter gives interesting personal information about her life in Carlisle, particularly her fondness for children and the shiftlessness of her second husband, John McCauley.

Wing states in his opening paragraph that he secured most of his information by talking to Mary Hays McCauley's neighbors and relatives. As such, his account of her actions at the battle and life in Carlisle largely reflect the testimonies given in Chapter 8 below.

Note that Wing's account is careful to say that Molly's husband was struck down, not killed, at Monmouth. This is because her neighbors and relatives were well aware that her husband survived the war and was not killed at the battle. Note also that Wing cites differing variants in the story, since his informants did not agree as to how many cannon shots she fired and whether she met Washington on the day of the battle or later.

The story that Wing tells about Molly saving one of her friends from the burial pits after the battle is unique to this account. It sounds somewhat like the story Isabella C. McGeorge tells of Molly saving a soldier named Dilwyn, a friend of her husband's, at the battle of Princeton (see No. 4A).

Wing cites a family bible as his evidence that Molly was born under the name Mary Ludwig. Unfortunately, this bible does not survive to confirm his statement. The absence of this confirmation is critical, since several later sources follow Wing's lead and say that Molly was born of German origin as Mary Ludwig, but give different variations of her origin. For example, Dr. William H. Egle in 1893 wrote that Mary Ludwig was born on October 13, 1844 in Lancaster County, Pennsylvania, as the daughter of John George Ludwig (No. 3J) while C. Malcolm B. Gilman wrote in 1964 that Mary Ludwig was born of the same parentage, but was christened at Trenton, New Jersey on October 13, 1754 (No. 5F). Egle gives no source for his statement, but Gilman cites baptismal records at the Lawrenceville Presbyterian Church.[12]

Wing states that Mary Ludwig married John Hays, a barber, before the Revolution, but does not cite his evidence. Several later sources also believe that she was married to John Hays, including Dr. Egle (No. 3J) and William S. Stryker (No. 3L). Egle does not give his source, but Stryker cites a July 24, 1769 marriage bond he located between Mary Ludwig and "John Casper Hays."[13] The actual marriage bond, however, is between Mary Ludwig and Casper Hays, not John Hays.[14] Some sources claim that this marriage bond was taken out in Carlisle, but this is not stated in the source cited.[15] In fact, there exists a marriage record from St. Michael's and Zion Church in

Philadelphia dated the next day, July 25, 1769, between "Caspar Hayes (formerly Haas) and Mary Ludwick [Ludwig}, Wid."[16] Since it would seem very odd if there were two couples named Casper Hays and Mary Ludwig, one of whom took out a marriage license in Carlisle on July 24 and the other of which got married in Philadelphia on July 25, these two sources must refer to the same pair. These records do not, however, help us identify Mary Ludwig's parentage.

These documents establish that Mary Ludwig married Casper Hays, not John Hays as stated by Wing, Egle, Stryker and others. This is a significant lapse. The fact is that no soldier named Casper Hays is known to have fought in the Pennsylvania artillery at Monmouth, which is an element essential to the Molly Pitcher story. However, there was, or at least Stryker and others thought (see Commentary to No. 3L), a John Hays in the artillery at Monmouth. For this reason Stryker, and probably Wing and Egle before him, found it necessary to hypothesize that Casper Hays enlisted in the Revolution under the "soldier name" of John Hays.[17] This is significant, because it shows that Mary Ludwig's husband Casper Hays was not in the army or at Monmouth. Therefore Mary Ludwig Hays could not have been at Monmouth either, and so could not be our Molly Pitcher.

More recent research, as pointed out by Jeremiah Zeamer and Samuel S. Smith, has established that Mary Hays McCauley was actually married to a soldier named William Hays in 1778. William Hays served in Proctor's Pennsylvania artillery, and so could well have been Molly Pitcher's husband at Monmouth in June 1778 (see Chapter 12).[18]

This evidence is disturbing because it brings into serious question Wing's claim to have read in Mary Hays McCauley's bible that her maiden name was Mary Ludwig.

Wing cites the correct year of Mary Hays McCauley's death as 1832; her tombstone as originally erected read 1833 by mistake and was later corrected to 1832. However, he cites her age at death as 89, whereas the tombstone says 79 (see No. 9A). This change in numbers may have been cited in order to give Mary Hays McCauley a birth year of 1844, rather than 1854 as the tombstone numbers would suggest.

This is the only source to say that Mary Hays McCauley's son John was born in Trenton, New Jersey. Samuel S. Smith believes that he was born in Carlisle.[19]

CONCLUSION

This is a significant account for being the first to claim that Mary Hays McCauley (Molly Pitcher) was born with name Mary Ludwig. Wing says that he obtained this information from a family bible. But other evidence is clear that Mary Ludwig married a man named Casper Hays, not John Hays. In addition, Mary Hays McCauley's husband at the time of Monmouth was William Hays, not John Hays. Therefore Mary Hays McCauley could not have been born as Mary Ludwig.

This account gives a good summary of the Molly Pitcher story as it was believed by residents of Carlisle shortly after her tombstone was erected in 1876. It contains a significant variant to the story by claiming that Molly saved one of her friends from the burial pits after the battle of Monmouth.

This is the only source to say that Mary Hays McCauley's son John was born in Trenton, New Jersey.

3F. E.M. Woodward, History of Burlington County, New Jersey, 1883.

The author is indebted to J. O'Heir, ordnance sergeant U.S.A. in charge of post Carlisle Barracks, Pennsylvania, for the following interesting item: MollyPitcher, the daughter of John Hanna, of Allentown, and the wife of a cannoneer named John Maban, who obtained her sobriquet from her carrying water to the soldiers of her husband's battery during battle, lies buried in the old cemetery at Carlisle. The following is the inscription upon the tablet erected over her grave:

Mollie M'Cauley
Renowned in History as
Mollie Pitcher,
The Heroine of Monmouth,
Died January, 1833,
Aged 79 years.
Erected by the citizens of Cumberland County,
July 4th, 1876.[20]

COMMENTARY

This account follows that of Sarah Smith Stafford (No. 3A) in claiming that Molly was born in Allentown, New Jersey, as the daughter of Mark Hanna. It mentions John Maban as her husband, a point that Stafford suggests, but goes a step farther and claims that Maban was her husband at the time of the battle of Monmouth. Woodward's source, Sergeant O'Heir, is not otherwise known. Nor do we know if he came upon this information independently, or got it from Stafford or elsewhere. The date cited for Molly's death, 1833, was put on her tombstone incorrectly, and was later corrected to read 1832 (see No. 9B).

CONCLUSION

This is another source claiming that Molly was born in Allentown New Jersey as Molly Hanna. It is the only source to claim that John Maban was her husband at the time of Monmouth.

3G. J.A. Murray, article in the Carlisle *American Volunteer*, 1883.

MOLLY MCCAULEY

As the State of New Jersey has taken steps to erect a monument on Monmouth battle ground, Mr. Isaac Craig, who had been desired to investigate the Molly Pitcher tradition, has applied to Dr. Murray for some information on the subject, for if found authentic, it is intended to recognize the heroine; and the material part of the information, furnished by Dr. M., we here give as something of interest to the community. – Ed.

I know something relating to Molly McCauley's monument, I believe the facts are following: Many years ago we had living in Carlisle a person named Richard Miles, a cooper and auctioneer; I remember him well. At one time Molly McCauley kept house for him. He had a son named Wesley, who became a prominent school teacher, an intelligent man, who has been living for several years past in Williamsport, Pa.; and who occasionally writes for one of our papers, giving his recollections of persons and things at or near Carlisle. He wrote such a letter about the time of our national centennial, in which he spoke of Molly as having been buried here years previously. And that there was no stone to indicate her grave. Immediately Peter Spahr (a native of this place and a brickmaker, a man of strong sense and energy and enterprise, and who remembers Molly very well) resolved upon the work of erecting a monument on her grave, and of having the undertaking completed on the 4th of July of that (centennial) year. When he so determined, it was equivalent to a success. He at once had a subscription paper prepared, to raise one hundred dollars, as he learned that a suitable marble monument could be erected for that amount, and he commenced by putting his own name down for $5. Three other persons- Mr. Henry Saxton, Judge Watts and Geo. Metzer, Esq.- each gave $5, and then the subscriptions were all smaller sums. Mr. Spahr was so interested in the matter that he would have paid half the entire amount sooner than have failed. But he secured the whole amount necessary.

The foregoing narrative I had from himself, since I received your letter—as I went to see him on the subject, and I read to him your letter. He assured me that there was no "Monument Association" existing here, as quoted by you, excepting what existed in his own brain. So also has Mr. Wm. Parks informed me, as he was about the first man made aware of Mr. Spahr's intention, and was himself very well acquainted with Molly—who had been quite intimate to his father's family. The monument was gotten and paid for through the personal efforts of Peter Spahr, who also got a leading member of our Bar, Samuel Hepburn Jr., to prepare the chaste and honorable inscription, and Capt. Vail to deliver the admirable address at the unveiling of it—which was most appropriately done by Mrs. Polly McCleester, the aged granddaughter of the Heroine of Monmouth.

I gathered from these gentlemen the following additional items, some of which I have known or heard before. After her husband, John Hays, had entered the service of his country, he sent word to her to come and join him, which she promptly and cheerfully did, willing to render whatever aid and comfort she could, and she remained with him throughout the war, nursing the sick or wounded, and making herself generally useful. At the battle of Monmouth she rendered valuable services—cheering and encouraging the men as well as carrying water to the excited and thirsty soldiers in the regiment to which her husband belonged, and hence received the familiar name of Molly Pitcher. Hays was not killed on that occasion, but knocked down and rendered insensible. She, however, supposed he was killed, and instantly handled his weapon and did what she could to supply his place at the cannon. He afterwards revived, recovered and returned to duty. After the war ended they came to Carlisle, where Hays died. McCauley, who had been a fellow soldier with her husband and knew her well, subsequently married her. She survived her second husband, and had issue only by her first husband. Mr. Spahr told me that she was a very masculine person, alike rough in appearance and character—small and heavy, with bristles in the end of her nose, and that she could both drink whisky and swear. Very distinctly do I remember her son, John L. Hays, he was tall and straight and had also stiff hairs on the end of his nose. He was called "Sergeant Hays" as he occupied that position in the old infantry company and was in the War of 1812. By the by, a similar military title had been given to his mother, and the fact has been perpetuated in the verse of a poem that the writer has in his collection and written by his friend since boyhood days. The Rev. Dr. Geo. Duffield of Michigan:

> "Moll Pitcher she stood by her gun,
> And rammed the charges home, sir.
> And this on Monmouth's bloody field,
> A sergeant did become, sir" etc.

Sergeant John L. Hays died there nearly thirty years ago, in the old stone house at the northeast intersection of East and South streets, and was buried with the honors of war. On that occasion, at the request of Capt. Samuel Crop and Lt. Wm. Parks, of the Carlisle Infantry, Captain May of the U.S. army. commanding of the Barracks, furnished the band of music and a large escort—as the deceased had served his country honorably in the late war with Great Britain. He has two sons living in Carlisle, John and Frederick. William and George are dead, and all his daughters are dead, excepting Mrs. Polly McLeester. John is our present street commissioner, an honest son of toil, and a gray-headed man, who has also a family.

Mr. Parks, as did also Mrs. McCleester, informed me that Molly had lived in the family of Dr. George D. Foulks, and other families, as well as faithfully served other persons in Carlisle, and though she generally wore a petticoat and short gown, and could drink grog and use language not the most polite, yet she was a kindhearted woman, and helpful to the sick and needy. A woman—"for a' that."

John Hays, Molly's grandson, could not tell me just when his grandmother died, but, after reflection, said: I am now 84 years old, and was somewhere about 10 or 12 years old when she died and she died in the old stone house near Lockridge's corner, at the south east intersection of North and Bedford streets. He spoke of her as a short, thick, heavy woman, and often heard her say that, if it had not been for her the battle of Monmouth would have gone against us! He could not tell me positively that she ever received a pension but thought that towards the close of her life she had gotten something of the kind but referred me to his widow sister, Polly McCleester, who is the oldest of the family. She is in her 81st year. I saw her, and though advanced in life, she is still somewhat vigorous, tall and slender like her father. After repeated and direct questions relative to the pension matter, she said that her grandmother had often tried unsuccessfully to get a pension, and had at last received one payment of $24 a short time before she died. It was the first she had received, and she was promised more if she lived. Polly however, could not tell me whether it was from the State or general government. She was not then living with her grandmother or in Carlisle, but with her husband in Papertown, several miles south of Carlisle, and hence she appeared to know the less about her. As the aged heroine received this amount the same month in which she died, even as a "pension," with the promise of more if she lived, and as there is not anything to show for it in the records of the Pension office at Washington or

Harrisburg, according to the explicit statement in your letter, may it not be possible, that, at that time of her life, feeble in health and in humble circumstances, some charitable and patriotic person in Carlisle made up a purse of $24 which was given to her with the conditional promise of more.

While Polly did not remember the year in which her grandmother died, she was certain it was in the month of January, adding, that her son, who was now about 54 years old, was then about 3 years old. She seemed to be indignant at Mr. Wesley Miles for stating that her grandmother came from Ireland, and said that "she was as Dutch as Sauer Kraut, and her maiden name was Mary Ludwig!" (Though her family name indicates her Teutonic origin, her married name certainly suggests a Celtic descent, and such a mistake could be easily made.) Thence I visited our old cemetery and Molly's monument. Altogether it is about six feet high, with a base and its cap each of suitable size, and the surmounted stone rounded at the top is 4 feet high, 2 feet wide and 6 inches thick, bearing the following inscription:

Molly McCauly,
Renowned in History as
Molly Pitcher,
The Heroine of Monmouth.
Died Jan. 1833
Aged 79 Years.
Erected by the Citizens of
Cumberland County,
July 4, 1876.

I examined the files of two of our local papers at that time, the *American Volunteer* and the *Carlisle Republican,* but did not see a notice of her in either of them. But, but by referring to a file of the previous year, I found the following:

"DIED—On Sunday last in this borough, at an advanced age, Mrs. Molly McCauley. She lived during the days of the American Revolution, shared its hardships and witnessed many a scene of "blood and carnage." To the sick and wounded she was an efficient aid, for which, and being the widow of an American hero, she received during the latter years of her life, an annuity from the government. For upwards of forty years she resided in this borough, and was during that time recognized as an honest, obliging and industrious woman."

The preceding has been carefully copied from the *Volunteer* of Thursday, Jan. 20, 1832. Hence she must have died on the 22nd of that month and in that year; and the statement on the monument, that it was in "1833," is one of those grave(stone) mistakes that will sometimes occur. It is greatly regretted that the very corner of the *Volunteer* containing the above obituary is torn off and lost, by which mutilation about half of the notice is apparently wanting. Among the death notices in the *Republican* of Thursday, Jan. 26, 1832, is this one: "On Sunday last, in this borough, at an advanced age, Mrs. Molly McCauley." The date is the same in each paper, and is a year previous to that given on her monument in our old cemetery.

Gen. Wm. Irvine's home was at Carlisle during the Revolution and for some time opposite to that of Gen. Armstrong. He married a daughter of Robert Callander, who lived near Carlisle and had ten children. (I have a number of letters and orders written by them while here.) Dr. W.A. Irvine, of Warren county, Pa., is a grandson. Years ago I was most credibly informed by a venerable friend, Mr. James Loudon, that it was in Gen. Wm. Irvine's family that Mary Ludwig lived, in Carlisle, when she first saw and married John Hays, who was a barber by profession, as well as an enlisted soldier. Recently, too, have I been told the same thing by her aged namesake, Polly McCleester, who detailed to me with manifest interest and pleasure what she so distinctly recollected of hearing her grandmother say in regard to their short and amusing courtship, which commenced when she was sweeping in front of the Irvine home, dressed in her petticoat and short gown. Soon afterward they were married. And she was still working in the Irvine family when she was summoned to join her husband in the army. Polly cannot tell to which company or regiment her grandfather belonged. If she ever knew, she has forgotten.Nor can I tell. But, by referring to the *Pennsylvania Archives,* second series, Vol. X, it will be seen that Wm. Irvine was Colonel of the Seventh Regiment, Continental Line. One of the companies in said regiment was commanded by Capt. John Alexander, and among his men occurs the name of "John Hays," but that it clearly refers to the husband of Molly, I cannot now certainly say, though it seems to point in that direction.

Sometime before the appearance of the letter in the Pennsylvania Magazine, III, 109, to which you refer, a friend in Harrisburg wrote to me for some data respecting Molly McCauley as he proposed writing an article about her. Accordingly I sent him a package of matter, printed and other wise, all I had, including a picture of Molly, (in an illustrated periodical) at Monmouth battle, standing near the cannon, with the rammer in her hand, and cheering the men. I do not know that the article has been written, but the package has not been returned, and I have not anything more to communicate.

It may here be added, that Peter Spahr, Wm. Parks, Polly McCleester and John Hays—among the very best informed persons in Carlisle in regard to the life and character of Molly McCauley—have been made acquainted more or less fully, with the contents of this communication, and not one of them has objected to any of it.

J.A.M. Carlisle, Pa., Sept. 4, 1883

P.S.—In "Near to Nature's Heart," published some years ago, the writer speaks of Molly's courtship and marriage to Larry O'Flaharty, but this I regard as romance and not veritable history. In June of 1876 Mr. Miles wrote several interesting letters for the *Volunteer* and the *Herald.* In one of these he gives his authority for saying that Molly was Irish and that her husband was actually killed at Monmouth, which is here given:

Barnes says: "During the day, an artilleryman was shot at his post. His wife, Molly Pitcher, while bringing water to her husband from a spring saw him fall and heard the commander

order the piece to be removed from the field. Instantly
dropping the pail, she hastened to the cannon, seized the
rammer and with great skill and courage, performed her
husband's duty. The soldiers gave her the name of Major
Molly. On the day of the battle she was presented to
Washington and received a Sergeant's commission with half
pay through life."

Goodrich says: "In the beginning of the battle of
Monmouth, as one Molly Pitcher was carrying water from a
spring to her husband, who was employed loading and firing
a cannon, the husband was suddenly killed before her eyes.
An officer came along and ordered the vacant cannon to be
put out of the way. To his great astonishment, however,
Mollie took her husband's post, and performed faithfully his
duties, and Congress, as a reward, gave her half pay for life."

Lossing says: "At Monmouth on one of the hottest days
ever known, they had a terrible battle. It lasted from 9 o'clock
a.m., until dark. Fifty soldiers died of thirst that day. One
soldier who was firing a cannon was shot dead. His wife, a
young Irish woman, named Molly, who had been bringing
water to him, took his place at the gun and kept firing it all
through the battle. Washington was so well pleased with her
for this act of bravery, that he gave her the pay of her
husband after that, and she wore his soldier clothes and was
called Captain Molly as long as she lived."

Bernard says: "It was the 28th of June (1778). The day
was excessively hot and sultry and the battle lasted until
night. During the day a soldier having charge of a cannon was
shot down at his post. His wife, a brave Irish woman, was at
the time bringing him water from a neighboring spring. She
saw her husband fall. Instantly dropping her pail, she seized
the rammer and stationing herself by the gun, performed her
husband's duty with great skill and courage during the action.
The soldiers nick-named her Major Molly."

Nevertheless, as previously stated, the aged kindred and
friends living here maintain that Molly was a German, and
that her husband—though felled and rendered unconscious
for some time—was not killed in the battle, but revived, and

ultimately died in Carlisle. The local testimony is strong and emphatic.

Concerning the question of pension, the Hon. J.B. Linn (lately secretary of the commonwealth) informed Mr. Miles, that "Molly drew a pension from the State for her services commencing Feb. 21st, 1822, and ending Jan. 1st, 1832; and as no application was made after that date, the presumption is she died in 1832." As stated above, according to our file of the Volunteer, she died Jan. 22nd, 1832 and this statement of Mr. Linn the writer accepts as good authority."

Sept. 12, 1883. J.A.M.[21]

COMMENTARY

This article by Rev. Murray contains a good amount of information not presented elsewhere, particularly concerning the family of Mary Hays McCauley.

It begins with a revisionist view of how the marker at Mrs. McCauley's grave was erected in 1876. There was no "Monument Association," as some accounts have stated, but instead the monument was erected almost solely through the efforts of Peter Spahr. Murray also explains how the incorrect death date was originally engraved, and how he determined that the correct year of her death was 1832, not 1833 (see No. 9B).

Murray described the life and appearance of Mary Hays McCauley's son, John L. Hays, and insists that the middle initial "L." stood for Ludwig, after his maternal grandfather. This claim is not made by any other source. Young Hays served in the War of 1812 and died in Carlisle around 1845, according to Murray. He actually died in 1856 (see No. 8A).

Murray spoke with two of Mary Hays McCauley's grandchildren, John Hays and Polly McCleester. He records a significant quote from John Hays the grandson that he "often heard her say that if it had not been for her the battle of Monmouth would have gone against us." Polly McCleester had a fuzzy and inaccurate memory of her grandmother's pension. She tells a most interesting story on how her grandmother met Mr. Hays, her future husband, while she was working for the Irvines in Carlisle. Polly McCleester was particularly angry at those who stated her grandmother was Irish, and insisted "she was as Dutch as Sauer Kraut, and her maiden name was Mary Ludwig." This evidence is very difficult to interpret, since written records clearly show that Mary Hays McCauley was not the Mary Ludwig who married John Hays in 1769, because her husband's name was William Hays, no John, Casper or John Casper (see above Commentary to No. 3E).

Murray speaks in passing of an incorrect story circulating at the time that Molly was at one time married to a man named Larry O'Flaharty. He then closes with a series of quotations from Lossing and other sources concerning Molly's actions at Monmouth.

CONCLUSION

Murray's article is significant for the personal background he provides on Mary Hays McCauley's son John L. Hays and grandchildren John Hays and Polly McCleester. He also gives good information on Wesley Miles and on Peter Spahr and his role in erecting the tombstone at Mrs. McCauley's grave in 1876. Murray says that John Hays the grandson recalled his grandmother speaking about Monmouth. He also says that her granddaughter Polly McCleester insisted that her grandmother was born under the name Mary Ludwig and was "as German as Sauer Kraut."

3H. Edwin Salter, Letter, June 22, 1886.

Washington, D.C.
June 22, 1886

Major Yard,
Dear Sir:

My files of the [Monmouth] Democrat are scattered owing to recent moving and I cannot now find the papers with the corrected version of Molly Pitcher story. I think it was republished in 1878 in Monmouth Battle Year.

However, I enclose your letters that will recall the matter to your mind. And also a version which you can amend, alter or shape to suit yourself. It will hardly answer to let Mollie Pitcher pass off as "Dirty Kate." The Democrat has done her justice.

I presume this correction would do in an "appendix."

Yours truly,
Edwin Salter

Captain Molly Pitcher, the heroine of the Battle of Monmouth, was a daughter of John Hanna of Allentown, N.J. [illegible] was Mary or Molly Hanna and she was born about 1754. For a short time before the Revolution she was a servant in the family of James Bruere of Col. Lawrence's Monmouth regiment. She afterwards, it was said, married John Maban a soldier in the war. And after his decease she married again; her last husband was named McCauley.

She spent the last years of her life in Carlisle, Pa. Mr. W. Miles of Williamsport, Pa., but a native of Carlisle, in his young days was personally acquainted with Molly Pitcher who at one time attended his [illegible] mother. In the early part of 1876 Mr. Miles in a letter to Major J.S. Yard, gave many interesting reminiscences of the old lady. He was then engaged in the laudable effort of raising funds to have a monument erected to her memory to be [illegible] Centennial.

Mr. Miles said that he well remembered when she died. She was buried (in January 1833) with military honors by the volunteer companies of Carlisle—the "Guards,""Artillery" and "Infantry." It drew out the largest [illegible] of people ever seen in one place. It was a military funeral in all its detail—pall bearer, soldiers, muffled drums, arms reversed and the usual salute fired at the grave.

Mr. Miles' efforts to have a monument erected were successful and the Carlisle papers duly [illegible] the ceremonies. Mr. Miles himself thus describes the affair in a private letter dated July 31, 1876.

"I was present. An immense crowd thronged the old graveyard, patiently waiting for two hours in the terrible heat, for the arrival of the immense procession of friends, societies, etc. It [illegible] headed by the speakers and Carlisle band. Of the number in our carriage one was a granddaughter of Mollie's aged 75 years, named Polly McLaester, who unveiled the monument. Captain Vale delivered an excellent oration, recounting the scenes of Monmouth, the army movements. Mollie's devotion to her husband, her death and she taking his place at the cannon, her subsequent history, death and burial.

"You may be assured Lossing's 'dirty Kate' who died near Hudson Highlands, was not our New Jersey Molly Pitcher. Oh! No. Her bones repose in the old graveyard in Carlisle. She was well known by scores of my associates when we were boys; one was a member of the military guard who buried her. Her heroic deed at Monmouth was known and appreciated."

On her tombstone at Carlisle is the following inscription:

Mollie M'Cawley
Renowned in History as
Mollie Pitcher
The heroine of Monmouth
Died January 1833
Aged 79 years
Erected by the Citizens
Of Cumberland County July 4, 1876

Edwin Salter[22]

COMMENTARY

Edwin Salter was born in 1824 and died in 1888. He was a local historian of note and the author of two significant books, *Old Times in Old Monmouth* and *History of Monmouth and Ocean Counties, N.J.*[23]

Salter wrote this letter to Major James S. Yard, owner and editor of the *Monmouth Democrat,* in 1886. It is part of a chain of correspondence that is lost, since it makes reference to other letters that are not preserved. His primary purpose was to dispute the tradition, begun by Benson Lossing, that Molly spent her last days in the Hudson Highlands under the sobriquet "Dirty Kate" (see No. 2J above and its Commentary). As evidence, he cites a letter by Wesley Miles of Carlisle referring to Mary Hays McCauley, who was thought to be Molly Pitcher by the citizens of Carlisle (see Chapter 8). It is interesting, though, that Salter refers to Molly as "Captain Molly," a title more often applied to Margaret Corbin.

Salter follows Sally Smith Stafford's account that Molly was born in Allentown, New Jersey, as the daughter of John Hanna, and was at one time married to a soldier named John Maban (see No. 3A).

His significant addition is the birth date of "about 1754," for which he gives no source. It is notable that he does not make mention of this lineage or date in either of his two books on the history of Monmouth County (see No. 3I).[24]

Molly's death date is incorrectly cited as 1833 on her tombstone as quoted here. It was later corrected to read 1832 (see below No. 9B).

CONCLUSION

Salter rightly points out Benson Lossing's error in confusing the later life of Margaret Corbin ("Captain Molly"), who died near the Hudson Highlands in New York, with that of Mary Hays McCauley (Molly Pitcher), who died in Carlisle. He follows Sally Smith Stafford's otherwise unsubstantiated claim that Molly was born in Allentown, New Jersey as the daughter of John Hanna. He makes a significant addition by giving Molly's birthdate as 1754, but does not cite his evidence.

3I. Edwin Salter, A History of Monmouth and Ocean Counties, 1890.

CAPTAIN MOLLY PITCHER
HER BRAVERY AT FORT CLINTON AND MONMOUTH
–

HER SAD END

From various articles relating to this noted woman the following are selected:

"The story of a woman who rendered essential service to the Americans at the battle of Monmouth is founded on fact. She was a female of the masculine mould, and dressed in a mongrel suit, with the petticoats of her own sex and an artilleryman's coat, cocked hat and feathers. The anecdote usually related is as follows: Before the armies engaged in general action, two of the advanced batteries commenced a severe fire against each other. As the heat was excessive, Molly, who was the wife of a cannonier, constantly ran to bring her husband water from a neighboring spring. While passing to his post she saw him fall and on hastening to his assistance, found him dead. At the same moment she heard an officer order the cannon to be removed from its place, complaining he could not fill his post with as brave a man as had been killed. "No," said the intrepid Molly, fixing her eyes upon the officer, "the cannon shall not be removed for the want of some one to serve it; since my brave husband is no more, I will use my utmost exertions to avenge his death." The activity and courage with which she performed the office of cannonier, during the action, attracted the attention of all who witnessed it, and finally of Washington himself, who afterwards gave her the rank of lieutenant and granted her half pay during life. She wore an epaulette and was called ever after Captain Molly." –*Howe's Collections.*

Lossing in the Field Book of the Revolution mentions Molly Pitcher:

"Captain Molly was a stout, red-haired, freckle-faced young Irish woman with a handsome, piercing eye. The French officers, charmed by the story of her bravery, made her many presents. She would sometimes pass along the French lines with her cocked hat and get it almost filled with crowns."

The same writer visited the locality of Forts Montgomery and Clinton on the Hudson, where Molly Pitcher ended her days and there found old residents who remembered the famous Irish woman called Captain Molly, the wife of a cannonier who worked a field piece at the battle of Monmouth on the death of her husband. She generally dressed in the petticoats of her sex, with an artilleryman's coat over. She was in Fort Clinton with her husband when it was attacked in 1777. When the Americans retreated from the fort, as the enemy scaled the ramparts her husband dropped his match and fled. Molly caught it up, touched off the piece, and then scampered off. It was the last gun the Americans fired in the fort. Mrs. Rose remembered her as "Dirty Kate," living between Fort Montgomery and Buttermilk Falls, at the close of the war, where she died a horrible death from syphilitic disease. Washington had honored her with a lieutenant's commission for her bravery in the field of

Monmouth nearly nine months after the battle when reviewing its events."[25]

COMMENTARY

For biographical information on Edwin Salter, see the Commentary to No. 3H.

This excerpt simply quotes two earlier sources, Barber and Howe (No. 2G) and Benson Lossing (No. 2K, but with a few slight change sin wording). It is odd that Salter does not give Molly's birth place or date as he believed them to be; he says she was born as Mary Hanna in Allentown, New Jersey, in the 1886 letter quoted above (No. 3H).

CONCLUSION

This passage simply quotes two earlier sources, and does not include all the information the author had at hand.

3J. William H. Egle, "Two Heroines of the Revolution," 1893.

Mary Ludwig Hays

Mary Ludwig, the daughter of John George Ludwig, was born in Lancaster county, Pennsylvania, October 13th, 1744. Her parents were emigrants from the Palatinate, Germany. Mary's early years were spent in the family of afterwards Gen. William Irvine, then residing at Carlisle. Here she became acquainted with John Hays, to whom she was married July 24th, 1769. When the struggle for independence began, John Hayes enlisted in Capt. Francis Proctor's independent artillery company. With almost every command a certain number of married women were allowed, who did the washing, mending and frequently the cooking for the soldiers. Among these was the wife of John Hays, who gladly availed herself of the privilege of sharing the privations and dangers of war with her husband. Two years had passed, of march, bivouac and battle, and the devoted wife followed the fortunes of her partner in life. It was reserved for her, however, to immortalize her name by one heroic deed. It was in the action at Monmouth that her conduct became conspicuous. Sergeant Hays, who had charge of one of the guns, was severely wounded, and being carried away, the wife took his place in the forefront, and when the conflict was over assisted in carrying water to the disabled. This won her the soubriquet [sic] of "Moll Pitcher." There may have been other "Moll Pitchers," but this heroine of Monmouth was none the less than Mollie Hays. For her brave conduct upon coming to the attention of the Commander-in-Chief, Gen. Washington, he personally complimented her, as she departed for her home in Pennsylvania with her wounded soldier, to show his appreciation of her virtues and her valuable services to her country. Hays never returned to the army, and died a few years after the close of the war due to the effect of his wounds. Owing to the fact that other women were credited with this brave heroic act at Monmouth the State of Pennsylvania, as well as the Federal Government, in recognition of her distinguished services as herein set forth, granted her annuities for life. Mrs. Hays subsequently married George McCauly, and was afterwards familiarly known as Mollie McCauly. She was highly respected by the citizens of Carlisle, and at her death, January 22, 1833, was buried with the honors of war. In 1876 the patriotic people of Cumberland county appropriately marked her grave, and the day is coming when the name of Molly McCauly will be honored and revered by patriotic throughout the land. Inured to hardships, privations and sufferings in her life, she was a true matron of the Revolutionary era. Poor, it is true, but conspicuous in her loneliness and poverty. Peace to her ashes.[26]

COMMENTARY

Dr. William H. Egle was born in 1830 and died in 1901. He was a noted Pennsylvania genealogist and historian, being editor of the immense *Pennsylvania Archives* series as well as author of the 1876 book *An Illustrated History of the Commonwealth of Pennsylvania.*[27]

This article was reprinted, with a few minor spelling variations, in Egle's 1898 book *Some Pennsylvania Women During the War of the American Revolution.*[28]

Egle was a distinguished genealogist, but unfortunately did not chose to include any footnotes to cite his sources. However, his line of thinking and some of his references can be secured from William S. Stryker's similar account written by 1899.[29]

Egle, like Wing (No. 3E) and Stryker (No. 3L), believes that the Mary McCauly (McCauley) who died in Carlisle in 1833 [1832] was the actual Molly Pitcher of Monmouth fame, accepting the evidence of her friends and neighbors in Carlisle (see Chapter 8). His account is significant for stating that Mary Hays McCauley was born as Mary Ludwig on October 13, 1744, but he does not cite a source. He also does not give his source for saying that she was born in Lancaster County, Pennsylvania. Wing believed that she was born in Germany, but suggests but does not state that she was born in 1844 (No. 3E).

Egle states that Mary Ludwig married John Hays in 1769, and then followed him to war when he enlisted in the artillery during the Revolution. She took the place of her husband when he was badly wounded at Monmouth, and then took water to the wounded troops, thereby earning the nickname "Moll Pitcher."

Egle's argument on Molly's alleged origin breaks down on several key points, as has been pointed out by Jeremiah Zeamer and Samuel S. Smith.[30]

The first point is Mary Hays McCauley's date of birth. Her obituary and tombstone (Nos. 7O, 7P and 9B) state that she died in January 832 at the age of 79 years. This would place her birth date in 1753 or 1754, which is a decade later than Egle's 1744.

Secondly, there is no evidence that Mary Ludwig ever married John Hays. Records show that a marriage bond was issued between Mary Ludwig and Casper Hays on July 24, 1769[31] and that a marriage took place on July 25, 1769, at St. Michael's and Zion Church in Philadelphia between "Casper Hays (formerly Haas) and Mary Ludwick, wid."[32] Apparently Egle chose Casper Hays to be Mary's husband, since he could not find a John Hays; it was necessary to have her married to John Hays because Egle found records for John Hays serving in the Revolution, but not Casper. Therefore Egle invented a fictional character "John Casper Hays" to be Mary Ludwig's husband, a man who used the name Casper Hays on his marriage certificate and the name John Hays on his enlistment papers.

Thirdly, there is no evidence that a John Hays fought at Monmouth in the artillery (see discussion in Commentary to No. 3L).

Fourthly and most importantly, it does not matter who married Casper Hays or what battles John Hays fought in, because the real name of Mary Hays McCauley's first husband was William Hays. Court and tax records from Carlisle show that Mary Hays was the widow of Williams Hays in 1788, with a five year old son, before she married John McCauley sometime between 1789 and 1793.[33]

For these reasons, it is certain that Molly was not born under the name of Mary Ludwig. Whatever background information that Egle found on Mary Ludwig, including her date of birth, place of birth, and national origin, is not relevant to Molly Pitcher.

There is also no evidence to show that Molly took home her wounded husband after the battle of Monmouth, as Egle claims. Egle also errs on citing Mary Hays McCauley's death date. It was originally inscribed as 1833 by error, but was later corrected to read 1832 (see below No. 9B). It should also be noted that not everyone in Carlisle held Mary Hays McCauley in high respect, as Egle claims. According to Jeremiah Zeamer, a number of them thought that she was "a vulgar and profane old woman, uncouth in appearance and notoriously fond of grog."[34]

Egle incorrectly gives the name of Mary Hays' second husband as George McCauley instead of John McCauley.

CONCLUSION

Egle accepts that Mary Hays McCauley was the Molly Pitcher of Monmouth. He believes she was the daughter of John George Ludwig and was born in Lancaster County, Pennsylvania, in 1744, and then married John Hays in 1769. None of these points can be proven; she was married to William Hays and was more likely to have been born around 1754, place and parentage unknown. Egle expands on many of the points first proposed by Wing in 1878 (No. 3E) and shares many of the same arguments used by Stryker in 1899 (No. 3L).

3K. Frank R. Stockton, *Stories of the Revolution,* 1896.

MOLLY PITCHER

At the battle of Monmouth, where Lord Stirling so distinguished himself for the management of his artillery, another person of an entirely different station in life, of different nationality, and even different sex, played a very notable part in the working of the American cannon on that eventful day.

This was a young Irishwoman, wife of an artilleryman. She was a different disposition from ordinary women, who are glad enough to hide themselves in places of safety, if there is any fighting going on in their neighborhood. Molly was born with the soul of a soldier, and, although she much preferred going to war to staying at home and attending to domestic affairs. She was in the habit of following her husband on his various marches, and on the day of the Monmouth battle she was with him on the field.

The day was very hot. The rays of the sun came down with such force that many of the soldiers were taken sick and some died; and the constant discharges of musketry and artillery did not make the air any cooler. Molly devoted herself to keeping her husband as comfortable as possible, and she made frequent trips to a spring not far away to bring him water; and on this account he was one of the freshest and coolest artillerymen on the ground. In fact, there was no man belonging to the battery who was able to manage one of these great guns better than Pitcher.

Returning from one of her trips to the spring, Molly had almost reached the place where her husband was stationed, when a bullet from the enemy struck the poor man and stretched him dead, so that Molly had no sooner caught sight of her husband than she saw him fall. She ran to the gun, but scarcely had reached it before she heard one of the officers order the cannon to be wheeled back out of the way, saying that there was no one there who could serve it as it had been served.

Now Molly's eyes flashed fire. One might have thought that she would have been prostrated with grief at the loss of

her husband, but, as we have said, she had within her the soul
of a soldier. She had seen her husband, who was the same to
her as a comrade, fall, and she was filled with an intense
desire to avenge his death. She cried out to the officer not to
send the gun away, but to let her serve it; and, scarcely
waiting to hear what he would say, she sprang to the cannon,
and began to load it and fire it. She had so often attended her
husband, and even helped him in his work, that she knew all
about this sort of thing, and her gun was managed well and
rapidly.

It might be supposed that it would be a very strange thing
to see a woman on the battlefield firing a cannon; but even if
the enemy had watched Molly with a spyglass, they would
not have noticed anything to excite their surprise. She wore
an ordinary skirt, like other women of the time; but over this
was an artilleryman's coat, and on her head was a cocked hat
with some jaunty feathers stuck in it, so that she looked
almost as much like a man as the rest of the soldiers of the
battery.

During the rest of the battle, Molly bravely served her
gun; and if she did as much execution in the ranks of the
Redcoats as she wanted to do, the loss in the regiments in
front of her must have been very great. Of course, all the men
in the battery knew Molly Pitcher, and they watched her with
the greatest interest and admiration. She would not allow any
one to take her place, but kept on loading and firing until the
work of the day was done. Then the officers and men
crowded about her with congratulations and praise.

The next day General Greene went to Molly - whom he
found in very much the condition in which she had left the
battlefield, stained with dirt and powder, with her fine
feathers gone and her cocked hat dilapidated - and conducted
her, just as she was, to General Washington. When the
commander in chief heard what she had done, he gave her
warm words of praise. He determined to bestow upon her a
substantial reward; for any one who was brave enough and
able enough to step in and fill an important place, as Molly
had filled her husband's place certainly deserved a reward. It
was not according to the rules of war to give a commission to

a woman; but, as Molly had acted the part of a man, Washington considered it right to pay her for her services as if she had been a man. He therefore gave her the commission of a sergeant, and recommended that her name be placed on the list of half-pay officers for life.

Every one in the army soon came to hear of the exploit of Molly Pitcher, and it was not long before she was called Captain Molly. The officers of the French regiment on the American side were particularly pleased with this act of heroism in a woman, and invited Molly to review their troops; and as she walked down the long line of soldiers, nearly every man put a piece of money in the cocked hat which she held in her hand.

This was the last battlefield on which Molly Pitcher appeared, but it had not been her first. Not long before, she had been with her husband in Fort Clinton when it was attacked by a very large force of the British. After a vigorous defense, the Americans found that it was impossible to defend the fort, and a retreat was ordered. As the soldiers were rushing out of the rear of the fort, Molly's husband turned away from his gun, threw down his match - a piece of rope soaked in combustible substances, and slowly burning at one end, which was used in those days for discharging cannon - and ran for his life. Molly prepared to follow him; but as she saw that her husband's gun was loaded, she could not resist the desire to take one more crack at the enemy. So she stopped for an instant, picked up the match, touched off the gun, and dashed away after her husband. The cannon which then blazed out in the face of the advancing British was the last gun which the Americans fired in Fort Clinton.

Molly did not meet with the reward which was recorded so many other Jersey women who were of benefit to their State and country. She died not long after the close of the war; and if she had known that she was to be famous as one of the heroes of the Revolution, there is no doubt that she would have hoped that people would be careful that it was a man's service that she did to the country, and not a woman's.[35]

COMMENTARY

Frank R. Stockton was born in 1834, a member of the distinguished Princeton family that included Richard Stockton, a signer of the Declaration of Independence. He was noted as a writer of children's stories, which were "characterized by their imaginative, fanciful character and long episodic plots." His *Stories of New Jersey* was intended to be part of a series covering all the states, written by writers of note, but only two other titles in the set ever appeared (on Ohio and Georgia). *Stories of New Jersey* is best viewed today as a period piece whose stories are "rambling, yet curiously effective." Stockton died in 1902.[36]

Stockton recounts the major lines of the myth with embellishments and details from his own story telling style. His source appears to be primarily Lossing's *Pictorial Field-Book of the Revolution* (Nos. 2J and 2K above).

CONCLUSION

This account is an embellished version of the standard myth, as derived from Lossing.

3L. William S. Stryker, *The Battle of Monmouth,* 1899.

The story of Molly Pitcher is related in many different ways.

In Barber and Howe's *Historical Recollections of New Jersey* the episode is told somewhat in this manner: During the engagement Molly, the wife of a cannonier, was busy carrying water from a neighboring spring to refresh the weary artillerists. While engaged in this work her husband fell dead at his gun. An officer about this time ordered the gun to the rear. "No," said the woman, "the cannon shall not be removed for the want of someone to serve it; since my husband is no more I will use my utmost exertions to avenge his death." She then performed the duties of cannonier and attracted the attention of all in sight. Washington gave her the rank of Lieutenant, and half-pay for life. She wore an epaulette afterward and was called Captain Molly.

Custis, in his *Recollections,* relates very much the same story but gives this as the woman's expression, "Lie there, my darling, and I will avenge ye."

The version of the story given by Lossing in his *Field Book* and in his notes to Custis' *Recollections* makes her a young Irishwoman, twenty-two years of age and a sturdy camp-follower. When she heard the order for the removal of the gun, she seized the rammer and with skill and courage tried to avenge her husband's death. The next morning, covered with blood and dirt, she was presented by General Greene to General Washington, who gave her a piece of gold and conferred upon her a commission as sergeant. The fame of "Sergeant Molly" spread throughout the army and the French soldiers, interested in her story, filled her chapeau with silver coin as she passé din front of the ranks.

The Journal of Doctor Albigence Waldo, dated in camp opposite Brunswick on July 3, 1778, gives probably the most accurate account of the incident in these words: "One of the camp women I must give a little praise to. Her gallant, whom she attended in battle, being shot down, she immediately took up his gun and cartridges and like a Spartan heroine fought with astonishing bravery, discharging the piece with as much regularity as any soldier present. This a wounded officer, whom I dressed, told me he did see himself, she being in his platoon, and assured me I might depend on its truth."

Now this statement of Doctor Waldo represents the woman as the sweetheart of an infantry soldier, who fell dead in his platoon, instead of the wife of an artillerist, serving his cannon. A most diligent search of the pension records of the Old War Office at Washington fails to show a pension given, or half-pay for life allowed, to any woman for the death of her lover or husband at the Battle of Monmouth under any of the names by which Molly Pitcher has been known—Molly Maban, Molly Hanna, Molly Hayes or Molly McCauley.

An incident of a similar character occurred at Fort Washington, November 16, 1776. The Supreme Executive Council of Pennsylvania on June 29, 1779, directed that an order be drawn "in favour of Margaret Corbin for Thirty Dollars to relieve her present necessities she having been wounded and utterly disabled by three Grapeshot, while she filled with distinguished Bravery the post of her Husband, who was killed by her side, serving a piece of Artillery at Fort

Washington." In the *Pennsylvania Colonial Records* we find that after reciting her services in the language just stated, the Council ordered, "that she be recommended to a further consideration of the Board of War, This Council being of the opinion, that notwithstanding the rations which have been allowed her, she is not Provided for as her helpless situation really requires." In the Second Series of *Pennsylvania Archives* we find her name in Colonel Lewis Nicolas' Invalid Regiment as discharged at the close of the war in April 1783, and thus Margaret Corbin must have been carried on the regimental rolls of the Continental Army for all those years after her heroic exploit in November 1776.

Mention should also be made of the record concerning "Captain Molly" which is found in Boynton's *History of West Point* (page 166). In this work the story is told of her firing the last gun at the British when Fort Clinton was taken October 6, 1777. Then follows the anecdote of her good conduct at Monmouth, nine months afterwards, in the same language as given in Barber and Howe's *Historical Collections of New Jersey*. In addition to this story, however, extracts are given from manuscript notes made at the Academy by Major George Fleming, Ordnance and Military Storekeeper. These notes are dated October 7, 1786, April 21, June 12 and July 8, 1787, and relate to lodging and food furnished her at the village of Swinstown, now called Buttermilk Falls. This clearly shows that four years after the Revolution the Secretary of War, General Knox, attended to the maintenance of a woman called Molly Pitcher at the government's expense.

The story which is now generally believed, which has same incidental record proof and which is likely to be regarded in the future as the true account, may be related in this wise: Mary Ludwig, daughter of John George Ludwig, who came to this country with the Palatinates, was born October 13, 1744. In the year 1768 she was employed as a domestic in the family of William Irvine, of Carlisle, Pennsylvania, afterward a distinguished general in the Revolutionary War. On July 24, 1769, Mary Ludwig married John Casper Hayes, a barber of Carlisle. On December 1,

1775, her husband, his soldier name being John Hayes, enlisted in Colonel Thomas Procter's First Pennsylvania regiment artillery and served therein one year. He then enlisted in January, 1777, in Captain John Alexander's Company of Colonel William Irvine's Seventh Pennsylvania regiment. It appears that Molly Hayes followed her husband to the war, as we have seen was the custom in the British Army, and to some extent in the American troops. These women nursed the sick and assisted in the cooking and washing. Private Hayes was probably detailed on the battlefield of Monmouth from infantry service to help one of the batteries. His wife was aiding the cause by caring pitchers of water for the heated and wounded men. When John Hayes was wounded at the gun she took his place and performed some act of unusual heroism. On the death of John Hayes after the war Molly Hayes married a worthless fellow named John McCauley. Molly McCauley, known familiarly in Carlisle as "Molly Pitcher," lived on the corner of North and Bedford Streets in a house which since has been demolished. On February 27, 1822, the Pennsylvania Legislature granted her the sum of forty dollars and an annuity of the same amount. She died January 22, 1832, and is buried in the old Carlisle cemetery. On the one hundredth anniversary of the Declaration of Independence the citizens of Carlisle erected a neat monument over the heroine's grave, with the following inscription:

MOLLY MCCAULEY
RENOWNED IN HISTORY AS
"MOLLY PITCHER,"
THE HEROINE OF MONMOUTH.
DIED JANUARY 22, 1833
AGED SEVENTY-NINE YEARS.
ERECTED BY THE CITIZENS OF CUMBERLAND
COUNTY, JULY THE FOURTH 1876[37]

COMMENTARY

William S. Stryker was born in 1838 and died in 1900. After serving assorted duties in the Civil War, he was appointed brigadier general and adjutant general of the state of New Jersey in 1867. He compiled massive rosters of New Jersey soldiers in the Revolution, War of 1812, and Civil War, and also wrote a history of the battles of Princeton and Trenton, as well as this monograph on Monmouth. The Monmouth study was completed in 1899, but still had not been published when Stryker died. The manuscript was given by Mrs. Stryker to Professor William S. Miers at Princeton, who edited it and saw it published in 1927.[38]

Stryker gives an excellent summary of the accounts of Molly given Custis (No. 2D), Barber and Howe (No. 2G), and Lossing (No. 2K). His quotation of Dr. Albigence Waldo's diary (No. 1B) is our only current source for this passage. Stryker discusses the story of Margaret Corbin as "an incident of similar character" to Molly Pitcher, but uncritically accepts Lossing's claim that Molly Pitcher resided at Buttermilk Falls in the Hudson Highlands in the late 1780s, an account properly describing Margaret Corbin (see Commentary to No. 2I above). Stryker also accepts the story of Molly's presence at the battle of Fort Clinton in 1777.

Stryker follows the theory of E.P. Wing and William H. Egle that Molly Pitcher was born under the name Mary Ludwig (Nos. 3E and 3J). Since Egle does not cite footnotes to show his sources and Stryker does, the validity of this Ludwig claim will again be discussed here. Wing cites a family bible to show that Molly was born as Mary Ludwig, but Stryker chooses not to cite him as a source.

Stryker accepted that the Mary McCauley who died in Carlisle in 1833 was the actual Molly Pitcher of Monmouth fame, accepting the evidence of her friends and neighbors in Carlisle (see Chapter 8). Since Mary McCauley's obituary stated that "Her first husband's name was Hays who was a soldier in the Revolution" (No. 7P), Stryker looked in the War Offices for records of a pension being issued to either Mary Hays or Mary McCauley for the death of her "lover or husband" at Monmouth. None could be found. He also looked for a similar pension for either Mary Hanna, the birth name for Molly Pitcher suggested by Sarah Smith Stafford, or Molly Maban, another possible married name for Molly Pitcher suggested by Stafford (No. 3A), but could not find one either.[39]

Stryker then looked for any evidence of a woman named Mary marrying a man named Hays in Carlisle just before the Revolution. Following Egle, he located a marriage bond issued on July 24, 1769 between Mary Ludwig and "John Casper Hayes, a barber of Carlisle."[40] Stryker then searched Revolutionary war muster rolls and found that John Hayes served in Colonel Thomas Procter's First Pennsylvania artillery in 1775-1776. In 1777 he enlisted in Colonel William Irvine's 7th Pennsylvania Regiment, which was present at Monmouth.[41] Stryker then suggests that Hays was helping to man one of the batteries when he was wounded, and Molly, who had been bringing water to the men, then "performed some act of unusual heroism." Her husband, according to Stryker, had been only wounded, not killed, as all earlier accounts of the story state.[42]

Stryker fleshes out Molly's background by following information printed by Egle: she was born on October 13, 1744 as Mary Ludwig, daughter of John George Ludwig, who had come to America from the "Palatinates" in Germany. Curiously, Stryker does not give a birthplace for Mary Ludwig, whereas Egle claims she was born in Lancaster County, Pennsylvania. He follows Egle and Wing to state that Mary was in Carlisle in 1768 as a servant to the family of William Irvine, who later served as a general in the Revolution. It was there she met and married John Casper Hayes in 1769.[43]

Stryker's account is significant for accepting a German origin to Molly Pitcher (Mary Ludwig Hays), following the account published by Egle in 1893. This lineage rivals Sarah Smith Stafford's claim that Molly was born as Mary Hanna, an Irish woman from Allentown, New Jersey. However, his argument breaks down on a number of points, as has been shown above (see Commentary to No. 3E).[44]

The first point is Mary Hays McCauley's date of birth. Her obituary and tombstone (Nos. 7O, 7P and 9B) state that she died in January 1833 at the age of 79 years. This would place her birth date in 1753 or 1754, which is a decade later than the 1744 date proposed by Stryker and Egle and suggested by Wing. Most notable is the fact that Stryker and Egle give an exact date for her birth, October 13, 1744, but do not cite any evidence for it. This is particularly unusual, since Stryker was a thorough historian and gives detailed footnotes for most of the other facts cited in the section of his book where he deals with Molly Pitcher. Also, it should be noted that Stryker does not offer a birthplace for Mary Hays McCauley, even though Egle claims she was born in Lancaster County, Pennsylvania.

Second, and most critical, is the matter of the 1769 marriage bond. The actual bond cited by Stryker was between a Mary Ludwick and Casper Hays. It is reasonable to accept that "Ludwick" is a variant spelling of "Ludwig." But it is not reasonable to accept that Casper Hays' full name was "John Casper Hays," as Stryker claims. This was a step that Stryker, like Egle, found necessary to take because he could not find any evidence of Casper Hays serving in the Revolution. He did, though, find evidence of John Hayes being in the Revolution. Since it was necessary for Mary to be married to a Revolutionary soldier, Stryker invented the persona he needed, "John Casper Hayes."[45]

However, Stryker's fictional "John Casper Hayes" did not quite fill the bill either.

Stryker claims that when "John Casper Hayes" enlisted in Procter's Artillery in 1775, he used his "soldier name" of John Hayes. There is absolutely no other evidence to support this assertion. Stryker also claims that this John Hayes is the same individual who enlisted in the 7th Pennsylvania regiment in 1777 as John Hays. This assumption cannot be otherwise supported, either, even without examining the difference of spelling in "Hayes" and "Hays." This equation is necessary in order to place "John Casper Hayes/Hays" at Monmouth in 1778. But because the John Hays of the 7th Pennsylvania was serving in the infantry, and the husband of Molly Pitcher was clearly a member of an artillery unit, Stryker has to make one more assumption, that "Private Hayes was probably detailed on the battle-field of Monmouth from infantry service to help with one of the batteries."[46]

These assumptions cause the theory of Wing, Egle and Stryker to fall apart, as Jeremiah Zeamer and Samuel S. Smith have pointed out. Mary McCauley was not married to John Hays/Hayes at the time of Monmouth, and was not born of German blood as Mary Ludwig. Whatever background Stryker found on the Mary Ludwig who married Casper Hays in Carlisle in 1769, relates to a different person than the Mary Hays McCauley who was known in Carlisle as Molly Pitcher until her death in 1832. It is now clear that the Revolutionary soldier to whom Mary Hays McCauley was married was named William Hays, a man who can be shown to have been a member of a Pennsylvania artillery unit at the time of the battle (see Chapter 12).[47]

Molly's death date is incorrectly cited as 1833 on her tombstone as quoted. It was later corrected to read 1832 (see below No. 9B).

CONCLUSION

Stryker believed that Mary Hays McCauley was the Molly Pitcher who fought at Monmouth. His claim that she was born as Mary Ludwig is based on research first published by C.P. Wing and William H. Egle that includes a contrived interpretation of a 1769 marriage between Mary Ludwick (Ludwig) and John Casper; likewise he invented the persona of "John Casper Hayes/Hays" in order to place Mary Ludwig's husband at Monmouth. In addition, Stryker's John Hayes/Hays was a member of the infantry in 1778, not the artillery. Though Stryker's book *The Battle of Monmouth* was not published until 1927, he had written it by 1899 and freely shared his interpretations with other scholars at the time.[48] Wing's and Egle's theory, as explicated by Stryker, was accepted by numerous later scholars, most notably John Landis (see No. 4E), and remains today the principal source for the widely held belief that Molly Pitcher was born under the German name of Mary Ludwig.

"Moll Pitcher, The Heroine of Monmouth," by Currier and Ives (see No. 2H)

4. SECONDARY SOURCES, 1900-1912

4A. Isabella Crater McGeorge, "A New Jersey Heroine of the Revolution," 1900.

Of the many Jersey women who rank as heroines in the Revolutionary War—those who actually fought the British, those who outwitted them, those who nursed the wounded, those who acted as guides and those who did without tea, using as a substitute that vile decoction of *Ceonothus Americanius,* Jersey tea—all merit full recognition and deserve unstinted admiration, credit and honor; But it is my design to call attention to but one brave and patriotic woman on New Jersey's brilliant constellation, Mary Ludwig Hays, and, if possible, to eradicate some erroneous impressions. Very few know of her by her correct name and fewer of her nationality and that she was by birth a Jersey woman.

On a small dairy farm that lay between Princeton and Trenton, in Mercer County, New Jersey, there was born in 1754, of German parentage, Mary Ludwig. As is the manner in German households, Mary was taught first obedience without question; to work willingly and cheerfully; to utilize what was at hand, and make the most of circumstances; when times bettered not—to thank God they were no worse.

It is said that she was not pretty, but had Titian hair, blue eyes, small features and was rather short in stature—but was so strong that with ease she could carry a three-bushel bag of wheat across her shoulder and deposit the same in the upper room of the granary. As was the custom of the times, she wore the "short gown and petticoat." This consisted of a sack like upper garment, and her preference was for a blue and white cotton skirt.

A lady from Carlisle, Pennsylvania, said to be the wife of General Irving, of French and Indian war fame, was visiting at Trenton in 1774, and being advised that Mary Ludwig would be satisfactory help, hired the girl and took her to Pennsylvania.

In Carlisle, Mary met her first fate, an Englishman, one John Hays, the barber; they were married and Mary worshiped her husband with the whole devotion of the German nature.

When the echoes of Lexington, penetrating Pennsylvania's woods, reached that peaceful village, John Hays was among the first to take the war fever, and soon joined the continental army. Small pay and frequently no pay at all—there was nothing to send the wife, so Mary Hays continued in the service of the Irvings—baked, brewed, spun, washed and preserved. The neighbors teasingly reminded her that she "had lost her pretty barber" and that she "would never again lay eyes on him."

But one July morning of that same year, after hanging her wash upon the lines, she went to a hillside to gather blackberries. She noticed a horseman "riding like lightning to General Irving's" (her own words, as she aftertime related the occurrence to her granddaughter, Polly McLaester). To the house she went hoping there might be word from the army. There was a letter from John Hays and great news indeed—for it said that she was to take horse with the bearer and return to New Jersey, where she was to go to her parents near Princeton; that they wanted her, and also being there he could sometimes have the chance of seeing her. Without a moment's hesitation she unpegged her own clothing from the lines, and she said they were "quite wet;" made them into a bundle, which was attached to the pommel of the saddle, mounted the horse behind the messenger and started for home. A most novel proceeding. The clothes were quite dry before she reached her New Jersey home and upon a real horse! To Mrs. Irving's credit be it said she made no objection to the loss of so valuable a servant, but aided her departure, bidding her God-speed.

Under her father's roof her child, John Hays Jr., was born, and there she lived quietly and industriously, as became a wife and mother. Those who have regarded her as a camp follower—flinging coarse jokes at the boys and being generally a hale fellow, none too clean personally or morally—most cruelly misjudge this kind-hearted woman. The fact that her husband desired her to visit him in camp is sufficient. She did whenever she had the chance, and no doubt considered it "good form." She saw him at Trenton and before Princeton on January 2, 1777.

General Washington quietly left the Trenton camp and surprising the three British regiments remaining at Princeton, took three hundred prisoners. Deeming it wise to leave before Lord Cornwallis could arrive wither reinforcements, he slipped off to Morristown, New Jersey—the noise of the cannon being mistaken at Trenton for thunder. Here was where Mary L. Hays had the chance to distinguish herself. After the continental army had gone she came to hunt among the wounded and slain for her husband's friend, as John Hays had charged her to find Dilwyn dead or alive and care for him. She came across a cannon charged and with a lighted fuse near by. This was a piece of rope soaked in some combustible substance, and slowly burning at one end, which was used for discharging cannon. The gun is said to have been a British cannon which was too cumbersome for the continental army to drag to Morristown. Mary Hays could not resist the impulse to take a hand—so she touched the gun off at just the right moment—for Lord Cornwallis's advance guard was within range. Fearing a trap, they were delayed an hour in hunting for the concealed foe, and when they swarmed into the enclosure they could find no gunners, never suspecting the red-headed German girl, who was carrying away a dead soldier. It was Dilwyn, but he was not dead. Mary had seen a moving hand and pulling away the obstructions had rescued her husband's friend by throwing him across her shoulder, as she used to do with the wheat bags, and carrying him to her father's house two miles distant. Here she nursed him back to health. In grateful acknowledgement, he sent her a box of fine dress goods, which she never made up, but cherished as being too lovely to mar with scissors.

The delay of the British at Princeton was of great advantage to the continentals, who rapidly pushed northwest, and by midnight were eighteen miles away. This was bitterly cold weather, and after a hard fight was considered a remarkable achievement. The soldiers had no food since the night previous, and it is said that they fell asleep as soon as they halted, so overcome were they.

In the meantime, Lord Cornwallis rushed on to New Brunswick to save the British stores at that point, and finding them safe gave up pursuit. General Washington went into winter quarters at Morristown, New Jersey.

Mary Hays stayed at her father's until June 27, 1778, then, as the army came her way, the chance to see her husband was not to be neglected, and Mary Ludwig Hays became the heroine of Monmouth.

That Sunday, June 28, 1778, was a blazing day, the thermometer stood at 96 degrees. General Lee had blundered and rightly deserved the censure of the commander-in-chief. Confidence being restored by the appearance of General Washington upon the scene the "continentals wheeled into line, altho' under fire, and took position as if on parade." Colonel Monckton's grenadiers, attempting to drive them back, were repulsed by General Knox's artillery with great slaughter, A second and third attempt were made, when Colonel Monckton received his death wound and fell from his horse. General Wayne came up with a force of farmers, their shirt sleeves rolled up as if at harvest (and it was indeed a harvest for death) and forced the British back, leaving the body of their commander on the field. After the battle, the continentals buried Colonel Monckton's body in the churchyard near-by and later the place was marked with a neat stone.

In the west ravine is the spring from which Mary L. Hays carried water for her husband's cannon and for his heated comrades of Knox's artillery. She used the cannon's bucket, a fixture of the gun of that age. She said that when she came up with a full bucket of water, the men would call out "here comes Molly with her pitcher," which was probably a bit of pleasantry on their part, and that when the battle grew fiercer, they abbreviated the call to "Molly Pitcher," and from that time always spoke of her by that name.

Overcome by fatigue and heat, Sergeant Hays dropped beside the cannon he was working—not killed as was so often told, for with his wife's efficient care he came out all right by evening. General Knox ordered the removal of the gun, but when the men came to take it away, they found the gunner's wife

"loading, firing that six-pounder,
And she bravely, 'till we won, worked the gun....
Tho' like tigers fierce they fought us,
to such zeal had Molly brought us,
That tho' struck with heat and thirsting,
Yet of drink we felt no lack;
There she stood amid the clamor,
Swiftly handling sponge and rammer,
While we swept with wrath condign, their line."
Thomas Dunn English

General Greene complimented her on the field, but when General Washington sent for her the next morning, she was in a predicament—her clothing was so torn and soiled. Some one solved the difficulty by putting on her a soldier's coat, which covered a multitude of rents and served to make her more presentable. From this circumstance arose the tradition that she fought in a man's clothing. The fact is, it was so excessively hot that day, the soldiers threw off their coats and fought in their shirt sleeves, and it is not unlikely that with her frequent trips to the spring for water and her arduous work at the guns that she would put on an additional covering.

Sergeant Hays was very proud of his wife that day, and he lived to tell how Washington praised her and conferred the brevet of captain on her, hence her title, Captain Molly. He also said that she should have half-pay for life. Then the grand French officer General Lafayette, asked that his men "might have the pleasure of giving madam a trifle." Although there were no French troops on the field at that date, yet there were many French officers who had volunteered in American regiments. The Frenchmen are ever appreciative of heroines who have worsted the English and they showered their extra silver upon the 'brave Marie'"—the trifle proving to be a hatful of coin.

After the close of the war, Mary with her husband and child returned to Carlisle, Pennsylvania, where they lived happily. John Hays took up his trade and his wife did washing—and with the annuity of $40.00 granted by congress they managed comfortably until the death of John Hays in the early part of the nineteenth century.

In a few years Mary again married and her second venture was most unfortunate. McCauley was a brutal, intemperate Irishman. It is said that he frequently cursed and beat her and that he cared more for her pension, pittance that it was, than for the fame she had won. Fortunately she outlived McCauley, and so for several years had respite from his cruelty.

An instance of the tender-heartedness of Mary has been related by her granddaughter. Upon one occasion the great-grandchild, infant son of Polly McAlester was very ill, the great-grandmother, our Monmouth heroine, though well advanced in years lay upon the floor all night to keep the cradle constantly rocking wit the gentle touch that was so comforting to the babe. A more uncomfortable position could not have been found, yet this old woman faithfully kept it up the entire night and felt amply repaid by the recovery of the child.

In January, 1833, she died of pneumonia contracted at the wash-tub, aged 79 years. She was buried, at her request, in the same grave as her first husband, John Hays, in the village cemetery at Carlisle, Pennsylvania, quietly and without military honors. Forty-three years later, on July 4, 1876, the citizens of Cumberland County, Pennsylvania, placed a handsome slab of Italian marble over her grave. Upon it is inscribed the time of her death and that she was the heroine of Monmouth.

At Freehold, New Jersey, November 13, 1884, there was unveiled the Monmouth battle monument, a granite structure over a hundred feet high, that cost $40,000. At the base of the shaft are five bronze tablets, each five feet high by six in width, commemorative of that famous battle. One of these is called the "Molly Pitcher," and shows Mary Hays using that six-pounder; her husband lies exhausted at her feet, and General Knox is seen directing the artillery; the Tennent church is seen at her left. Thus two communities remember her fittingly.

The placed marked as Molly Pitcher's well on the Amboy division of the Pennsylvania railroad, an account of which recently appeared in several of the eastern dailies, is a good half-mile southwest of the point where Knox's division Was stationed on June 28, 1778. The well so marked was not dug until in the eighteen hundred and fifties, some twenty-two or more years after the death of Mary Hays.

So mistakes are cumulative. Mary Ludwig Hays was not Irish, not a camp-follower, but an unselfish mother, a successful nurse, a woman who had the genius to perceive a critical situation and to act at once, and she was a Jersey woman. Her enthusiasm was a potent factor on that June day and the victory at Monmouth strengthened and sealed the French alliance. Thence the continental army moved on to victory, and left us their heirs.

> "Nor while the grass grows on the hill, and streams flow
> through the vale,
> May we forget our father's deeds or in that covenant fail;
> God keep the fairest, noblest land that lies beneath the
> sun,
> Our country, our whole country and our country ever
> one."[1]

COMMENTARY

McGeorge believes that Molly Pitcher was Mary Hays McCauley, who died in Carlisle, Pennsylvania, in 1832. In this she is in agreement with a number of other scholars. However, McGeorge claims that Molly was not Irish, but was of German origin. Specifically, she claims that Molly was born in 1754 under the name Mary Ludwig, "on a dairy farm that lay between Princeton and Trenton, in Mercer County, New Jersey."

These claims need to be looked at one by one.

The 1754 birth date first was put forward by Edward Salter in the 1880s in connection with his claim that Molly was born under the name Mary Hanna in Allentown, New Jersey (see No. 3H above). McGeorge appears to have followed Salter's date, but changed Molly's maiden name and place of birth.

McGeorge's claim that Molly's maiden name was Mary Ludwig follows a theory first put forward by C.P. Wing in 1879 (No. 3E) and followed by Wiilliam H. Egle in 1893 (No. 3J) and also William S. Stryker by 1899 (No. 3L). Wing (No. 3E) cites a family bible that said that Molly's maiden name was Mary Ludwig. This claim is suspect, though, because no later accounts make mention of it (see Commentary to No. 3E). Neither Egle (No. 3J) nor Stryker (No. 3L) cite their source for Molly having a maiden name of Ludwig.

McGeorge may have been familiar with a baptismal certificate seen by C. Malcolm B. Gilman showing that a Mary Ludwig was baptized at the Presbyterian Church in Lawrenceville, New Jersey, on October 13, 1754.[2] However, this birth certificate cannot be located today (see Commentary to No. 5F).

McGeorge is the first account to place Molly's birth between Princeton and Trenton. This may be through confusion on the location of Allentown, New Jersey, in upper Monmouth County, as cited by Salter, but may also have been assumed because Lawrenceville is located in that part of Mercer County. Having Molly be at her father's farm in Mercer County in 1777-1778 also makes her conveniently available to join her husband during the Monmouth campaign, rather than be a common "camp follower," which is a term with negative sexual overtones.

This account uses General Irving's wife as the means to get Molly to Carlisle before the Revolution. Wing, Egle and Stryker also connect Molly with the Irvines in (using the more proper spelling of their name).[3]

McGeorge, like Wing, Egle and Stryker, claims that Molly married John Hays, an Englishman and a barber, in Carlisle before the war. This is one the most demonstrable shortcomings of her entire account. Jeremiah Zeamer and Samuel S. Smith have ably demonstrated that Mary Hays McCauley was married to William Hays of Carlisle at the time of the Revolution, not John Hays.[4] The removal of John Hays (and Casper Hays) from the account negates the possibility that Molly was born under the name Mary Ludwig (see Commentary to Nos. 3E and 3L).

McGeorge seems to amplify Wing's account by stating that Mary Hays' son John Hays Jr. was born "under her father's roof" in Mercer County New Jersey, apparently around the year 1776. Wing simply states that her son was born in Trenton (No. 3E).

This account is the first appearance of the story that Molly saved her husband's friend Dilwyn at the battle of Princeton on January 3, 1777. McGeorge does not give a source for the story. It does, however, appear to have some similarities with the story told by Wing of Molly saving a friend from the burial pits after the battle of Monmouth (No. 3E). Her account of Molly finding an abandoned and loaded cannon on the field and then firing it at the British advance guard at the close of the battle of Princeton, is also not related by any earlier source. It sounds somewhat similar to the story first appearing in Lossing that Molly fired the last cannon short at the battle of Fort Clinton (see No. 2J).

McGeorge follows Wing and Egle to state that Molly's husband was a Sergeant at the battle of Monmouth (Nos. 3E and 3J).

McGeorge is the only account to have Molly getting water for the troops from the west ravine during the battle. This would not be likely because the west ravine was between the contending lines for much of the battle (see Chapter 13 below). In addition, McGeorge's account is the only one to place Molly's husband in Knox's artillery at the battle. Most early accounts place him in one of Procter's batteries (see Chapter 12 below).

This account is interesting in that it has Molly's husband collapse from heat exhaustion instead of being killed. This is probably an effort by McGeorge to account for the presence of Molly's husband, Mr. Hays, in Carlisle after the war. McGeorge, though, states that Mr. Hays survived to the early 1800s. This is clearly an error. Court records from Carlisle show that Molly's husband probably died in 1787, since she appeared in Orphan's Court in 1788 as a widow seeking relief for herself and her five year old son.[5]

McGeorge's mention of General Greene complimenting Molly after the battle is reminiscent of Custis' account (No. 2D). The story of Lafayette and the French soldiers giving her a hatful of coins is also told by Lossing (No. 2K), based on information he received from the widow of Alexander Hamilton (No. 2I). McGeorge has Molly being given the rank of Captain by George Washington, whereas most other accounts say she was commissioned either a Sergeant (Lossing, No. 2K) or lieutenant (1837 *New-Jersey State Gazette* article, No. 2B, and Barber and Howe, No. 2G).

Molly's death date on her tombstone is incorrectly cited as 1833. It was later corrected to read 1832 (see below No. 9B).

CONCLUSION

McGeorge's is a long and unique account. It contains significant new material not previously cited elsewhere, most notably concerning her presence at the battle of Princeton. Unfortunately she gives no sources for this information. McGeorge believes that Mary Hays McCauley was the historical Molly Pitcher, and follows the theory of E.P. Wing, William H. Egle and William S. Stryker that her maiden name was Mary Ludwig. The Ludwig theory, though, can be shown to be false.

McGeorge says that Molly was married to John Hays at the time of the battle of Monmouth, but evidence shows that her husband at the time was William Hays. McGeorge follows Egle to place the birth of her son in Mercer County, but errs concerning the death date of her husband. She rationalizes some of the elements of the myth, explaining the names "Molly Pitcher" and "Captain Molly," and cleansing her of the status as camp follower.

McGeorge's purpose is clearly stated in her final paragraph: she is anxious to show that Molly Ludwig Hays was from New Jersey and was not Irish or a camp follower. Her account has played a key role, along with those of Wing (No. 3E), Egle (No. 3J), Stryker (No. 3L) and Landis (No. 4E) in perpetuating the belief that Molly Pitcher was born under the name Mary Ludwig.

4B. Francis B. Lee, New Jersey as a Colony and as a State, 1902.

Molly Pitcher, rightly Mary Ludwig, daughter of John George Ludwig, a German Palatine; *b.* in Pa., probably at Carlisle, Oct. 13, 1744; married John Hays 1769, a gunner in Proctor's 1st Pa. Art.; she followed him into the field, and when he was shot at Monmouth took his place; "served nearly eight years in the army," placed on list of half pay officers; married Sergeant George McCauley, or McKolly; died Jan. 22, 1833, and buried with military honors.[6]

COMMENTARY

This account follows the theory begun by Wing, Egle and Stryker (Nos. 3E, 3J and 3L) that Molly was born of German birth as Mary Ludwig. This theory breaks down because Mary Hays McCauley was first married to William Hays, not John Hays, as demonstrated above (see Commentaries to Nos. 3E and 3L).

CONCLUSION

This account is unique for placing Molly's birth in Carlisle. There is no evidence to support this statement.

4C. Frank R. Symmes, History of Old Tennent Church, 1904.

One of the thrilling stories about the Battle is that of Molly Pitcher called the "heroine of Monmouth." Her maiden name was Mary Ludwig, of German descent, born in 1754 in New Jersey on a farm situated between Princeton and Trenton, and married John Hays, of Carlisle, Pa., who joined the Continental army, and Mary came back home to live with her father. As the army came across New Jersey she visited her husband and was with him on the Sunday of the Battle. During the Battle she aided her husband and the gunners in Gen. Knox's artillery by carrying water in the cannon's bucket for the thirsty men, who in pleasantry called her "Molly Pitcher." Her husband, overcome with fatigue and heat dropped down by the cannon, when his wife jumped forward and helped "work the gun." A bas-relief on the monument gives this scene showing her as "an ideal woman of great muscular power. Her (exhausted) husband is at her feet, and Gen. Knox is seen in the background directing his artillery line. A wounded soldier uses his right hand instead of left in thumbing the vent. This, it is readily seen, improves the composition of the picture. The Old Tennent Church, still standing as a memorial of the battle, is seen on the extreme left of the relief." Molly soon nursed her husband to his usual strength after the battle. Gens. Washington, Greene and Lafayette complimented her. Congress bestowed on her an annuity of $40. After the death of her first husband she married a man by the name of McCauley. She died Jan. 1833, and was buried at Carlisle, Pa. Years afterwards on July 4, 1876 the citizens of Cumberland Co., Pa., placed a handsome Italian marble stone over the grave. She was not a coarse campfollower, as sometimes has been said, but a robust, industrious, kind-hearted woman, faithful as a wife and mother. Mrs. Isabella (Crater) McGeorge has written a fine sketch of this subject in the American Monthly Magazine of Nov. 1900.[7]

COMMENTARY

Frank R. Symmes was born on October 24, 1856. He graduated from Princeton University in 1881 and from Princeton Theological Seminary in 1886. He was ordained as the fifteenth Pastor of Old Tennent Church in 1890 and served there until his death on March 28, 1928. His account of Molly Pitcher's origin and actions closely follows that of Isabella Crater McGeorge (No. 4A), his acknowledged source.

CONCLUSION

Symmes' account is derivative form McGeorge's and adds nothing new to the story of Molly Pitcher.

4D. Jeremiah Zeamer, "Molly McCauley Monument," 1905.

Molly McCauley Monument
Why Expend $5,000 Upon Her Memory and Nothing
Upon Cumberland County's Real
Revolutionary Heroes?

A bill appropriating $5,000 from the State treasury for a monument at Carlisle to the memory of Molly McCauley "renowned as Molly Pitcher," has passed the State Senate and is in a fair way of also passing the House. If it reaches the Governor he should before appending his signature, inquire fully into the merits of it, for it does not appear that the members of the Legislature have done so.

The grave of Molly McCauley in the Old Graveyard at Carlisle is already appropriately marked, having a large and elegant marble headstone, provided by the citizens of Carlisle and unveiled by them with public ceremony on July 4, 1876. Besides this it is reported that the patriotic orders have secured from the War Department the promise of a cannon with which to mark the spot of her interment still more conspicuously. Considering the small and doubtful service Molly McCauley rendered the country this is about all the respect that can be awarded her memory in justice to history.

Molly McCauley is neither the historical nor moral character to hold up to young Americans for emulation. Her only claim to distinction was won on the battle of Monmouth, and that the imaginative space writers—who never investigate—have magnified and glorified out of all resemblance to the actual deed—carrying water for the soldiers of the battery to which her husband belonged. There is nothing anywhere in the records, or in the early prints, to authenticate, or to make plausible, the claim that she helped to man the gun after her husband was disabled. For forty years prior to her death she lived in Carlisle, and up until recently it was an easy matter to find old citizens who knew her personally. Some of these often heard her tell of the Revolution, and of having been in it, but not one of them ever heard her tell of helping to man a gun at Monmouth, or of meeting Washington, or Wayne, or of receiving a commission for gallantry. Had anything so remarkable occurred she certainly would have felt sufficient pride in it to remember it and sometimes speak of it. Had the young people who associated with her in her late years believed that she had performed extraordinary deeds in battle they would have asked her to tell them. Two newspapers in Carlisle at the time of her death published brief obituary notices of her, but neither made any reference to the Monmouth incident. Had she really fired a cannon upon that occasion it would have been such an extraordinary performance that the newspapers would have known of it at the time of her death when the incident was yet comparatively fresh and corroboration easy. The fact that they made not the slightest allusion to anything of the kind should be satisfactory proof that it did not occur.

The late Rev. Dr. Wing, in a footnote in his history of Cumberland County, briefly relates the regulation story concerning her but states that it has been embellished. In after years he acknowledged to the late Bennett Bellman, Esq.—as Mr. Bellman records in the Carlisle Herald of June 2, 1897—that "the evidence on Molly McCauley is too unsatisfactory to be put down as legitimate history." To erect a public monument upon such unauthenticated and doubtful history is simply pandering to a morbid sentiment upon which sensational space writers have been ringing the changes ad nauseam for the past twenty-five years. It would be a reproach to the section in which it is proposed to erect it, for Cumberland has

Revolutionary achievements to her credit much more glorious than those claimed for Molly McCauley.

But there are other reasons why Molly McCauley does not deserve so great a mark of honor and distinction. Whatever she may have been in her youth in her latter years—in the period when the late old people of Carlisle knew her—she was a vulgar, profane old woman, uncouth in appearance and notoriously fond of grog. When drunk she would make exhibitions of herself on the streets and naturally was much guyed by the rude gamins of that day. It was from the Carlisle bad boy of seventy-five and eighty years ago that she received the titles of "Sergeant Molly" and "Captain Molly," and not form any commission that was ever bestowed upon her. She was so repulsive in manner and appearance that children were afraid of her. For some years she lived at the corner of North and Bedford Streets, a locality—as stated in a paper read before the Carlisle Civic Club and published in the Carlisle Herald of March 4, 1902—was then known as "Hell Street," presumably because of the nature of its inhabitants. It is said that she nursed women in sickness, and for this her admirers extol her much, but she more frequently was employed to boil soap, whitewash fence and do other rough work congenial to her rough nature. It is not known that she belonged to any church. Woman addicted to vulgarity, profanity and grog never have religious scruples. Neither do they make good nurses for the sick.

These are not idle assertions, but established facts, authenticated by persons who nearly had a friendly leaning towards Molly, and therefore made their representations as favorable as the truth permitted.

In 1876 Wesley Miles wrote in the Carlisle Herald that she "was prone to indulge in passion and profanity." Molly nursed Mr. Miles' mother in her last illness and after her death kept house for his father, which gave the boy Wesley special opportunities of knowing her. She was a heroine in his eyes and he would have shielded her but her "passion and profanity" were so pronounced that he could not shield them and he did not attempt it.

Peter Spahr, whose efforts secured the monument that now stands upon her grave, described her as "a every masculine person, alike rough in appearance and character, small and heavy, with bristles at the end of her nose, and she could both drink whiskey and swear." This description he gave to the late Rev. Dr. Murray, who embodied it in an article which he published in an article in the Carlisle Volunteer on September 12, 1883.

In the same article Dr. Murray relates that William Parks, and Molly McCleester, who was a granddaughter of Molly McCauley, both informed him that Molly drank grog and used language not the most polite, but"—in the way of extenuation added—"she was a kind hearted woman and helpful to the sick and needy."

The late Harriet M. Foulke, who died in 1898 at the age of 93, knew Molly well, as she worked in the Foulke family when Harriet was a little girl. Miss Foulke unhesitatingly pronounced her a vulgar, profane, drunken old woman, and would remonstrate personally with newspaper publishers for admitting to their columns so much trash concerning Molly McCauley, as people knowing the truth about the woman were sure to be disgusted with it.

Besides these there are others that might be quoted to show that the memory of Molly McCauley is not entitled to the extraordinary recognition that the bill in question proposes to give her. Morally the present generation owes as much to itself, and to the future, as to the past. To erect an expensive public monument to such a character as Molly McCauley, would have a baneful effect upon the young womanhood of this and upcoming generations. They would look upon its grandeur and reason thus: "Molly McCauley? Why she was vulgar, profane and fond of grog. Why be good? Goodness is not appreciated. Let us swear, be obscene, get drunk and raise Old Ned, for if, after we are gone, people would become possessed of the absurd notion that we helped to fire a cannon, they will see the monuments are erected over our graves at public expense."

Cumberland County has Revolutionary heroes who lived useful and respected lives and whose title to honor and distinction is not in doubt as is Molly McCauley's. Many of them fell in the memorable struggle while others lived through it to the end, acquitting themselves nobly and reflecting glory upon the section that sent them forth. What do the promoters of the Molly McCauley project propose to do to keep their memory green?

The remains of General Armstrong—friend and associate of Washington, hero of Kittanning and of the Revolution, "eminently distinguished in patriotism, valor and piety"—lie within a stone's throw of where Molly McCauley's lie, but his grave is to remain sufficiently marked by the plan stone slab that lies upon it.

The grave of Gen. William Thompson, Colonel of the first regiment Pennsylvania sent into the Revolution, is in close proximity to that of Molly McCauley, and less ostentatiously marked than General Armstrong's. If erected at her grave the proposed monument to Molly McCauley will cast the gloom of its evening shadows across General Thompson's tomb.

Adjacent to General Thompson's resting place is a memorial to Dr. George Stevenson, who as a Lieutenant distinguished himself at the battle of Brandywine; who with his command spent the memorable winter of 1777-1778 at Valley Forge, and as Captain of the Carlisle Infantry helped to subdue the Whiskey Rebellion. This memorial likewise will fall within the shadows of Molly McCauley's proposed monument.

The grave of General Henry Miller, Lieutenant in Colonel Thompson's regiment, who "risked his person in fifty or sixty conflicts," and in the war of 1812 was a Brigadier General, is also near by and marked only by a modest monument. To erect a great monument at the grave of Molly McCauley will dwarf General Miller's, which is neither just to his memory or the best way to promote patriotism.

Captain Andrew Irvine, in active service from the beginning to the end of the Revolution, and who carried to his grave the scar of a wound received at Paoli, is buried in the same vicinity, and his grave is less ostentatiously marked than Molly McCauley's now is marked. Captain Irvine was a brother of General William Irvine, in whose family before the war Molly McCauley was a servant.

General William Irvine, citizen of Carlisle before, during and after the Revolution, has not even the semblance of a memorial in Cumberland County. He was a devoted, patriotic and brave officer, but his memory is not honored as bit is proposed to honor the memory of a woman who ounce was a servant in his family.

Captain William Hendricks was the first officer from the west of the Hudson to fall in the Revolution; and Captain Walter Denny, another worthy son of Cumberland, laid down his life at the Battle of Crooked Billet, yet there is not as much as a wooden post in the entire county dedicated to the memory of either.

There were five Butler brothers from Cumberland County who served in the Revolution from start to finish, one rising to the rank of Colonel, one to Lieutenant Colonel and three to Captain. On the field of Brandywine one of them received the thanks of Washington for intrepidity, and at Monmouth the thanks of Wayne. They were illustrious in their lives and gave to the country illustrious families, but they have no memorials to their memory in this part of the country nor is it proposed to erect any. The proposed monument to Molly McCauley will belittle "the fighting Butlers" and their glorious records.

Colonel Robert Magaw, Col. Ephraim Blaine and Gen. Frederick Watts wrought nobly in the struggle for American independence, and Cumberland county should feel a glow of pride in their patriotism and valor, but their graves are unmarked and the whereabouts of them in doubt. Why is it not proposed to erect memorials to them at the public expense, instead of to a profane, vulgar, bibulous woman whose memory long ago received abundant recognition for the little she is said to have done in the Revolution?

In the cemetery where Molly McCauley lies are interred scores of Revolutionary heroes whose graves are unknown. They were buried with the honors of war but have not the honor of marked graves. After the turf closed over them all knowledge of their final resting place faded out of the minds of those who buried them and it is now impossible to find them. But their names and deeds linger sweetly in the traditions of the section in which they lived and died and the great country for whose liberty they fought and bled owes them homage. Shall so much be bestowed upon the half mythical Molly McCauley and nothing upon the heroes whose patriotic dust hallows the ground around her? Must their deeds of suffering and sacrifice be lost from view in the glamour of a great monument earned neither by righteous living nor by undoubted heroism? I trust not. J. Zeamer. Carlisle, Pa. April 4, 1905.[8]

COMMENTARY

Jeremiah Zeamer was longtime editor of the Carlisle *American Volunteer* newspaper. His "revisionist" view of Mary Hays McCauley's character differs strongly with those of most of the commonly quoted statements given by Mary's neighbors in the late 1800s (see Chapter 8 above). His motivation for attacking Mary's character was clearly the expense and the lack of recognition given to the graves of other Revolutionary war heroes. Despite Zeamer's efforts, her grave was marked by a cannon, flag and flagstaff in 1905 (see No. 9C) and a large state monument in 1916 (see Nos. (9D and 9E).

Zeamer's claim that not of Mary Hays' McCauley's neighbors remembered her speaking of fighting at the battle of Monmouth is contradicted by the 1895 of Susan Heckendorn (No. 8H). ·

For Zeamer's views on the claims that Mary Hays McCauley was born as Mary Ludwig, see No. 4F below.

CONCLUSION

Zeamer's statements create a coarser, more crass picture of the character of Mary Hays McCauley, but do not refute her possible presence at Monmouth.

4E. John Landis, A Short History of Molly Pitcher, 1905.

A SHORT HISTORY OF MOLLY PITCHER
The Heroine of the Battle of Monmouth
Together with an Account of the Ceremonies incident to
the Unveiling of the Cannon implanted over her grave

in the Old Graveyard in Carlisle, Pennsylvania,
by The Patriotic Order of Sons of America,
on June 28, 1905

Many and confusing have been the stories of "Molly Pitcher." If by competent testimony and authentic records we may relieve the story of her life from uncertainty, we shall do but simple justice to her memory.

She is said to have been born in New Jersey, and she is said to have been born in Pennsylvania. She has been called Irish and she has been called German. She is said to have "thrown a wounded man over her shoulder" and carried him off the battle-field "as she sued to carry bags of wheat;" and this notwithstanding her father was a dairyman and not a farmer, and that from the age of fifteen until marriage she was a domestic in the home of a physician.

She is said to have been commissioned by Washington on the battle-field and recommended half pay for life. It has been said she was buried at Carlisle in the "Potters' Field," and, to have been buried there "in the same grave as her first husband;" while it has further been claimed that she was buried on the banks of the Hudson.

In a series of ten papers on her life, it is stated in five that her husband was wounded at Monmouth, in one that he was mortally wounded, in three that he was killed, and in one that he died form the heat. No less a writer than the late beloved Frank R. Stockton, in his "New Jersey," (Appleton's Stories from American History), states that, a "bullet from the enemy struck the poor man and stretched him dead." Even Harper's Encyclopedia of United States History says that her husband was killed, and that his young wife took his place, "to avenge his death." We are told that she was barefooted at Monmouth, and caught the ammunition in her petticoat as it was thrown to her. But they did not use cartridges in those days, and an attempt to catch a cannon ball in that way might have caused her serious discomfiture.

She was not as devout as Joan of Arc, nor as fair as the wife of Tyndarus, nor as spectacular as Boadicea. But she was a woman, and such as she was it is the purpose of this article to show.

The name, "Pitcher," was not an unusual one. We may find it among the names of revolutionary soldiers. But our heroine's name was not "Pitcher" at all, but Ludwig; and at the time she earned her well known soubriquet she was the wife of an artilleryman. Her father, John George Ludwig, came to this country from the Palatinate. He made a settlement in Mercer County, New Jersey, not many miles from Trenton, where he engaged in the occupation of a dairyman. It was here his daughter Mary was born, on October 13th, 1754; and here among the surroundings of her father's home were spent the youthful days of the future "Molly Pitcher."

Her story should include a reference to William Irvine, a young physician from Ireland, who settled in Carlisle, Pennsylvania, in 1763. He was an ardent patriot, and took an important part in the revolutionary struggle. He married Anna Callender, a daughter of Robert Callender who lived near Carlisle. Irvine must have been as ardent a lover as patriot, for in writing to his wife he always addressed her as "My dearest love." Mrs. Irvine. When visiting friends in Trenton, saw the youthful Mary Ludwig, and being pleased with her and in need of a domestic, took the young girl with her on returning to Carlisle.

With Mrs. Irvine, then, she found her new home at the susceptible age of about fifteen years. And here, a domestic in Dr. Irvine's home, on the corner where the First Lutheran Church now stands, she subsequently became the wife of a young man, who, like her master, became a soldier in the revolutionary ranks. The young patriot was John Casper Hays, of Carlisle, a barber, who kept his shop not far from the Irvine mansion. The presence of the youthful Mary attracted the young barber, and the tale of their courtship is told in pleasing story. When the patter of her fairy feet was heard on the Irvine steps, or the swish of her broom on the sidewalk, it was not long until John Casper Hays found himself gazing out of the window of his little shop. And Mary, it seems, found quite a good deal of work necessary outside the house. Both being frank and sincere, they found their devotion mutual, and Mary seems to have been a bride-elect at about sweet sixteen. Their marriage license was granted on July 24th, 1769, at Carlisle, the county-seat of Cumberland County. They were doubtless married on the same day as they lived near the Office where marriage licenses were issued. And so Mary Ludwig became Mary Ludwig Hays.

Waves of discontent were now sweeping the Colonies. No community was earlier in rising against the oppression of the Mother Country than the Scotch-Irish of the Cumberland Valley. None were more earnest and determined in standing out against the King. Finally these waves of discontent, rising higher and darker, broke in all the terrible dignity of war.

Carlisle was an important point of rendezvous during the revolutionary period, and had been a military post for many years previous. Here, in the center of the town, stood Fort Lowther, built by Colonel Stanwix, of the British Army, and a short distance north-east of the fort was the great square of "the Breastworks," or "Intrenchments." Here ran the great road leading from Philadelphia to the western frontier, over which marched the men, and over which were carried their stores, in expeditions for the protection of the western border. Through and across this valley ran the old Indian trails. Here the troops rendezvoused as late as October, 1794, preparatory to moving westward to quell the Whiskey Insurrection in Western Pennsylvania, and they were here reviewed by President Washington.

The patriotic and warlike surroundings with which Mary Ludwig Hays became familiar in those trying days doubtless nurtured the spirit she afterwards exhibited. Her husband and her master both soldiers, her heart was with them and her country, and she needed but the opportunity to show the mettle of which she was made.

A few years of quiet wedded life, disturbed only by the warlike preparations centered about the little town, and John Casper Hays became a soldier. He enlisted on December 1st, 1775, in Proctor's First Pennsylvania Artillery, in which he served as a gunner. His term of service expired in December, 1776. During the first year of his service we hear nothing of his young wife. In January, 1777, he re-enlisted in the Seventh Pennsylvania Regiment, Continental Line, in the Company commanded by Captain John Alexander of Carlisle.

Dr. Irvine, active in the preparations for resisting the demands of King George, in 1776 entered the field as Colonel of the Sixth Pennsylvania Line, under appointment of January 9th, 1776. Promotion followed, and he was commissioned Brigadier General on May 12th, 1779. Previous to this time, however, on the sixth day of June, 1776, he was captured at the unfortunate affair of *Trois Rivieres*. He remained a prisoner until his exchange on the 21st of April, 1778, when he assumed command of the Seventh Pennsylvania Regiment, in which John Casper Hays was a private. As Colonel of this regiment he participated in the battle of Monmouth.

After Hays left with his regiment, his wife remained employed at Colonel Irvine's. Some time thereafter, her parents, who still resided in New Jersey, sent a courier to bring her to their home. It is said that the horseman who carried the word to Molly had a letter begging her to come, as he might then get an opportunity to see her. With Mrs. Irvine's consent and blessing she set about her long and tiresome journey. With poor roads, and no means of travel except on horseback we can picture her weary ride. No doubt she was cheered with the thought of seeing her father and mother, and with the hope of meeting her husband.

We come now to the period when the episode occurred which made her famous. To prevent the movement of the British on New York, Washington marched his troops again into New Jersey, and the battle of Monmouth was fought on the 28th of June, 1778. At that time Molly Hays was a young woman of twenty-four years.

According to Alexander Hamilton and Colonel William Irvine, the decisive battle of Monmouth continued from eleven o'clock in the morning until half past four in the afternoon. The day was one of the hottest of the year. Lossing says the battle lasted from nine o-clock in the morning until night. Fifty soldiers are said to have died of thirst, and the tongues of many to have been so greatly swollen as to protrude from the mouth. While the battle was in progress Molly carried water for the thirsting soldiers from a neighboring spring, which is still pointed out on the historic spot. Back and forth she went, under shelter or under fire, supplying the much needed water. Possibly, as stated by some, it was carried in the cannonniers' bucket. In whatever way it was carried, the sight of Molly with her "pitcher" was a welcome sight to the weary and thirsty soldiers.

Molly's husband, as will be remembered, had served for one year in Proctor's Artillery, and though now an infantryman, had been detailed as a gunner in a battery that was engaged. Doubtless Molly was never out of sight of that battery. As she was coming toward the smoking lines with water she saw a soldier lying at his gun, whom she thought to be her husband, and hurrying on she found her husband wounded, and the dead man one of his comrades. It is stated that the cannon was ordered to the rear, and would have been taken off the field, had not Molly bravely sprung to her husband's place, and so kept the gun in action. Her husband recovered, but lived only a few years after the close of the war.

One of Molly's strong characteristics, exhibited in many and various ways, was her readiness to help others in time of need. Opportunity was all that was necessary. She was intensely interested in the war. A warm patriot and a warmer hater of redcoats, she could not see the poor soldiers in the heat and dust of battle suffering from thirst, without exposing her own life, if necessary, in their relief. How grateful must Molly's "pitcher" have been to those thirsting men, and how astonishing her bravery, as she seized the rammer and worked like an Amazon to save her husband's gun. She was dubbed "sergeant," by the soldiers, and was also called "Major Molly."

"Moll Pitcher she stood by her gun,
And rammed the charges home, sir,
And thus on Monmouth's bloody field,
A sergeant did become, sir."

How long, in the smoke and din of battle Molly stood by her gun on that hot and terrible day we do not know. But what time she carried water must be credited to the brave woman, as well as the time she was engaged with the battery.

Here let us allow the poet his license. He can paint the picture with the warmth of the color it deserves.

> "'Wheel back the gun,' the gunner said,
> When like a flash before him, stood
> A figure dashed with smoke and blood,
> With streaming hair, with eyes aflame,
> With lips that falter the gunner's name.
> 'Wheel back his gun that never yet,
> His fighting duty did forget?
> His voice shall speak though he be dead,
> I'll serve my husband's gun!' she said.
> Oh, Molly, Molly, with eyes so blue,
> Oh, Molly, Molly, here's to you!
> Sweet Honor's roll will aye be richer,
> To hold the name of Molly Pitcher!"

No imaginary heroine was Molly Pitcher, but a real buxom lass, a strong, sturdy, courageous woman. The roll of the world's heroines hardly contains her name, yet her conduct at Monmouth certainly contributed to the favorable results of that battle; and the victory itself was the beginning of a brighter era in the revolutionary period. It was celebrated with great rejoicing throughout the Colonies, and a vote of thanks was tendered Washington and his army by Congress. Some years ago the State of New Jersey was first to render her due to "Molly Pitcher." On the battle monument erected at Freehold on the historic field, one of the five tablets surrounding the base of the beautiful shaft commemorates her heroic act in enduring bronze.

As to Molly's personal appearance, not much that is reliable can be learned, except as she was remembered in her later years by several old persons. We have no description of her as a young girl and wife. We may be sure she was at least pleasing in her manner and appearance, as she favorably impressed so cultured a lady as the wife of General Irvine. That she was lovely in the eyes of at least one man, we can look to John Casper Hays to prove.

A revolutionary soldier is said to have described her, as, "rather stout and red" at the time of the battle of Monmouth and that she was a "coarse and uncouth looking female." His description may have been correct. Her appearance on that hot summer day, begrimed with smoke and dust, and barefooted like many of the soldiers themselves, may have justified his description. She was a rather stout woman with considerable color, and is by some described as of course features. Her form, of average height, muscular, strong and heavy set, became stooped in old age and her hair mixed with gray. She had a defective eye, the left, having met with an accident which finally caused its blindness. This was later in life, and was said to have been caused by a particle of lime entering the eye. Her ordinary dress was a blue and white striped "short skirt," a petticoat, a broad white cap with wide flaring ruffles, a sun bonnet, woolen stockings and heavy brogans. Such is her description as an old woman.

Some years after the death of her first husband, Sergeant John Casper Hays, she married George McKolly, another soldier and a comrade of Hays's, and she then became known as Molly McKolly. This name was also written "McAuley," and "McCauley," while on her tombstone it was cut "McCauly."

At the entrance to the grounds of the Carlisle Indian Industrial School, formerly for many years United States Barracks, still stands the old stone guard house with walls over four feet thick, which was built by the Hessian prisoners taken at the battle of Trenton, and which escaped the fire when the Barracks were burned by the Confederates in 1863. At this Post Molly lived for many years after the Revolutionary War, cooking and washing for the soldiers. Subsequently she kept a small store in the southeastern part of the town of Carlisle, not far from the house in which Major Andre and Lieutenant Despard were confined in 1776, after Andre's first capture near Lake Champlain. The latter years of her life were spent in a stone house near the southeast corner of Bedford and North Streets, in Carlisle, where she died on Sunday,

January 22nd, 1832. Her death was hastened by a stubborn cutaneous disease. She attended the Lutheran Church and was respected by her neighbors.

Her services to her country were recognized not only by her friends and neighbors. On the 21st of February, 1822, the Legislature of this State, by a Special Act, granted her an Annuity for services during the Revolutionary War, the sum of forty dollars immediately, and the same sum half yearly during life, from January 1st, 1822. The "Chronicle," of Philadelphia, about that date stated, in reference to the granting of the Annuity, that, "It appeared satisfactory that this heroine had braved the hardships of the camp and dangers of the field with her husband who was a soldier of the Revolution, and the bill in her favor passed without a dissenting voice." The "Pension" mentioned by many who have written of her was this Annuity.

To prove that this Annuity was granted on account of her own personal services, and not because she was the widow of a soldier, let us examine the proceedings of the Legislature.

On Thursday, February 14th, 1822, "The Clerk of the Senate being introduced, presented for concurrence the bills entitled," *inter alia*: "No. 265. An Act for the relief of Molly McKolly, widow of a soldier of the revolutionary war." It was read and laid upon the table. The following day, "On motion of Mr. Wadsworth and Mr. Cochran, the House resolved itself into a committee of the whole, Mr. Kirk in the chair, on the bill from the Senate, No. 265, entitled, 'An Act for the relief of Molly McKolly, widow of a soldier of the revolutionary war.'" The bill went on to a second reading and was ordered prepared for a third reading, "the title being amended by striking out these words, 'widow of a soldier,' and inserting in lieu thereof these words, 'For services rendered in,'" and so passed. And it was "Ordered that the Clerk return the same to the Senate and request their concurrence in the amendment thereto by this House." On Saturday, February 16th, 1822, "The Clerk of the Senate was introduced and gave information that the Senate had concurred in the amendment by this House." On Wednesday following, among others, the following was reported by Mr. Cassat as having been presented to the Governor for his approbation,' to wit: "I. An Act for the relief of Molly McKolly for her services during the revolutionary war." The next day, February 21st, 1822, the bill was signed by Governor Hiester. We see from this that the annuity was granted in recognition of her personal services, and that the Legislature considered the matter of sufficient importance to resolve itself into a committee of the whole on the Bill.

The statement that she received a pension from the United States is unsupported. Information from the Bureau of Pensions at Washington, D.C., states that neither the name "Molly Hays," nor "Molly McKolly" is found on the Pension Rolls. The law pensioning widows of revolutionary soldiers was approved July 4th, 1836, which was subsequent to Molly's death, and no Special Act is found granting her a pension.

For ten years she lived to enjoy the bounty of the Commonwealth, small though it may seem to us now, and to have the satisfaction of knowing that her act was in this way commended and appreciated.

She died on Sunday, the 22nd day of January, 1832, and was buried in the Old Graveyard or as then known, the English Graveyard, in Carlisle, where repose the remains of many of Carlisle's noted and eminent citizens. The "Carlisle Herald" of Thursday, January 26th, 1832, in its list of "Death Notices" has the following: "Died on Sunday last, Mrs. Mary McAuley, (better known by the name of Mary McAuley) aged ninety years. The history of this woman is somewhat remarkable. Her first husband's name was Hays who was a soldier in the war of the Revolution. It appears she continued with him in the army, and acted so much the part of a heroine as to attract the notice of the officers. Some estimate may be formed of the value of the services by her, when the fact is stated that she drew a pension form the government during the latter years of her life."

The "American Volunteer" of the same place and date has this notice: "Died on Sunday last, in this Borough at an advanced age, Mrs. Mary McCauley. She lived during the days of the American Revolution, shared its hardships, and witnessed many a scene of 'blood and carnage.' To the sick and wounded she was an efficient aid: For which and being the widow of an American hero, she received during the latter years of her life, an Annuity from the Government. For upwards of forty years she resided in this borough, and was, during that time, recognized as an honest, obliging, and industrious woman."

In the Spring of the year 1876, an article on Molly Pitcher appeared in the "American Volunteer," a weekly newspaper published in Carlisle. The article was written by Miss Agnes M. Graham, a daughter of Hon. James H. Graham, for twenty years President Judge of the Courts of Cumberland County. Her communication closed with the suggestion that it would befit the celebration of the Fourth of July on the essential year to erect a headstone to the memory of Molly Pitcher.

Peter Spahr, a well known citizen of Carlisle who died September 28. 1884, eagerly seized the suggestion of Miss Graham and carried it into execution, and the stone at present marking her grave was erected, and unveiled on the Fourth of July, 1876. Mr. Spahr knew her well and was present at her funeral. He knew where she was buried, tho her grave had been unmarked. This was in the graveyard mentioned, on the southeastern corner of the lot of John Noble, who died in 1804. Her age and the date of her death were fixed by Mr. Spahr from memory and were not entirely correct. Attention was called to the error in the date of her death, and it was subsequently correct ed from 1833 to 1832, by the Civic Club of Carlisle. Her age was therefore seventy-eight instead of seventy-nine years.

The stone is inscribed as follows:
MOLLIE MCCAULY
Renowned in History as
"MOLLIE PITCHER"
The Heroine of Monmouth,
Died January, 1832.
Aged 78 years.
Erected by the citizens of
Cumberland County,
July 4, 1876.

At the time of the unveiling appropriate ceremonies were held, a band played patriotic airs and an address was delivered by Captain Joseph G. Vale, a veteran officer of the war of the rebellion. This address contained much of interest, but unhappily no copy of it seems to have been preserved.

As the house in which she lived for many years and up to the time of her death there can be no question. At the southeastern intersection of Bedford and North Streets in Carlisle, is original town lot No. 240, formerly known as Loughridge's corner. On this lot stood two small houses; a log house fronting on Bedford Street, and adjoining it on the east a stone house somewhat larger fronting North Street. Apparently these houses were communicating in an early day. Only a few years since, when the log house was torn away to afford space for a brick building, a door frame in the back wall adjoining the stone house stood in its original position, fastened to the logs with heavy wrought iron spikes fully nine inches long. The stone house, which before had been reconstructed mainly of brick, had a depression in the western wall corresponding quite if not altogether with the door frame in the log house. These conditions point to communication between the buildings.

In the rear of the stone building the original wall remains, The western window in this wall is pointed out as the window of Molly Pitcher's room.

Abundant testimony fixes the stone house as that in which she lived during the latter years of her life, and where she died in 1832. The two houses being both on the corner lot, it has lately been claimed that the log house was Molly's home because it was on the corner of the lot. But the uniform testimony of numerous competent witnesses fixes the stone house on the corner lot as the true Molly Pitcher house. The fact is now beyond dispute. Besides the testimony of her grandson, she lived there with her up to the time of her death, and of others who often visited her there, we have the same statement made by the Reverend Joseph A. Murray, D.D., late of Carlisle; the late Reverend James A. McCauley, D.D., a former president of Dickinson College; and by Benjamin M. Nead, Esq., of Harrisburg, Pa.,; all of whom have written excellent articles on Molly Pitcher, and by all of whom the stone house has been designated as her residence.

It would seem proper, and may be of interest, to hear the testimony of some of the persons who knew her. The following facts are from the depositions of the parties, duly signed and sworn to.

John A. Hays, who died at his home on East Penn Street in Carlisle in 1896, at the age of seventy-four, was Molly's grandson, and nearly eleven years old when she died. He was born in the stone house near the southeast corner of Bedford and North Streets, in Carlisle, Pa., and lived there with Molly up to the time of her death. His father John Ludwig Hays, was said to have been born in a tent on the battlefield of Monmouth after the battle; but this he afterwards said was uncertain. In her old age he heard her speak a great deal about her army experiences, and often heard her speak a great deal about her army experiences, and he often heard from her own lips the story of the battle of Monmouth, and of her participation in it, giving the facts as they have been already detailed He often heard her speak of her early life and the time she spent among the soldiers. He was at home with her when she died, was present at her funeral, and at her grave when she was buried. He stated that the stone now marking her grave in the Carlisle graveyard stands on the spot where she was buried.

Mrs. Susan Heckendorn, a very intelligent old lady residing in Carlisle, whose deposition was taken in 1895, when she was seventy-nine years of age stated that she had lived in Carlisle since 1828. She was a young lady of sixteen when Molly Pitcher died. She often saw her at the house of her son, John L. Hays, near the corner of Bedford and North Streets, and knew her very well. She said Molly was a rather large woman with a florid complexion, her hair mixed with gray. She attended the Lutheran Church. She often told this deponent and her girl friends the story of her army life, and her experiences at the battle of Monmouth, and said to them, "You girls should have been with me at the battle of Monmouth and learned how to load a cannon." Mrs. Heckendorn further stated that Molly died about 1832, and was buried in the public graveyard at Carlisle. She was present at the burial. It was in the southeast corner of the Noble lot, where the stone was erected in her memory in 1876. She had great admiration for the hero-woman, often visited her grave, and was much interested in seeing it properly marked; feeling that the resting place of so brave a woman should not be forgotten.

Miss Harriet M. Foulke, who a few years ago died in Lancaster, Ohio, a very intelligent old lady, testified in 1896, that she lived in Carlisle from 1809 to 1861. Her father, Dr. George M. Foulke, a prominent physician of Carlisle, attended Molly in her last illness. At that time Miss Foulke was nearly twenty-three years of age. Her description of Molly accords with that given before. She says Molly had a defective eye, which was also distinctly remembered by Mrs. Spangler, an aged lady of Carlisle, who recalled her appearance with great distinctness. Molly was often employed at Dr. Foulke's home in various kinds of house work, during a number of years, She was homely in appearance, not refined in manner or language, but ready to do a kind act for any one. She was of average height, muscular, strong and heavy-set. She was a very busy talker. She wore a short gown, white or calico, a Lindsey striped skirt, very short and full, woolen stockings, heavy brogans, and a broad white cap with wide flaring ruffles. Miss Foulke further stated that she was so well known as the "Molly Pitcher" of Monmouth, that no effort seems to have been made to perpetuate a fact which all seemed to recognize.

I will quote one more witness, Mrs. Barbara Park, who died in Carlisle, December 16th, 1896, where she had lived since she was nine years old. She knew Molly very well. She was a girl of about twelve years old when the corner stone of the present Episcopal Church was laid on September 8th, 1826. A quarry on the public square, from which stone for the foundation had been taken was still open at the time. She and a younger brother were on their way to see the ceremonies, and passing too near the quarry both fell in. She was somewhat hurt. The first person to help them, notwithstanding her age, was Molly Pitcher, who first assisted her brother out and then herself. The occasion of the laying of the corner-stone of the church was a public one. The military of the town, and numerous organizations were drawn up in parade. To the ladies who were admiring the military demonstration, Molly said, "This is nothing but a flea bite to what I have seen." Mrs. Park was about nineteen years old at the time of Molly's death. Her appearance and dress she described the same as Miss Foulke. She said Molly was a brave woman, and had a kind word for everyone. She was known as "Molly Pitcher" from her having carried water in a pitcher to the soldiers at the battle of Monmouth; and from her having assisted in firing the cannon, became known as "The heroine of the battle of Monmouth." She died at the home of her son, John L. Hays, in the stone house previously mentioned.

Molly McKolly left few effects. Such as remain today are principally in the hands of the family of John A. Hays and other relatives in Carlisle, and of Mrs. Martz, of Ogden, Utah. Most of her effects were destroyed by fire at the time of the occupation of Carlisle by the Confederates in 1863, when they burned the house in which her grandson lived.

The facts above recited, all from authentic sources, the more material of which are supported by affidavits of competent witnesses, must set at rest any question as to the home and burial place of the real "Molly Pitcher."

Many reminiscences are related of Molly, which, however, can not be verified by competent testimony. At the battle of Monmouth she was personally complimented by General Washington for her bravery. On one occasion, before she knew Washington, while she was engaged in cooking and washing for the soldiers, having a kettle over the fire which she wished to remove, she called upon a passing soldier to assist her. Struck with the soldier's prompt compliance and kind manner, she asked his name, and was so greatly astonished that she almost dropped the kettle when he answered, "I am General Washington."

She carried a wounded soldier from the battlefield, and nursed him into speedy recovery. His name was Dilwyn. She found him lying amongst the dead, where he was left for burial with the rest. Finding that he was still living, she carried him off the battlefield, and nursed him back to life. When an old woman, she lay upon the floor by the cradle of a sick child an entire night, and watched and cared for the little one.

Some time after the close of the Revolutionary War two old Army officers arrived in Carlisle on horseback. They inquired for Molly, and upon meeting her, the three were moved to tears. One of them was said to have been a soldier whom Molly nursed back to life, after he had been left for dead on the battlefield. This may refer to the Dilwyn rescue.

Molly was an ardent admirer of Washington, and believed there was no other so brave and good a man in the world. In this view she has been followed by the many millions of her countrymen. She had often heard complaints from the soldiers during the dark periods of the war, but she never shared them; instead, she went about doing good, and always giving words of encouragement. She was very much interested in the presence of President Washington and the soldiers who rendezvoused at Carlisle, at the time of the Whiskey Insurrection in Western Pennsylvania. In 1812 when Captain Squires' Carlisle Company of soldiers marched out the turnpike on their way to Baltimore, Molly accompanied them several miles.

The real Molly, then, was a young woman of German parentage, living among the Scotch-Irish, imbibing the patriotic fervor of the day, and loyal to her husband and to her country. With true German fidelity she followed her husband into the army. Not only an account of her courage is she to be remembered, but because that courage took practical form and led her to do more than could have been expected of a woman. Many might have shown as much bravery on sudden impulse; but not many would have continued in patient persistence through those long and terrible hours to minister to the wants of the weary soldiers. When water was needed by the thirsty men she supplied it to keep them at the front; but when a man was needed she dropped the pitcher and filled the artilleryman's place. When she found Dilwyn still living, she at once took him into her own care. When, in the quiet of domestic life, as in the cases of the sick child and of the boy and girl who fell into the quarry, she exhibited the same qualities, we see one of the characteristics of Molly Pitcher.

This quality seems to have been the key to the strongest trait of her nature. Helpfulness inspired her life until strength failed to support a willing heart. Her rough, homely attire, and her brusque manner and speech, made a surface impression of coarseness, which it is hard to believe was the real character of the woman.

Let us leave her memory, then, in the hearts of her generous countrymen. Let us remember the times in which she lived and the scenes through which she passed, and then, it may be, the plainness of her face, and frankness of her speech, will be forgotten in the tenderness of her heart, and the usefulness of her life.

There remain a few facts which will settle any questions as to whether the body was removed from its first resting place in the old graveyard.

A number of years ago, Mrs. Patton of Carlisle, an aged lady who died on November 26, 1895, a daughter of Mr. Noble, had a tablet prepared to place over the unmarked graves of a brother and sister who had died in infancy. She located these graves in a corner of the Noble lot where the Molly Pitcher monument stood, and there was not sufficient space for the tablet. The Molly Pitcher grave, she averred, was somewhat further southward on the adjoining Hays lot. As the burial of these children at the spot indicated seemed sufficiently determined by Mrs. Paton, arrangements were made with a stone cutter to move the Pitcher stone to another position, on the theory that Mr. Spahr might have been slightly mistaken as to the exact location of the grave, The new foundation for it was already prepared, when a notice was served upon the stonecutter, R.H. Owen, of Carlisle, by the Patriotic Order of the Sons of America, who had retained legal counsel, warning all persons against moving the stone. The Hays family, descendants by Molly's first husband, also demurred to the proceeding. Mr. Noble's daughter, however, insisted that she was right as to the location of the children's graves, while the Hays family were equally sure that they were right, and the matter bid fair to get into the Courts.

Upon consultation with Mr. Hays and others interested it was agreed that the spot should be dug up, and if children's remains were found the tablet should be placed over them if not, then the stone should remain. On Tuesday, the 3rd of May, 1892, James Martin, the curator of the graveyard, opened the grave in the presence of Mr. Frederick Hays, Molly's great-grandson, and Mrs. Patton's attorneys. After digging down between three and four feet he came upon the remains of small coffins, and the fact was demonstrated that children had been buried there. He had a "digging iron" in his hands, and probing the ground with it unexpectedly pierced to a greater depth just along the southern edge of the small graves, He dug on and found a grave very close by the side of the small ones.

This he carefully opened when a skeleton was exposed to view. An examination proved it to be the skeleton of an adult female. The skull, the pelvic bones and some of the larger bones were examined, They were then carefully replaced, the earth filled over them, and all that remained of Molly Pitcher was shut out from the light of the world forever, and her "Monument" remains on the spot where she was buried in 1832.

A SOUVENIR OF MOLLY PITCHER
State of Pennsylvania, County of Cumberland.

Before me a Notary Public in and for said State and County, personally appeared Mary E. Wilson, who, after having been by me duly sworn according to law, doth depose and say that she is now forty-eight years old and resides in Carlisle, where she has lived all her life, that she is the daughter of Fred'k McCleaster, who was the son of John and Polly McCleaster, the said Polly McCleaster was the daughter of John Hays, who was the son of Molly McKolly, otherwise known as "Molly Pitcher" (whose maiden name was Molly Ludwig), and whose first husband was John Hays. She further says that she has had in her possession, since the death of her grandmother, Polly McCleaster, the pitcher, which was formerly the property of "Molly Pitcher," which was presented to her, the deponent, by her grandmother, Polly McCleaster, at the time of her death, with the strict admonition that she should be very careful to preserve it because it had been the property of her grandmother, Molly McKolly, alias "Molly Pitcher." She further says that her grandmother, Polly McCleaster, raised her the deponent, from her childhood up until the time of her marriage, and that she lived constantly in her family, and that her grandmother told her frequently that the pitcher concerning which this affidavit is made, was presented to her personally by her grandmother, Molly McKolly, and that she had been charged by her to be very careful of it as it was a favorite piece of ware, and as her grandmother stated frequently, that because her grandmother had given her such strict instructions about preserving the picture she often cautioned me about handling it at all. She, the deponent, further says that she frequently heard and saw her grandmother show this pitcher to her friends and neighbors and explain to them that it was the pitcher that belonged to her grandmother, "Molly Pitcher."

Deponent further says that her grandmother died April 28th, 1884, at which time she, deponent, came into possession of the pitcher, which by reason of the admonitions given her by her grandmother, she has been very careful to preserve intact, until this date, when now she disposes of it to be cared for by the Cumberland County Historical Society and deposited with its collection. A description of the pitcher, which is the subject of this affidavit, is as follows, to wit: It is ewer shaped, wide mouth, standing eight and one-fourth inches to the top of the handle and seven and seven-sixteenth inches high to the centre of the mouth and four inches in diameter at the base; the figures on the outside of it are brown in color on a white base, and are made up for the most part of Chinese or Japanese pagodas, and something resembling fortifications with the figures of two men on these fortifications, one holding in his right hand something in the shape of a three-leafed clover and the other man apparently suspended in the air and pointing upward, around the handle and the top of the pitcher it is edged with blue.

My grandmother often told me about her grandmother Molly McKolly alias "Molly Pitcher" telling her about being in the army and about carrying water to the wounded and dying.

Witness my hand this 13th Aug., 1903, Mrs. Mary E. Wilson

Sworn and subscribed before me this 13th of August, 1903.

John R. Miller, Notary Public, Carlisle, Pa.

My commission expires April 18, 1907.

The Unveiling of the Cannon planted over the
Grave of Molly Pitcher in the Old Graveyard in Carlisle, Pa.,
by the District of Cumberland County P.O.S. of A.
of Pennsylvania on June 28, 1905

Action of Patriotic Order Sons of America
Obtaining of Cannon
Services on Placing Cannon on Grave

A District convention of the Patriotic Order Sons of America of Cumberland County, was held in Carlisle in the camp room of local camp No. 171 at the corner of E. Main and Market House Square, October 9, 1904. Mr. W.A. Rupp of Carlisle, Pa., the appointed District President of Cumberland County, in his address at the convention urged upon the convention the taking of some action looking to the placing of a cannon on the grave of Molly McKolly, renowned in history as "Molly Pitcher," who lies buried in the Old Graveyard in Carlisle. On motion of the District President, a committee was appointed as follows: A. Grant Richwine, of Mechanicsburg, W.A. Rupp, of Carlisle, D.M. Graham, of Carlisle, and C.W. Heyd, of Camp Hill. The committee at once too up the matter of securing a cannon from the War Department. A petition was presented to the Council of Carlisle which was approved unanimously. The Council of Carlisle who approved the petition was as follows: Ed. J. Weidman, President; Chas. H. Kutz, Secretary; Dr. H.M. Boyer, Louis C. Faber, Sr., Con. Faller, J.A. Hildebrandt, C.P. Humrich, W.M. Kronenberg, John Lindner, T.M. Mauk,

Geo. W. Rinesmith, J.S. Searight, S.B. Sadler. The same was approved by Congressman M.E. Olmsted, of this district, and through Major A.H. Russel of the Ordnance Department of Washington, D.C., the committee secured a twenty-four pound howitzer cannon from the Watertown Arsenal, Watertown, Mass., as a gift to the Patriotic Sons of America, to be placed on the grave of "Molly Pitcher" at Carlisle. A special convention was called of the Patriotic Order Sons of America of Cumberland County, Pa., which was held in the camp room of Camp 164, Hauck building, in Mechanicsburg, Pa., for the purpose of taking action to secure an appropriation from the State of Pennsylvania for a monument to mark the grave of "Molly Pitcher." On motion of D.M. Graham, Esq., of Carlisle, seconded by W.E. Keefer, of Mechanicsburg, the following resolution was passed: "Resolved, That the Legislature at its coming session be memorialized and petitioned to appropriate the sum of $5000 for the purpose of erecting a monument in the Old Graveyard at Carlisle, Pa., to perpetuate the memory of the patriotism and valor of "Molly Pitcher" the heroine of Monmouth; That the State Secretary of the Pennsylvania Patriotic Order Sons of America be requested to communicate the above resolution to each of the camps in the state and request their cooperation in bringing the matter to the attention of their Senators and Representatives and in urging them to aid in passing the said appropriation." The said resolution was passed unanimously. An Act was drawn by D.M. Graham, Esq., and the same committee appointed as at the meeting held in Carlisle., October 9th, 1904, who set to work to have the suggested appropriation passed by the Legislature. The Legislature passed finally a bill appropriating $2000, which however was vetoed by the Hon. Samuel W. Pennypacker, Governor of the Commonwealth of Pennsylvania. The executive committee of the Patriotic Order Sons of America of Cumberland County went to work making the arrangements to dedicate the cannon they had secured from the War Department as a memorial on the grave. They finally fixed on the 28th day of June, 1905, to unveil said cannon. It being the 127th anniversary of the battle of Monmouth. The gun carriage was made at Gettysburg, and weighs two thousand five hundred pounds. The cannon was placed upon the grave facing North, the muzzle overhanging the grave. The plate upon the carriage bears this inscription:

"Erected in memory of
Mollie McKolly
renowned in history as
Mollie Pitcher,
by the P.O.S. of A. of
Cumberland County, 1905."

This celebration, which was held in Carlisle, will go down in the history of the town as one of the most successful and important historical events ever held in that old and historic place. Long before 6:30 p.m. the hour for the parade to move, the streets were thronged with people, the weather was most favorable and the evening was perfect. The town was crowded with people brought there by the Cumberland Valley Railroad and the various trolley lines which enter it, and at the graveyard fully five thousand gathered to hear the speaking and to see the unveiling of the cannon. Not since her burial had so many visited the grave of Molly Pitcher. The credit of this demonstration belongs to the Patriotic Order Sons of America of Cumberland County and the various newspapers cheerfully accorded it. The parade was as follows:

Carlisle police force.
Chief Marshal Harry Hertzler of Carlisle, Pa.; Aids John S. Searight and Joseph Einstein, Carlisle, Oa.
Carriages drawing Chairman A. Grant Richwine of Mechanicsburg, Pa.; Hon. Marlin E. Olmsted, Harrisburg, Pa.; Hon. W.I. Swope, Clearfield, Pa.; Capt. J.B. Landis, Carlisle, Pa;
Carriage drawing Nellie Kramer, great-great-granddaughter, who unveiled the cannon, and Rev. J.E. Kleffman, Carlisle, Pa.
Carriages drawing Burgess H.G. Brown and the City Council of Carlisle, Pa.

Post G.A.R. Carlisle, Pa., and invited guests with Post cannon.

Major W.G. Speck, Eighth Regiment National Guards of Pennsylvania.

Adjutant, J. Adair Herman, 8th Regiment N.G.P.

Eighth Regiment Band, Sergeant W.M. Kronenberg commanding.

Company G Eighth Regiment National Guards of Penn., Capt. E.M. Vale,

Commanding.

Company C Eighth Regiment National Guards of Pa., Chambersburg, Capt. Samuel Bowers, commanding.

Jr. United American Mechanics, of Mt. Holly Springs and County.

Carlisle Indian School Cadets, Major W.G. Thompson, commanding.

United States Indian Band, Capt. C.M. Stauffer, commanding.

Patriotic Order Sons of America from Carlisle, Shippensburg, Newville, Dickinson, Mechanicsburg, Boiling Springs, New Cumberland, Camp Hill, New Kingston, Lemoyne, Leesburg, Harrisburg, and the neighboring counties.

The parade formed on the square and marched down East High Street to Bedford, out Bedford to North, up North to West, down West to High, down High to Hanover, out Hanover to Penn, countermarched at Penn, down Hanover to the Old Graveyard, where the unveiling took place. Seated upon the platform were the following persons: Chairman A. Grant Richwine, of Mechanicsburg, Pa., the Hon. Marlin E. Olmsted, of Harrisburg, Pa., the Hon. W.I. Swoope, of Clearfield, Pa., Capt. J.B. Landis, of Carlisle, the Rev J.E. Kleffman, of Carlisle, Pa., Miss Nellie Kramer, Carlisle, Pa., Hon. D.M. Graham, Carlisle, Pa., the Hon. J.H. Brinkerhoff, Leesburg, Pa., John W. German, of Harrisburg, Pa., C.W. Heyd, of Camp Hill, Pa., Col. H.C. Demming, Post 58, G.A.R. Harrisburg, W.A. Rupp, District President of Patriotic Order Sons of America of Cumberland County, Pa., and Burgess H.G. Brown and the City Council of Carlisle. At the salute by the Post G.A.R. cannon, Miss Nellie Kramer, great-great-granddaughter of "Molly Pitcher," who was attired in white, gracefully pulled a rope which raised the handsome flag off the cannon and sent Old Glory to the top of the staff as the Indian School Band played the Star Spangled Banner. Rev. J.E. Kleffman, Pastor of the Grace U.B. Church of Carlisle, and himself a P.O.S. of A. man, offered a fervent prayer, after which Chairman Richwine introduced the first speaker, Hon. Marlin E. Olmsted, Congressman in this district, who said:

One hundred and twenty-seven years ago today, beneath the burning rays

Of a blazing summer's sun, there was fought on the field of Monmouth one of the fiercest and most decisive battles of the American revolution. Before the rising of another sun the British army, under Sir Henry Clinton, defeated and dismayed, had silently stolen away.

> "The fires were bright in Clinton's camp,
> But long ere morning's dawn,
> His beaten host was on the tramp,
> And all the foes were gone.
> Never again may cannon sweep.
> Where waves the golden grain;
> And ne'er again an army sleep,
> Upon old Monmouth's plain."

Aided by Lafayette, that distinguished son of France, whose name is written upon our hearts and in our country's history, the immortal Washington there rendered services which turned defeat into victory and subsequently received acknowledgement in a vote of thanks by a grateful Congress; our own "Mad Anthony" Wayne gallantly earned most honorable mention in the official report of the commanding general; and she who there gained the sobriquet of "Molly Pitcher," performed those deeds of valor so often told in story and in song, and in commemoration of which we place upon her grave today this appropriate and enduring monument.

So fierce and so oppressive was the heat that the parched tongues of many soldiers were swollen speechless. Numbers of either army, receiving no wound, perished from the heat alone. The faces of those who died turned almost instantly black and the dead and dying lay in heaps like sheaves upon the harvest field.

MOLLIE PITCHER APPEARS

Upon this terrible scene of carnage a young woman, fearless of the leaden hail which fell about her, repeatedly appeared with water from a nearby spring wherewith she relieved the sufferings of the wounded and gave to the living strength to continue the fight. While she was thus heroically engaged the artilleryman, John Hays, her husband, whom she had followed into battle, was severely wounded. For want of another gunner to man the six-pounder of

which he had been in charge, it was ordered removed, lest it fall into the hands of the British. But she, whom the grateful soldiers had now style "Molly Pitcher," sprang forward, declaring her ability and desire to take her husband's place and demanding permission in a tone that brooked no denial, was given charge of the gun. At that critical period she renewed its deadly work upon the advancing enemy. Her act aroused, almost to frenzy, the enthusiasm of those about her and held the wavering soldiery in line.

At a later period finding in a pit among the dead a soldier yet alive, she carried him in her arms to the hospital and nursed him to recovery.

Great courage conspicuously exhibited in a great cause has in all ages commanded the unbounded admiration of mankind. That admiration is fitly expressed in lasting monument commemorating the deed and encouraging emulation of its notable example.

HER APPROPRIATE MONUMENT

But perhaps never before has such a monument as this we dedicate today been chosen to commemorate the deeds or mark the final resting place of a woman. The glorious achievements of "the man behind the gun" are often told. The woman behind the gun is exceptional and unique. The glories and successes of the gentler sex are not usually achieved by the aid of gunpowder. We do not commonly associate the deadly roar of the cannon with the low, sweet voice which all agree is so excellent a thing in a woman. Brave and patriotic and self-sacrificing as were our forefathers, they did not in any single noble attribute exceed our foremothers, But the courage which the women displayed; the patriotism which animated them, and the sacrifices which they made, were exhibited in the less conspicuous field of home life, where after all, we most love to think of woman, and where, from her throne upon her own hearthstone, her influence is greatest.

Verily, "the hand that rocks the cradle moves the world," but the monuments it achieves are most frequently found in the hearts of loved ones, friends and neighbors. In those trying days of the revolution, patriotism and bravery were so common in both men and women as almost to be taken for granted and excite no comment. It was only the unusually conspicuous deed that attracted attention. In bringing succor to the wounded; in quenching the thirst of her husband and his fighting comrades; the ministrations of Molly Hays, or, as she was then baptized, "Molly Pitcher," were distinctly feminine; and were rendered under conditions of imminent and deadly peril, requiring even greater intrepidity of soul upon the part of an unarmed woman than of an active participant in the fighting, in charge of her fallen husband's cannon, shows that she had that iron in the blood and dauntless courage so essential to great deeds.

A PENNSYLVANIA GERMAN GIRL

Mary Ludwig (for such was her maiden name) is properly classed with the Pennsylvania Germans, who at that time comprised three-fifths of the population of Pennsylvania, and whose thrift and industry had done much to place it among the foremost in material prosperity of all the American colonies. If in these days the Pennsylvania German did not give much attention to politics; if he was less aggressive and pugnacious than the Scotch-Irish; if he was patient and conservative; if he was pre-eminent in the acquisition and tenacious in the holding of lands; devoted to agriculture and to his home life; he was, nevertheless, patriotic, loyal and courageous. Her husband, though of humble means, had the fighting blood of the Irish and the Scotch.

The fires of patriotism, everywhere kindled, burned nowhere with more fervent heat than in this old county of Cumberland (the sixth in age of all the counties of the Commonwealth) and throughout the entire Cumberland Valley. Small wonder that shortly after the marriage of Mary Ludwig to John Hays he found himself a gunner in the service of his country or that his young wife, as was not unusual in those day in her rank of life, followed the fortunes of her husband, kept near him in the army and was thus present on the eventful twenty-eighth day of June.

Upon the death of Hays she married Sergeant McKolly. But with her subsequent life it is not necessary that we here concern ourselves.

Her name is perpetuated upon the bronzes of the battle monument near the old Monmouth court house.

STATE RECOGNIZED HER HEROISM

During the first session of the Legislature of Pennsylvania, in the old (then new) capitol, recently destroyed by fire, at Harrisburg, a committee of the Senate acting upon a petition presented by Senator Alexander Mahon, representing Cumberland and Perry counties, reported a bill, which promptly and unanimously passed the Senate, entitled, "An act for the relief of Mary McKolly, widow of a soldier of the Revolutionary war." It required the State Treasurer to pay her $40 immediately and granted her a continuing annuity of the same amount, payable semiannually. The House of Representatives passed the bill with equal promptness, but amended the title so as to make it distinctly show that the annuity was granted to her not because her husband had been a soldier, but "for services rendered in the Revolutionary war" by herself.

The petition presented by Senator Mahon was, unfortunately, not preserved. But its character is indicated by the descriptive title "Revolutionary Heroine," which appears after he name in the Journal of the House of Representatives. Governor Joseph Hiester, himself a Pennsylvania German, approved the bill upon the 21st day of February, 1822. The records of the State Treasury show that for the next ten years the annuity was paid to her regularly, sometimes under the name of Mary M'Kolly and sometimes under the name of Mary McCaulley.

THE CHANGE IN THE NATION

Noble deeds never die. More than a century and a quarter have passed since that eventful battle. That war was ended and other wars have been fought. Thirteen small colonies have grown into forty-five great States, bound together in one mighty and indissoluble union. The flag, which then was new to three millions of people, is now the emblem of peace and protection to more than eighty millions; and yet the fame of Molly Pitcher remains undimmed. That patriotism still abounds and fills the hearts of men and women and is witnessed by this vast assemblage gathered here in memory of gallant deeds performed.

Such occasions as this are the foundations at which, from time to time, our patriotic strength is renewed. It is well that the younger generation, in particular, shall now and then pause in the crowding activities of modern life and reflect upon the struggles, the sufferings, the endurance, the stern devotion to duty, the high ideals, the abiding confidence, and the enduring victory of those who made possible American independence.

We do well to keep green the memories of those eventful days following the determination of thirteen feeble colonies expressed in their world-famous Declaration "to assume among the powers of the earth the separate and equal station to which the laws of nature and of nature's God entitle them."

Behold, to what station they have attained. James Anthony Froude writing in 1864, said: "Washington might have hesitated to draw his sword against England could he have seen the country which he made, as we see it now." Ah, but could he have seen it as we see it to-day, with its continental vastness of domain, its unbounded prosperity and its glorious history. How his anxious heart would have been cheered; his toil made easy and his bosom filled with pride, that he in all ages and in all lands should be known as the Father of such a country. We live in a wonderful age, in a wonderful land and under a wonderful government. We cannot stop. We must go forward. We must struggle upward and help others upward. We must shun war but always prefer it to national cowardice or to peace without honor. We rejoice that our government is the greatest agency for peace the world has ever known, and equally rejoice that it never has been and never will be, a dastard in war. But unless we diligently strive we shall neither advance nor keep what the patriotism of the fathers laid up for us.

The stronger nations push the weaker to the wall. So it has been from the beginning, and so it may be to the end. We do not seek to push, but we must not be pushed. Therefore we must be strong; not merely in numbers or in wealth, "Ill fares the land, to every ill the prey. Where wealth accumulates and men decay;"—but strong in all that makes a nation great—in vigilance, in watchfulness, in enterprise, in perseverance and in principle; - in unyielding fortitude, in undying patriotism and in high exalted civic virtue. While we prosper materially we must also progress morally. In this vast audience I see descendants of revolutionary sires; I see men who fought for the Union in the sixties, I see men who upheld the Stars and Stripes as they freed ten millions of people from the medieval rule of Spain, and I see hundreds who would rally to their support should danger threaten. Not one in this great throng, of any nationality, any religion, any creed, or any political persuasion would hesitate to do so. I say to you all that for the protection of our beloved country, from open foe without or corruption and decay within, we must be ever ready to gird

our loins and pledge anew "our lives, our fortunes and our sa-
cred honor." May our starry banner be ever an emblem of
Virtue as well as of Liberty and Independence.

There are many flags in many lands.
There are flags of every hue;
But there is no flag in any land
Like our own Red, White and Blue.

At the conclusion of Congressman Olmsted's address,
which was eloquent, forcible and interesting, Chairman A.
Grant Richwine introduced Capt. J.B. Landis, of Carlisle,
who gave a most interesting history of Molly Pitcher which
already has been given in full. At the conclusion of his address, the Chairman introduced the Hon. W.I. Swoope, of
Clearfield, Pa., President of the greatest patriotic organization
in the State of Pennsylvania, the Patriotic Order Sons of
America, who delivered the following address: [There follows an eight page oration on patriotism and liberty.][9]

COMMENTARY

John B. Landis, known as "Captain Landis," was the historian
of the Patriotic Order of the Sons of America, and wrote this booklet
in 1905 at the time his organization dedicated a cannon at the grave of
Mary Hays McCauley in Carlisle. The historical section of this booklet, less the second half containing the ceremonies at the time of the
cannon's dedication, was published in *The Journal of American History* in 1911, with the addition of a new one page introduction (see
No. 4I below).[10]

Landis believes that Mary Hays McCauley was the historical
Molly Pitcher. He bases his conclusion on a collection of statements
he collected from neighbors who knew Mary Hays McCauley personally, including Susan Heckendorn (No. 8H), Harriet Foulke (No. 8I),
Barbara Park, and her grandson John A. Hays.

He also believes that Mary Hays McCauley was born on October 13, 1754 in Mercer County, New Jersey as the daughter of John
George Ludwig. She then came to Carlisle as a servant in the Irvine
family, and there met and married John Casper Hays, who served in
Proctor's artillery and then in the 7th Pennsylvania during the Revolu-

tion. His account closely follows that of Isabella Crater McGeorge (No. 3A), with the significant addition of a birth day and month (October 13) not cited by McGeorge. Interestingly, this day and month are the same given by William S. Stryker for Mary's birth, but Stryker cites the year 1744 and not 1754 (see No. 3L above).[11] Significantly, neither Stryker, McGeorge nor Landis cite a source for this birth date. Landis' belief that Mary Hays McCauley was born under the name Mary Ludwig is not valid for the reasons discussed in the Commentary to Nos. 3E and 3L above. Landis also includes the story of Molly saving the life of her husband's friend Dilwyn at the battle of Princeton, an episode first related by McGeorge (No. 4A).

Landis offers a variant to the traditional story of Molly at Monmouth by having her husband be wounded, not killed; he says it was another man whom she saw killed. He also says that she may have received her nickname "Molly Pitcher" because she was carrying water to the men in a cannonier's bucket.[12]

Landis is the first account to attribute the rank of Major to Molly Pitcher.[13]

Landis' purpose in writing this booklet was to establish that Molly Pitcher was a historical person to be identified with Mary Hays McCauley, at whose grave his organization, The Patriotic Order of the Sons of America, was dedicating a cannon in 1905.

CONCLUSION

This account marshals a number of statements by residents of Carlisle who knew Mary Hays McCauley after the Revolution. At least one remembers her talking about her presence at the battle of Monmouth (Susan Heckendorn). Landis' belief that Molly was "a young woman of German origin living among the Scotch Irish" cannot be proven by the evidence he cites.

4F. Jeremiah Zeamer, "'Molly Pitcher'" Story Analyzed," 1907.

"MOLLY PITCHER" STORY ANALYZED
She was Wife of William Hays,
Not John Casper Hays
She Fired No Cannon at the Battle of Monmouth

A bill is now pending in the Legislature asking for an appropriation of $10,000 for the erection of a monument to

"Molly Pitcher, the heroine of Monmouth." It is stated in the newspapers that the measure has the support of a patriotic order that is very strong throughout Pennsylvania, and that a determine effort will be made to have it passed. Two years ago a bill appropriating $2000 for the same object passed the Legislature but was vetoed by Governor Pennypacker.

Naturally the effort to this honor a woman, whose claim to distinction never has been authenticated, arouses inquiry. The people whose money it is proposed to expend so liberally have a right to know whether it is expended worthily.

The "Molly Pitcher" that this legislation will bring into public notice, during the last 50 years of her lifetime, was a resident of Carlisle and her remains are interred in Carlisle's principal burying ground, where her grave is conspicuously marked by a large and beautiful tombstone, contributed by the citizens of the town and also by a cannon and a large flag pole. At this late day persons who believe in the romance concerning her prefer calling her "Molly Pitcher," but at Carlisle she has always been better known as Molly McCauley, her last husband having been John McCauley. It does not appear by the public records, or anywhere by the public prints, that she was called "Molly Pitcher" until about 40 years after her death. So far as has been ascertained the name "Molly Pitcher," as applied to this particular woman, is a modern invention.

In the past 35 years much has been written about this "heroine," but no effort at all made to authenticate the extravagant and absurd claims that have been made for her. Her biographies seem to have been written more with a view to please the prevailing morbid desire for sensational literature than to record an historical incident that actually happened. To "relieve the story of her life from uncertainty" the patriotic order referred to has recently had printed and circulated a history of her, written by the late J.B. Landis. Bearing the endorsement it does it is probably intended as the official story of "Molly Pitcher," and as such is entitled to review. Besides a ten thousand dollar monument is involved and it is important that consideration be given it, and with the kind permission of the "American Volunteer" we will do so.

Briefly stated the life of "Molly Pitcher," as related in this little history, is as follows: "She was Mary Ludwig, the daughter of John George Ludwig, who was born at Trenton, N.J., October 13, 1754; was brought to Carlisle at the age of 15 by Mrs. General William Irvine; lived in the Irvine family from the age of 15 until her marriage; and she and a John Casper Hays, a barber, obtained a marriage license at Carlisle, July 24, 1769, and were married on the same day. John Casper Hays enlisted on December 1, 1775, in Proctor's Artillery; reenlisted in January, 1777, in the 7th Pennsylvania Infantry, in a company commanded by Capt. John Alexander of Carlisle; at the battle of Monmouth he was detailed from the infantry to a battery of artillery; that while serving a gun he was wounded and one of his comrades killed; that the gun for lack of gunners to man it was about to be moved off the field, but that Molly, who was carrying water in a pitcher to the soldiers at the tome, bravely sprung to her husband's place and kept the gun in action, thus contributing to the favorable results of the battle."

Now, how will this story bear analysis?

Mary Ludwig was born on October 13, 1754, and married on July 24, 1769; that is married at the age of 14 years and 9 months, yet she lived in the Irvine family "from the time she was 15 until her marriage."

That a marriage license was granted at Carlisle to John Casper Hays and Mary Ludwig is not borne out by the Cumberland county records. In fact it does not appear that marriage licenses were granted in Cumberland county at that early date. Marriage bonds were filed in court but among the marriage bonds remaining in the Court House at Carlisle there is none of this couple. Besides there was no John Casper Hays in Cumberland county at or near that time, Nor was they're a John Hays that fits into the case.

She was brought to Carlisle at the age of 15—that is in 1769—by Mrs. General William Irvine. That cannot be true. The Anne Callender, who became Mrs. William Irvine, was born February 8, 1758, and consequently was three years younger than Mary Ludwig. In 1773, at the age of 16, she married Dr. William Irvine, but that was not until four years after Mary Ludwig had married John Casper Hays. There, then was no Mrs. General Irvine that could have brought Mary Ludwig to Carlisle at or near the time named.

In 1897 the author of the aforesaid little "history" published in the Carlisle newspapers an article on "Molly Pitcher" in which he states that Mary Ludwig was born on October 13, 1744. Dr. Egle, Rev. A. Stapleton and other writers also give that date as their preference, and it is more likely that she was born in 1744 than in 1754. If born in 1744 she was 13 years younger than General Irvine, which makes her a grotesque misfit in the Irvine family prior to the war of the Revolution. The truth of the matter is that this woman was not in Carlisle prior to the Revolution and could not then have had any association with the Irvines.

And it is doubtful whether "Molly Pitcher's" maiden name was Mary Ludwig.

On the Carlisle tax list of 1783, the year the War of the Revolution ended, there stands the name of

   ·   William Hays, barber, 1 House and Lot.

For the year 1784 there is no assessment on record, but in that of 1785 there appears,

William Hays,
1 House and Lot, rented,
1 House and Lot, his own,
1 Cow.
In 1786 it again is
William Hais, barber,
One-half lot and Cow.

This is his last appearance, but in 1787 appears,

Mary Hais, widow,
2 Houses and Lot,

and the records in the Register of Wills office show that letters of administration on the estate of William Hays were issued to Mary Hays on October 3, 1787.

These different entries show that from 1783 to October 1787 there was in Carlisle a William Hays, who by occupation was a barber, and that his wife's name was Mary. During that time there was no John Casper Hays, nor John Hays, nor any other Hayses on the records of Carlisle.

On page 37 of Orphan's Court docket No. 3, is recorded that on February 12, 1788, Mary Hays, administratrix of William Hays, deceased, petitioned the court, setting forth that her husband died leaving her a widow, and a son John aged five years, to survive him, and praying that an order be granted empowering her to sell a part of her deceased husband's real estate to maintain said orphan son agreeable to the acts of assembly. The order was granted and the real estate sold and return made as by record fully appears.

Mary Hays, widow of William Hays, deceased, then, had one son; his name was John; he was an only child and he was five years old in February, 1788.

Among the records in the Carlisle court house there is no assessment for 1788, but that of 1789 contains the name of

Polly Hays,
1 House and one-half Lot.

This is the woman's last appearance on the Carlisle tax list as Mary Hais, Mary Hays, or Polly Hays.

In the aforesaid little "history" it is stated that some years after the death of her first husband, Sergeant John Casper Hays, "Molly Pitcher" married George McKolly. "McKolly" is merely an effected form of McCauley and the name George is an error.

After 1789 there is no Cumberland county assessment recorded until 1793 and in that year there appears on the Carlisle list,

John McCaley
House and one-half Lot and Cow.

The next assessment recorded is that of 1795 and on it stands
John McCawley
1 House and one-half Lot,
2 Cows,
One-half dozen Teaspoons.

The next assessment is in 1799, but upon it the name of this individual does not appear. After 1799 the assessments come regularly every three years, and among the Carlisle taxables of 1802 we find

John McCalla
1 House and one-half Lot.

After this no trace of him can be found and he probably died along about that time, but left a widow, for on the Carlisle tax list of 1814 is this entry:

Molly McCalley.
One House and one-half Lot.
In the assessment of 1817 we find again:
Molly McColly,
1 House and one-half Lot.

The reader will note that this woman in both these years is taxed with exactly the same real estate—1 House and one-half Lot—that John McCaley—McCawley—McCalla - was taxed with in three different assessments. He will also note that in 1789 Polly Hays was assessed with 1 House and one-half lot.

On page 90 of Book BB in the Recorder's Office at Carlisle is recorded a deed showing that on February 1, 1814, John L. Hays and Elizabeth his wife and Mary McCalla—McCaula—conveyed to Joseph Lynd a part of the lot on South Street, Carlisle, that descended from William Hays, "barber." That is, Mary McCalla, the widow of John McCalla—McCaley—McCawley—McColly—McKolly—formerly the widow of William Hays, the barber, joined John L. Hays—her son and only child—and his wife Elizabeth, to deed away what remained of the lot which, as the records remained of the lot which, as the records show, William Hays, "barber," bought from John Gray on August 28, 1784.

By documentary evidence, then, it is clearly established that Molly McCauley, the woman at whose grave it is proposed to erect a ten thousand dollar monument, was the widow of John McColly, and that when she married McColly she was the widow, not of John Casper Hays, nor John hays, but of William Hays, barber, who died in 1787. Now, was she ever Mary Ludwig? There is nothing anywhere in the records to show that she was.

The woman who is said to have kept a cannon in action at the battle of Monmouth was the wife of John Casper Hays. That her husband was John Casper Hays the author of the aforesaid "history" is morally uncertain, for in relating the story he repeats that name six different times.

In the Pennsylvania Archives, Second Series, Vol. XI, p. 176, it is recorded that a John Hays, on December 1, 1775, enlisted in Proctor's Artillery. In the Pennsylvania Archives, Second Series, Vol. X, p. 614 it is recorded that John Hays, in January, 1777, enlisted as a private in a company commanded by Capt. John Alexander, of Carlisle, which company became a part of the 7th Pennsylvania Infantry, commanded by Col. William Irvine , of Carlisle. Proctor's Artillery was not recruited at Carlisle, and it does not appear that the John Hays who enlisted in that command was from Carlisle, nor does it appear that the John Hays of Proctor's Artillery and the John Hays of Capt. Alexander's company were one and the same.

But it matters little whether they were the same or not for it has not been shown that a John Hays married a Mary Ludwig. In the Pennsylvania Archives, Second Series, Vol. II, p. 115, it is recorded that on July 24, 1769, a Casper Hays married a Mary Ludwig, and to give the story consistency and a semblance of accuracy, the romancers, without authority, combine the John and the Casper and name the man John Casper Hays. This leaves out of the account entirely William Hays, the barber, who, as Carlisle records show, was the husband of Molly McCauley when she settled at Carlisle, and it leaves out Mary Ludwig, too.

But no matter what the woman's name was, or how many husbands she had, or who they were, the query concerning her to be settled is.

Did she help to load and fire a cannon at the battle of Monmouth?

It is so alleged but the claim has never been authenticated, nor has any serious effort been made to authenticate it. Now that it is proposed to build a great monument to her memory it is important that the story be freely discussed and the doubts enveloping it cleared away, if possible.

For a woman to help load and fire a cannon in battle is an extremely improbable incident, and those who make the claim that it was done at Monmouth must accompany their statement with satisfactory proofs or it cannot and will not be accepted as history. In this age of intelligence and investigation people generally do not believe the absurd story of "Molly Pitcher" at the battle of Monmouth. They reason that if a woman had participated, as is alleged, it would have been so remarkable an occurrence that the entire army would have learned of it and been astonished at it. It would have become the leading topic of conversation in camp and on the march, and among the ten thousand American soldiers who engaged in the battle there would have been hundreds who would have written to their friends at home about it, and the survivors would have told it after returning to their homes. But no such letters were written and no such stories related, for if there had been some of them would surely have come to public notice long ago. Two days after the battle Gen. William Irvine wrote Col. John Davis of near Carlisle, a letter in which he referred especially to the cannonading done in the battle, but said not one word of a woman, who once was a servant in the Irvine family, having assisted in the cannonading. As an officer in the artillery it was Lieutenant-Colonel Oswald's duty, as well as his opportunity, to carefully observe and direct the work of the artillery, which he did so ably that soon after the battle General Knox pronounced him "one of the best officers in the army." Colonel Oswald afterwards published the "Independent Gazette" of Philadelphia, but never recorded in his paper anything of a woman having assisted in the artillery operations at Monmouth.

At the commencement of the Revolution there were 39 newspapers published in the United States, five of them in Philadelphia, and had a woman performed the remarkable feat attributed to Molly McCauley at Monmouth intelligence of it would certainly have found its way into some of these papers and been copied and recopied with the customary credit ever since. This was not done and the inference is that this never happened.

Because of the conduct of General Lee the details of the battle were discussed, officially and otherwise, as no other battle of the war was discussed, and a great mass of information concerning it got into the public archives and into the newspapers, but in all that mass there is not one reference to the Molly Pitcher incident.

In 1822 the Legislature of Pennsylvania granted Molly McCauley an annuity "for services rendered in the revolutionary war," but in the passage of the bill not a word was uttered and recorded intimating that she had loaded and fired a cannon. That was only 44 years after the battle of Monmouth was fought; its scenes yet lingered vividly in the minds of the American people and had she helped man a gun as claimed it would certainly have been recalled and extolled in the way of argument for the granting of the pension. It however was not so recalled and the conclusion is that no such thing happened.

Molly McCauley died in Carlisle in 1832 and two Carlisle newspapers published obituary notices upon her, speaking gently and kindly of her qualities and services, but not intimating in the slightest that she ever fired a cannon in battle. The editors of both papers were persons of intelligence—one a college graduate—and long resided in Carlisle and long known Molly McCauley, but they knew nothing of her having fired a cannon at Monmouth or they certainly would have placed such distinction to her credit in her obituary notices. Such silence, at the time of her death, on the very point that is now madder her chief claim to distinction, argues as conclusively as anything can that she never fired a cannon.

According to the obituary in one of these papers—the "American Volunteers"—Molly spent the last forty years of her life in Carlisle, and up until 1898 there were people living who in their youth knew her personally. They could distinctly recall how she looked and dressed and acted and swore, but not one of them, however severely questioned, could recall ever having heard her make the absurd claim that she helped to load and fire a cannon. For the purpose of obtaining material to make up for the aforesaid little "history," these old survivors were interviewed and their recollections written out and published, but the nearest any one of them heard Molly McCauley claim that she helped load and fire a cannon was a Mrs. Heckendorn, who testified that she heard Molly say: "You girls should have been with me at the battle of Monmouth and learned how to load a cannon," which is no claim at all that the woman herself helped to load a cannon. A distinction that Molly McCauley while living was not rash enough to claim for herself, some writers not acquainted with the records, or their subject, now persist in thrusting upon her.

The story of "Molly Pitcher's" exploit at the battle of Monmouth is a pure fiction, for there is not anywhere the slightest corroboration of it.

Respectfully submitted, J. Zeamer
Carlisle, Pa., Feb 16, 1907.

* On page 338, Vol. IX, 2d Series Pennsylvania Archives, appears a marriage notice as follows: "On July 25, 1769, in St. Michael's and Zion Lutheran Church, Philadelphia, Casper Hayes (formerly Haas) and Mary Ludwick, wid."[14]

COMMENTARY

Jeremiah Zeamer was a longtime editor of the Carlisle *American Volunteer* newspaper. For his revisionist views on the character of Mary Hays McCauley, see No. 4D, an article he wrote to express opposition to erecting a monument to her as Molly Pitcher.

Zeamer accepts the basic thesis that Mary Hays McCauley was the Molly Pitcher of history, but strongly objects to the romanticized versions of her story that were circulating in his time, particularly those put forward by John Landis in his 1905 booklet *A Short*

History of Molly Pitcher (No. 4E). He points out that Mary Hays McCauley was not idolized in Carlisle during her last years, nor was she known as Molly Pitcher during her lifetime. The title "Molly Pitcher" did not become commonly used, he says, until forty years after she died.

Zeamer may be correct that Mary Hays McCauley was not called Molly Pitcher in Carlisle during her lifetime. The first appearance of the name Molly Pitcher, however, appeared long before the 1870s. An article in an 1837 issue of the *New-Jersey State Gazette* shows that the story of Molly Pitcher was in common circulation in New Jersey just five years after Mary Hays McCauley died in 1832 (No. 2B).

Zeamer outlines the basic biography of Molly Pitcher as presented by Landis: that she was born as Mary Ludwig in Trenton in 1854; that she came to Carlisle with the Irvines; that she married John Casper Hays in 1769; that Hays was at Monmouth serving with the artillery; and that Molly brought water to the troops until she saw her husband wounded, whereupon she helped to "keep the gun in action." He then proceeds to question each of the points, particularly those concerning Molly's life before 1778.

First, concerning the marriage of Mary Ludwig and John Casper Hays in Carlisle in 1769. Zeamer states that no marriage licenses were issued in Cumberland County in that era, and that there is no record at the Cumberland County Court House of any marriage bond being issued to this couple. Nor are there any records to show either a John Hays or a John Casper Hays living in Cumberland County at the time. There is a marriage bond between Casper Hays and Mary Ludwig dated July 28, 1769 listed in the *Pennsylvania Archives* series, but it does not give their hometown.[15] In fact, there is another reference in the same publication that shows that a couple named "Casper Hayes (formerly Haas) and Mary Ludwick [Ludwig], wid." were married in St. Michael's and Zion Lutheran Church in Philadelphia on July 29, 1769.[16]

Zeamer accepts the 1744 birth date for Mary Hays McCauley presented by Landis and others, as opposed to the 1754 date proposed by Salter (No. 3H). His arguments that Molly was too old to serve in the Irvine household, and that Mrs. Irvine was too young to marry Dr. William Irvine at age 16 in 1774, are not followed elsewhere.

Zeamer's strongest argument is to show that Mary Hays McCauley was never married to a John Hays or a John Casper Hays from Carlisle. He cites a number of court and tax records from Carlisle to show that the name of Mary Hays McCauley's first husband was most certainly William Hays, a barber who died in Carlisle in 1787. Therefore Mary Hays McCauley, widow of William Hays, could not be the same person as the Mary Ludwig who married Casper Hays in 1769.

He then questions whether any resident from Carlisle named John Hays served in a Pennsylvania artillery unit at Monmouth. This point, Zeamer correctly points out, is actually no longer relevant, since Mary Hays McCauley was married to William Hays, not John Hays (or John Casper Hays) in 1778.

Zeamer's argument goes astray, however, when he strongly asserts that there would not have been any women on the battlefield, let alone any who would have been known how to fire a cannon. This statement was made because the idea of a woman fighting on the battlefield violated his sense of Victorian sensibility. The well documented case of Molly Corbin's participation in the battle of Fort Washington in 1776, where she was badly wounded while firing a cannon after her husband was killed, clearly shows his theory to be wrong (see Commentary to No. 2I). He is, though, correct in stating that none of the newspaper accounts that mention Mary Hays McCauley's 1822 pension mention that she ever fired a cannon or was at Monmouth (Nos. 7O and 7P).

Zeamer strongly states in his last paragraph that "The story of Molly Pitcher's exploit at the battle of Monmouth is pure fiction, for there is not anywhere the slightest corroboration of it." Here he clearly ignores the testimony of Mrs. Susan Heckendorn that she heard Mary Hays McCauley speak of firing a cannon at Monmouth (No. 8H). Zeamer is also unaware of the accounts of Joseph Plumb Martin concerning a woman firing a cannon at Monmouth (No. 1A) and of Rebecca Clendenin concerning a woman called Captain Molly bringing water to the troops at Monmouth (No. 1C).

CONCLUSION

Zeamer's article is significant for showing that Mary Hays McCauley was married to a man named William Hays at the time of the battle of Monmouth, not John Hays or John Casper Hays. For this reason Mary Hays McCauley could not be the same person as the Mary Ludwig who married Casper Hays in 1769. His citation of primary sources to prove his case was followed and expanded by Samuel S. Smith in his booklet *A Molly Pitcher Chronology* published in 1972 (No. 5G).

Zeamer's argument that no women would have been on the battlefield firing a cannon overlooks the well known example of Molly Corbin at the battle of Fort Washington. His claim that there is no evidence whatever for Molly Pitcher firing a cannon at Monmouth ignores the evidence of Joseph Plumb Martin and Mrs. Susan Heckendorn.

4G. Martin I.J. Griffin, "Irish Molly Pitcher," 1909.

"When will Congress erect some suitable memorial to a patriotic woman, for example, Irish Molly wife of an Irish gunner, who was personally complimented by Washington after the battle of Monmouth and conferred upon her the title of Lieutenant Colonel and half pay for life. I hope some day soon that Congress may remember the brave deed of Moll Pitcher, the true Irish wife from gallant Tipperary," [Mrs. Jolly.]

There is no evidence of any "Irish Molly, wife of an Irish gunner" being at Monmouth nor evidence of any woman there "being complimented after the battle." Washington was in no humor of giving compliments at that battlefield. It is there he is alleged to have sworn with a big D at General Lee for trying to have the army defeated.

Washington could not confer the title of Lieutenant-Colonel on any one nor order half pay. That was the province of Congress and Congress did not do either for any woman for any action at Monmouth or elsewhere.

So Congress is not now likely to erect a monument to "a heroine" when there is no evidence of the alleged action.

Irish orators claim Molly was Irish. The Germans claim her as their own and that her name was Mary Ludwig. In the *Pennsylvania Archives,* 5th Series, Vol. III, p. 1018, she is stated to have been the wife of Sergeant John Hays of Proctor's Pennsylvania Artillery.

She died at Carlisle, Pa., January, 1832, age 89, and was buried with military honors. The Editor of the *Archives,* in a footnote, states, "She was the celebrated Moll Pitcher who distinguished herself at the Battle of Monmouth. For this service she was pensioned by Pennsylvania."

Over her grave was erected in 1876 a headstone inscribed, "Molly McCauley, Renowned in history as Molly Pitcher." She was German. "Dutch, Dutch as sour crout," declared her granddaughter in 1883. It was not until 1876 the claim was made of her having taken her husband's place at Monmouth. She was there, however.

In 1905 a Bill appropriating $2000 "for the erection of a monument to the memory of Molly Pitcher, the heroine of Monmouth" passed the Pennsylvania Legislature, but was vetoed by Governor Pennypacker. In 1907 another Bill, supported by one of the "patriotic societies," appropriating $10,000 was offered but did not pass. *The American Volunteer,* in supporting the Bill, said her name was Mary Ludwig, born at Trenton, October 13, 1754, brought to Carlisle at age of fifteen by Mrs. General William Irvine in whose family she lived until her marriage to John Casper Hays, a barber, and other specifications.

Mr. J. Zeamer of Carlsile, Pa.,, has historically examined all the statements presented in favor of the alleged Molly Pitcher and found all incorrect and that she was the wife of William Hays and not John or John Casper Hays. He died in 1787. She then married John McCalla (McKolly). In 1822 the Legislature granted her an annuity for "Services in the Revolutionary War," but the nature of these services is not recorded. She died in 1832. The two Carlisle papers published obituary notices but no mention appears of the Monmouth incident, although she spent forty years of her life and persons were living there in 1898 but had never heard of the alleged gun firing claim. Mr. Zeamer concludes: "The story of 'Molly Pitcher's' exploit at the battle of Monmouth is a pure fiction, for there is not anywhere the slightest corroboration of it."

Because of the name McKolly she is claimed by the Irish—though she was a German.

There is another who seems to have a better title but is not known as "Molly Pitcher," and for whom there are official records to show her services. She is Margaret (or Margery) Corbin, of Pennsylvania, who at the British attack and captured of Fort Washington on the Hudson, November 16, 1776, took the place of her husband and was wounded in the arm and so disabled for life. The Supreme Executive Council of Pennsylvania on June 20, 1779, voted her thirty dollars and a suit of clothes yearly.

The Continental Congress of July 6, 1779, acted on the report of the Board of War of July 3d and "Resolved, That Margaret Corbin, who was wounded and disabled in the attack on Fort Washington, whilst she heroically filled the post of her husband who was killed by her side serving a piece of artillery, do receive, during her natural life, or the continuance of said disability, the one-half of the monthly pay drawn by a soldier in the service of these States; and that she now receive out of the public stores, one complete suit of clothes or the value thereof in money."

Additional records in her case may be read in the *Magazine of American History,* September, October and November, 1886.

So Margaret Corbin did really "fill the place of her husband who was killed by her side," but that was nineteen months [Nov. 16 1776—June 28, 1778] before the Battle of Monmouth.

Nevertheless, a "Molly Pitcher" who is alleged to have carried water to the soldiers at Monmouth and so got the name "Pitcher" and for whom it is claimed took the gun (cannon) of her husband after his death, loaded it and discharged it at the British, has a popular existence though she cannot be proven to have acted as claimed.

In the office of the State Treasurer of New Jersey at Trenton for many years hung a painting, said to have cost six thousand dollars, of "Molly Pitcher at Monmouth." In January, 1908, it was, on claim of heirs of Senator Crowell of Rahway, restored to Mrs. John H. Crovsk, his heir, as his personal property. It was painted about forty years ago.

Few battles of the Revolution have had the minutest incidents recited as has that of Monmouth. The late General Stryker, who compiled all the available information regarding the battle said he could not find a word about Moll Pitcher.

William Nelson, Esq., Corresponding Secretary of the Jersey Historical Society, the best informed of men concerning New Jersey events, never attached any importance to the story, regarding it as one of those myths which have prevailed in all countries and in all ages.

Mr. Zeamer, last April, showed that there was a "Moll Pitcher, the Fortune Teller of Lynn," Massachusetts, of whom John G. Whittier wrote "Moll Pitcher, a Poem," which he later endeavored to suppress. This "Moll" died in 1813, but no claim was ever made for her as being at the Battle of Monmouth.

Poets are not Historians. So William Collins had his imagination as the only basis for poem on Moll Pitcher at Monmouth, though it might apply to Margery Corbin at Fort Washington.

> "Quickly leaped she to the cannon,
> In her fallen husband's place,
> Sponged and rammed it, fast and steady,
> Fired it in the foeman's face.
> Flashed another ringing volley.
> Roared another from the gun:
> 'Boys, hurrah!' cried Irish Molly,
> 'For the flag of Washington'"

On 24 June, 1908, Elizabeth Delaff [Dehuff], of Carlsile, made Oath before John R. Miller, Notary Public, that she (Elizabeth White) was born February 18, 1818, that she knew Mollie McCauley who lived across the street from her; that she was often in her mother's house; was rough and uncouth in her expressions when she would tell about the battlefield; that her mother told her, "I won't have that kind of talk or swearing before the children"; that she would tell of the battlefield and how she used to carry water to the soldiers, and

when her first husband was killed she took his place at the cannon's mouth. "Yes, she did that. I remember it distinctly."
It is to be noted that the battlefield is not named.

Mr. Zeamer writes in THE RESEARCHES:

I rather incline to the theory that the Monmouth story was inspired by the story of the Maid of Saragossa [Zaragosa]. The two have marks of resemblance, viz.: the Maid was 22 years old, which, according to most writers, was the Monmouth woman's age; the Maid had a lover who fell at the gun and at Monmouth the woman had a husband killed.

The Siege of Saragossa took place in 1808-1809. Byron immortalized the Maid in his "Childe Harold," written in 1810 or 1811 and published in 1812. "Childe Harold" did not reach general circulation in America till years afterwards and it was not till the world was generally informed of the deed of Saragossa that it became known that a similar act had been performed by a woman at Monmouth. Geo. W.P. Custis was the first to put the story in print. He wrote in 1840, sixty-two years after the battle, and carefully abstained from telling where he got his facts. If there is an earlier reference to the incident in print than Custis's it is yet to be discovered. Probably the next earliest reference to it is by Barber & Howe in their *Hist.Colls. of N.J.* (1844).

I have a large collection of material bearing on the incident which I some day may publish in the form of a monograph. I can make the proof that no such thing happened at Monmouth much more conclusive than appears in anything that I have written yet.

Yours truly, J. Zeamer[17]

COMMENTARY

This article was written by Martin I.J. Griffin, editor of *The American Catholic Historical Researches,* for the "Errors Corrected" section of his October 1909 issue.

It does a good job of summarizing some of the issues concerning Molly Pitcher that were being debated at the time, particularly concerning the issue of whether she was Irish or German.

It begins with comments on a statement by a Mrs. Jolly, presumably from an earlier issue of the *Researches,* and includes comments on Margaret Corbin (see also No. the Commentary to No. 2I), Moll Pitcher (see Nos. 2A and 2C), and a poem by William Collins. Notes are also included on the researches of Jeremiah Zeamer (see Nos. 4D and 4F), and the article concludes with a short letter by Zeamer. Unfortunately, Zeamer never compiled all his work into a book, as he indicated that he intended to do.

CONCLUSION

This article includes comments on a number of topics does not come to a conclusion on any of them. It includes an informative section on the "Maid of Saragossa," a woman who played a key role in the defense of Saragossa, Spain during a famous siege in 1808-1809. She was commemorated in a poem by Lord Byron, which may have helped to contribute to the creation of the Molly Pitcher legend in some way.

4H. "Moll Pitcher," unsigned article in *The Pennsylvania German Magazine,* February 1910.

Prof. Faust in his "The German Element" repeats the well known story of "Moll Pitcher," a sketch of whom was given in THE PENNSYLVANIA GERMAN of July 1901. The Kutztown Patriot in the issue for January 22, in reviewing Prof. Faust's book dances about in high glee editorially at the "discovery" of the Germans and refers to historic Moll in these words:

"Of course, every school boy and every school girl knows the story of Moll Pitcher, who when her husband, at Monmouth, could no longer serve his gun, took his place and made the cannon do goodly service for the patriotic cause. The Irish have claimed Moll Pitcher. But that is wrong. She wasn't Irish at all. Her name wasn't Pitcher either. That was a nickname she got because she carried water in a pitcher to the thirsty soldiers during the battle. She was a German. Her husband was a German, William Hess by name, and so her name was Hess, too, a good German name. But she was a German by birth, Maria Ludwig she was before she married Hess. How pleasant it is for us to learn all this. Hurrah, hurray! At last we are discovered."

It looks as if we might be called upon to take "Moll Pitcher" from her pedestal and consign her to the scrap pile. One of our correspondents calls the account of the heroic deed a "baseless story" and is prepared to give reasons for his faith or rather lack of faith. He takes "the ground that no woman performed the cannon act at Monmouth." We hope to submit a statement by our correspondent in a subsequent issue. Before you take off your hat to cheer for "Moll" hear what our correspondent has to say.[18]

COMMENTARY

This article quotes an editorial from the *Kutztown Patriot* of January 22, 1910, showing great rejoicing and ethnic pride that Molly Pitcher was being claimed to be of German origin and not Irish. The preponderance of evidence today suggests that she was Irish, not German, and that she was not born under the name Mary Ludwig.

The "correspondent" cited in the last paragraph is probably Jeremiah Zeamer.

CONCLUSION

This article is an example of the controversy that started in the late 1800s, and still rages, as to whether Molly Pitcher was of German or Irish origin. It is unusual for claiming that Mary Ludwig's first husband was named William Hess (not Hays).

4I. Editor's Note to John B. Landis, "Investigation into American Tradition of Woman Known as 'Molly Pitcher,'" 1911.

This investigation into the identity of the American heroine known as "Molly Pitcher" develops many revelations of a popular as well as an historical interest. There has never been a popular idol in history with more or varied names than that of the woman who fought as a cannoneer in the American Revolution. She is given historical record as having been born in new Jersey, and as having been born in Pennsylvania. She is recorded by competent testimony as Irish and also

German. Her biographers state that she carried "a wounded man over her shoulder" from the battlefield "as she used to carry bags of wheat" from her father's barn. While others state that her father was a dairyman and not a farmer. And that from the age of fifteen until her marriage she was a domestic in the home of a physician. Even her own name and that of her husband and the place of her marriage have been in contention. She is said to have been commissioned by Washington on the battlefield and recommended half-pay for life, while other historians record that she was buried in the "Potter's Field" in Pennsylvania, only to have it further claimed that she was buried on the banks of the Hudson. In a series of ten papers on her life, it is stated in five that her husband was "wounded at Monmouth," in one that he was "mortally wounded," in three that he was "killed," and in one that he "died from the heat." No less an authority than the late Frank R. Stockton, in "Appleton's Stories from American History," says that "a bullet from the enemy struck the poor man and stretched him dead," while Harper's "Encyclopedia of the United States" says that her husband was killed and that his young wife took his place "to avenge his death." This investigation enters into an exhaustive endeavor to secure the truth and straighten out the mystery of "Molly Pitcher," this disentangling the various knots. The original evidence is deposited in Carlisle, Pennsylvania, with sworn affidavits, and is recorded in THE JOURNAL OF AMERICAN HISTORY by the authority of its curators.—Editor.[19]

COMMENTARY

This essay does an excellent job of summarizing the conflicting accounts of Molly Pitcher's life and activities that were current in the early 1900s. It serves an introduction to a reprint of the first half (pages 1-34) of John Landis' 1905 booklet, *A History of Molly Pitcher*. This article contains his arguments for Molly Pitcher's existence as Mary Hays McCauley of Carlisle (see No. 4E). It omits the second half of the 1905 booklet (pages 35-58) containing the dedicatory ceremonies for a cannon unveiled on June 28, 1905 at Mary Hays McCauley's grave in Carlisle by the Patriotic Order of the Sons of America.

The Craig House, built in 1746, is preserved today as a museum. Photograph by the author.

5. SECONDARY SOURCES, 1914-1972

5A. Samuel Craig Cowart, Address, Battle of Monmouth, and Poem, Patriot Sires of Monmouth, 1914.

The bravery of Mollie Pitcher at Monmouth is familiar to every student of Revolutionary history. When her husband fell mortally wounded, while serving one of the cannon, when Ramsey was defending his guns, the commanding officer directed the cannon to be withdrawn. She at once stepped forward and said she would avenge her husband's death by serving the cannon herself. She seized the ramrod and loaded and fired the gun during the rest of the battle. Her gallantry was an inspiration to the soldiers fighting by her side and was observed and rewarded by Washington himself, who gave her a Lieutenant's commission and she was known thereafter as "Captain Mollie." While her husband was serving as cannonier, the heat being excessive, she is said frequently to have gone to a neighboring spring to get water for him and his comrades. I am satisfied that this spring was in the edge of Gordon's woods near what is known as "Gordon's Bridge" on the Pennsylvania Railroad, and not where "Mollie Pitcher's Well" is pointed out, for the reason that Ramsey's guns in the third skirmish were near these woods and the well was not dug until long after the battle. Anyhow, it would have been too far away for convenient use that day. It was an intensely hot day and many soldiers on both sides died from the heat without suffering a single wound.[1]

COMMENTARY

Samuel Craig Cowart (1854-1943) was a lawyer of note in Freehold for most of his life. He owned for some time the "Craig House" on the battlefield, and was also noted as a local historian of the battle. Some of the stories he told, however, related family oral tradition rather than proven fact.

Cowart's brief account is reminiscent of the 1837 New-Jersey State Gazette article cited above (No. 2B) and Barber and Howe's 1844 account (No. 2G) by having Washington give her a Lieutenant's commission on the battlefield.

It was Cowart's belief that Molly's husband was killed while serving as a member of Ramsey's command. This caused him to place the scene at the incorrect spot (see No. 13B below). Molly's husband William Hays was serving with Proctor's battery on Perrine Hill (see Chapter 12 and the Conclusion to Chapter 13).

CONCLUSION

Cowart was a well known local historian, but his belief that Molly served a cannon in Ramsey's command and got her water from a spring in Gordon's Woods cannot be supported by current evidence.

5B. *History of Monmouth County, New Jersey, 1664-1920,* **1922.**

One of the most thrilling stories about the battle is that of "Sergeant" Molly Pitcher. She was of German descent, her name being Mary Ludwig, and born on a farm between Princeton and Trenton. She married John Hays, of Carlisle, Pennsylvania, who became a gunner in the Continental army, and Mary went home to visit her parents. When the army came across the State she visited her husband, and was with him on the Sunday of the battle. During the fighting she was of great assistance to the gunner of General Knox's batteries by carrying water to the thirsty men, who in pleasantry called her "Molly Pitcher." Her husband, overcome by heat and fatigue, dropped swooning by the cannon, when his wife sprang forward and assisted in loading and firing the gun during the remainder of the engagement.

General Greene presented her to General Washington on the morning after the battle and, in thanking her, he declared that, having done a soldier's duty, she was entitled to a soldier's reward and rank, and ordered that her name be enrolled as a sergeant in the army roster. General Lafayette and other officers publicly complimented her, and Congress voted her an annuity of $40. After the death of her husband she married a man named McCauley. She died in January, 1833, and was buried at Carlisle, Pennsylvania, where on July 4, 1876, the citizens of Cumberland county, Pennsylvania, placed a handsome marble monument over her grave. She was not a coarse camp-follower, as has been said; but a patriotic, industrious and kind-hearted woman. Mrs. Isabella (Crater) McGeorge wrote an excellent article concerning this heroic woman, published in the American Monthly Magazine of November, 1900.[2]

COMMENTARY

This account closely follows that of its stated source, Isabella Crater McGeorge's 1900 magazine article, "A New Jersey Heroine of the Revolution" (No. 4A). The author believes that Molly Pitcher was born in Mercer County, New Jersey, as Mary Ludwig, the daughter of a German farmer; that she was married to John Hays of Carlisle; that she brought water to Knox's artillerymen at Monmouth, where she helped fire a gun after her husband swooned from the heat; that General Greene presented her after the battle to General Washington, who gave her a commission as a sergeant.

CONCLUSION

This account is derivative from McGeorge's and adds nothing new.

5C. Randolph Keim, "Heroines of the Revolution," 1922.

Heroines of the Revolution
Mary Ludwig Hays, the Heroine of "Monmouth,"
and Margaret Corbin, the Heroine of Fort Washington

There exists a conflict of identity as to two heroines of the war for American Independence for which there can be no excuse except the carelessness of persons assuming to write history.

The case in point is the mistaken personalities of Mary Ludwig Hays, the heroine of "Monmouth," a Pennsylvania German, and Margaret Cochran Corbin of Pennsylvania, of Scotch Irish stock and Virginia-Pennsylvania parentage.

A local authority in the *Telegraph* of Harrisburg, Pennsylvania, March 5th, 1907, calls attention to this mix-up.

By way of comment the writer says:

Historian after historian in referring to the War for American Independence, makes mention of the valor of the patriots of the Revolution, and of the heroism of the one particular woman who is designated as "Moll Pitcher" from the services performed by her at Monmouth and Fort Washington in carrying water to the soldiers at the guns. One writer or another centers her brilliant actions around the former engagement, while others in narrating the events which led up to the surrender of Fort Washington, speak of "Moll Pitcher" as gallantly defending herself with that memorable event, by firing the last gun before its surrender. Investigation and research disclose the fact, that both women were not identical – and although belonging to or accompanying the same artillery force of the Continental Army, each earned the laurels which writers have heretofore failed to bestow on the right women. One of the most noted historians of the Revolution referring to "Captain Molly" in his account of the action at Monmouth states that "she was a sturdy, young camp follower, only twenty years of age, and in devotion to her husband, she illustrated the character of her country – women of the "Emerald Isle." The sketches which follow of these heroines of Monmouth and Fort Washington, give the facts of the courage and skill of two American women – one of them German, the other of Scotch-Irish lineage – records of duty which in any other country would be perpetuated in marble or bronze. Much fiction has been furnished relating to these events, but the narrative herein set forth has been furnished relating to these events, but the narrative herein set forth will tend not only to perpetuate the incidents but preserve the names of two of the most heroic womanly figures of the Revolution.

Molly Hays, The Heroine of Monmouth

Mary Ludwig, the daughter of John George Ludwig, was born in Lancaster County, Pennsylvania, October 13, 1744. Her parents were emigrants from the Palatinate, Germany. Mary's early years were spent in the family of General William Irvine, then residing at Carlisle. Here she became acquainted with John Hays, to whom she was married July 24, 1769. When the struggle for independence began, John Hays enlisted in Captain Francis Proctor's independent artillery company. With almost every command a certain number of married women were allowed, who did the washing, mending, and frequently the cooking for the soldiers. Among these was the wife of John Hays, who gladly availed herself of the privilege of sharing the privations and dangers of war with her husband. Two years had passed, of march, bivouac and battle, and the devoted wife followed the fortunes of her partner in life.

It was preserved for her, however, to immortalize her name by one heroic deed. It was in the action at Monmouth that her conduct became conspicuous. Sergeant Hays, who had charge of one of the guns, was severely wounded, and being carried away, the wife took his place in the forefront, and when the conflict was over assisted in carrying water to the disabled. This won for her the sobriquet of "Moll Pitcher." There may have been other "Moll Pitchers," but this heroine of Monmouth was none the less than Molly Hays. For her brave conduct, upon coming to the attention of the commander-in-chief, General Washington personally complimented her as she departed for her home in Pennsylvania with her wounded soldier, to show his appreciation of her virtues and her valuable services to her country. Hays never returned to the army, and died a few years after the close of the war from the effects of his wounds. Owing to the fact that other women were credited with this heroic act at Monmouth, the State of Pennsylvania. As well as the Federal Government in recognition of her distinguished services as herein set forth, granted her annuities for life.

Mrs. Hays subsequently married George McCauley, and was afterwards familiarly known as Molly McCauley. She was a woman highly respected by the citizens of Carlisle, and at her death, January 22, 1832, was buried with the honors of war. In 1876 the patriotic people of Cumberland County appropriately marked her grave, and the day is coming when the name of Molly McCauley will be honored and revered by patriots throughout the land. Inured to hardships, privations and sufferings in her life, she was a true matron of the Revolutionary era. Poor, it is true, but conspicuous in her loneliness and poverty.[3]

COMMENTARY

Keim authored only the five introductory paragraphs. The section on Molly Hays is almost word for word the same as the article on Molly Pitcher published by William H. Egle in 1893 (No. 3J) and 1898 (see Commentary to No. 3J).

CONCLUSION

This article is derivative from Egle and contributes nothing new.

5D. William S. Hornor, *This Old Monmouth of Ours,* 1932.

MOLLY PITCHER

The brave and patriotic service of "Molly Pitcher," who was born Mary Ludwig, in carrying water from the near-by Wemrock Brook to the batteries on Comb's Hill, in order that moistened swabs might extinguish smouldering tinder within the guns, and the guns themselves kept cool enough for continuous serving, is worthy of all praise, and she well deserves a high place on that day's roll-of-honor. But the student of history reads with regret the fulsome and fantastic legends that have grown up or been woven around her by over-enthusiastic creative imaginations. This misleading sign, "Molly Pitcher's Well," near the railroad is no credit to Monmouth. Her first husband, John Hays, an artilleryman, was killed at Monmouth. She married, secondly, Sergeant George McCauly. Her death took place in Carlisle, Pa., in January, 1833, at which time she was 79 years of age.

The real hero of Monmouth's battle was General Anthony Wayne.[4]

COMMENTARY

Hornor follows the Wing-Egle-Stryker tradition that Molly was born as Mary Ludwig and was married to John Hays at the time of the battle; the Ludwig lineage is erroneous and she was married to William Hays in 1778 (see Commentary to Nos. 3E, 3J and 3L). He states that her husband was killed at the battle, and then mistakenly gives the name of her second husband as George McCauly instead of

John McCauly (McCauley). Her death date was 1832, not 1833 as Hornor states (see No. 9B).

Hornor is unique in placing Molly's heroism on Comb's Hill, and in stating that she drew her water from Wemrock Brook. Battle evidence is that Procter's artillery, in which William Hays was serving, fought on Perrine Ridge, some distance from Wemrock Brook and Comb's Hill (see Chapter 13). He is correct in questioning the misleading "Molly Pitcher's Well" sign that is near the railroad (see No. 13C).

CONCLUSION

This account follows the Wing-Egle-Stryker tradition that Molly's birth name was Mary Ludwig and that she was married to John Hays (not William) at the time of the battle. It is unique in saying that Molly got her water from Wemrock Brook and fought on Comb's Hill.

5E. George E. Scheer, *Private Yankee Doodle,* 1962

Mary Ludwig Hays, wife of a Pennsylvania private whom she followed to war and who, this day, seems to have been assigned to a gun battery. A woman of no education who smoked, chewed tobacco, and "swore like a trooper," she won immortal fame as Molly Pitcher.[5]

COMMENTARY

George F. Scheer edited and wrote the introduction to the 1962 edition of Plumb Martin's commentary that was reprinted by Little, Brown and Company in 1962. In this brief note he accepts the commonly held belief that Molly Pitcher was born under the name Mary Ludwig. This theory, however, has been shown by Zeamer and Smith (Nos. 4F and 5G) to be invalid.

CONCLUSION

This is a more recent repetition of the incorrect interpretation begun by Wing in 1878 that Molly Pitcher's maiden name was Mary Ludwig (No. 3E).

5F. C. Malcolm B. Gilman, *Monmouth, Road to Glory,* 1964.[6]

Charles Malcolm Brookfield Gilman was born in 1898 and served in both World War I and World War II, rising to the rank of Colonel in the Army Medical Corps. He was educated at Columbia and then at Cornell, where he earned his M.D. His other books include *The Huguenot Migration, The Story of the Jersey Blues,* and *Surgery during the American Revolution.* Dr. Gilman, or Col. Gilman as he preferred to be called, resided in Middletown, New Jersey.

Gilman wrote *Monmouth, Road to Glory,* for the primary purpose of attempting to exonerate Major General Charles Lee from the blame he has received from many historians for his actions at the battle of Monmouth. Gilman's interest stemmed form that fact that one of his ancestors, Major Charles William Gilman, supported Lee's position after the battle, a stance for which he suffered personally after the war.[7] The book contains a reprint of the 1864 edition of Lee's court-martial, with numerous marginal notes made by Gilman at points that he believes support Lee's case.

Gilman also includes several other supporting chapters, including one entitled "Molly Pitcher, Mary Ludwig, Huguenot Heroine of the American Revolution."[8] Here he states that Molly Pitcher was the daughter of John George Ludwig, a dairy farmer near Trenton, and was born on October 13, 1754. She met Mrs. William Irvine in Allentown, New Jersey, and returned with her to Carlisle, Pennsylvania, where she met and married John Casper Hays, "the village barber," on July 24, 1769. When her husband joined the army during the Revolution, Mary rejoined her family in Allentown. During the Monmouth campaign she "joined her husband as the Army passed over from Valley Forge to Monmouth." At Monmouth she brought water to the troops "from a nearby spring on Wemrock Road" and then helped to fire one of Knox's cannons after he husband was seriously wounded. The next day she was given a parade with "mounted horse, continentals, Jersey Blues, artillery, militia, and flagbearers" as well as most of the army's top generals. There Washington gave her a commission as sergeant plus a pension.[9]

Gilman cites a number of new sources as evidence for his statements. He says that he found a christening record for Mary Ludwig at "The Lawrenceville Presbyterian Church, then the Church of Christ" dated October 13, 1754. However, the current church staff are not aware of the existence of this document. Published records of the Lawrenceville Presbyterian Church do not include record of any baptisms before 1821.[10]

Gilman then expands on Mary Ludwig's ancestry, and cites a Mr. West of Allentown for evidence that "She lived just outside Allentown on the road to Maidenhead [Lawrenceville]; she was a Huguenot all right – her mother's name was Susan Neau." This theory follows the line presented by Isabella Crater McGeorge in 1900 (No. 4A), with the added information about her mother's name. However, other sources, most notably Sally Smith Stafford, say that Molly Pitcher was born in the Allentown area under the name of Mary Hanna, and was of Irish lineage, not German (No. 3A).

To clarify her marriage with John Hays, Gilman cites a marriage records from the Church of Christ in Carlisle that reads as follows, "Married this day Mary Ludwig to John Hays. Mary is a simple kindly child of good faith."[11] It is interesting that this source, if accurate, is not cited elsewhere by supporters of the theory that Molly Pitcher was born as Mary Ludwig. In fact, the 1769 marriage bond published in *Pennsylvania Archives* states that Mary Ludwig was to marry Casper Hays, not John Hays.[12] The bottom, line, however, is that it does not matter whether Mary Ludwig married Casper Hays or John Hays, because the man to whom Mary Hays McCauley was married at the time of Monmouth was actually named William Hays, as Zeamer and Smith have shown (Nos. 4F and 5G).

Gilman's claim that Molly Pitcher served a cannon in Knox's command and got her water from a nearby spring on Windsock [Wemrock] Road cannot be substantiated by other evidence (see Chapter 13). There is also no other evidence for Molly being feted the day after the battle by a parade including Generals Washington, Knox, Wayne, Green [sic], Cadwallader, Lafayette, Poor, and Hamilton [sic].[13]

Gilman rightly points out the confusion between the stories of Molly Corbin and Molly Pitcher.[14]

He has either misinformation or a misprint when he cites Mary Hays McCauley's death date as January 1822; it should be January 1832.[15]

Gilman offers more than a few rationalizations about differences in the Molly Pitcher tradition. He suggests that those who say she was born in Pennsylvania were confused between Allentown, Pennsylvania and Allentown, New Jersey. He also suggests that the confusion about whether or not John Hays served in the artillery is irrelevant, because all Revolutionary war infantry regiments "according to the plan of 18th century warfare carried two pieces of artillery," a point that is patently incorrect concerning Monmouth. He also suggests that Molly's husband John Hays was serving with Dr. Irvine's regiment at Monmouth because Irvine wanted him in his command because he knew that Hays was a barber, and barbers in those days also doubled as surgeons.[16]

Gilman's account of Molly Pitcher is interesting, but is tainted by a number of his own personal biases. His primary purpose in writing this chapter was to show that Molly was "a Huguenot cannoneer, heroine of the American Revolution."[17] His interest in doing so can be plainly understand since he was at one time President General of The National Huguenot Society. For the same reason he found it necessary to show that Molly was a "fine woman" and an "affectionate wife," not a "drunkard, never-married, camp follower" who was "just a 'no-good tramp.'"[18] His claim that Molly was honored after the battle by a parade featuring the Jersey Blues and flag bearers who passed before her in a reviewing strand with Washington and his generals may be tainted by Gilman's desire to glorify the Jersey Blues, in which his ancestors served. It is no accident that the first item listed on Gilman's list of accomplishments on the title page of this book is "Governor-General, The Ancient and Honourable Order of the Jersey Blues." He also wrote books on the Huguenots and the Jersey Blues.

CONCLUSION

Gilman cites fresh evidence concerning Mary Hays McCauley's possible baptism as Mary Ludwig in Lawrenceville, New

Jersey in 1754 and her alleged marriage to John Hays in Carlisle in 1769. None of this evidence, though, can be firmly substantiated, and even it were, it would have no bearing on the life of Mary Hays McCauley, who was married to William Hays in 1778, not John Hays or John Casper Hays.

5G. Samuel S. Smith. *A Molly Pitcher Chronology* (1972).

This paper, being delivered before *The Battleground Historical Society,* at Freehold, New Jersey, on the 194th anniversary of the Battle of Monmouth, has the following objective. It is to present documented evidence that the person buried beneath the Molly Pitcher monument at Carlisle, Pennsylvania, is indeed the heroine of Monmouth, but that she has been incorrectly identified as Mary Ludwig, and incorrectly identified as the wife of John Casper Hays. To this end, the following Molly Pitcher chronology is given.

The first in print reference to Molly Pitcher, although not by name, was in the book ....*Some of the Adventures, Dangers, and Sufferings of a Revolutionary Soldier,* published in 1830. The author, Private Joseph Plumb Martin, in 1776, was living with his grandparents at Milford, Connecticut, when he enlisted in the American army. By 1778, Pvt. Martin was serving under Colonel Giles Russell in his 8th Connecticut Continental Regiment, which fought at Monmouth, where several men in the regiment were killed or wounded.

Following is Martin's colorful account: "One little incident happened during the heat of the cannonade, which I was an eyewitness to, and which I think would be unpardonable not to mention. A woman whose husband belonged to the artillery and who was then attached to a piece in the engagement, attended with her husband at the piece the whole time. While in the act of reaching a cartridge and having one of her feet as far before the other as she could step, a cannon shot from the enemy passed directly between her legs without doing any other damage than carrying away all the lower part of her petticoat."

While this on-the-scene account was being reported to American readers, there were some unprinted remembrances of Molly Pitcher, called by some, Captain Molly. In Rebecca

Clendenen's pension application, dated May 12, 1840, she stated that her husband, John Clendenen "often mentioned to this respondent the toils and fatigues which he underwent and related particularly that he was at the Battle of Monmouth, and suffered greatly with the heat and thirst, that a woman who was called by the troops Captain Molly was busily engaged in carrying canteens of water to the famished soldiers..."

Sergeant John Clendenen served in Captain Powers' company of Colonel Thomas Craig's 3rd Pennsylvania Continental Regiment. This regiment was heavily involved in the fighting at Monmouth during the later stages of the battle.

When Mary Clendenen gave her pension testimony, it was 62 years after the Battle of Monmouth. Hardly a man or woman was still alive who participated in that American victory. There were no more personal memoirs to be printed. Yet, the events at Monmouth would be retold again and again by a new generation of historians.

For example, there was the team of J.W. Barber and H. Howe whose work was published in 1844, titled *Historical Collections of the State of New Jersey.* Barber and Howe were the first, in print, to use the name, "Captain Molly," although Rebecca Clendenen had used the name four years earlier, in her pension application. But when Barber and Howe employed a direct battlefield quotes, at the cannon's mouth, it seemed a bit bizarre.

Another was Benson J. Lossing whose two volume work, *Pictorial Field-Book of the Revolution,* was published in 1851-52. Lossing's title was descriptive of his method of researching and writing history. He would go to the actual scene of events, examine the ground, and interview local historians or sons and daughters of veterans who might have some contribution to offer.

It was on one of these field trips in New York State that Benson Lossing met Mrs. Rebecca Rose who claimed that she earlier knew "Captain Molly," and was willing to describe her. The description, which Lossing published was of another woman, Margaret Corbin, and it will not be repeated here, because no purpose would be served in describing someone not the subject of this paper. For those who wish to know the full facts of this misidentification, the answers will be found in the well researched and well documented work of Edward Hagaman Hall published in 1932, titled *Margaret Corbin, Heroine of the Battle of Fort Washington, 16 November 1776.*

Six years later, in 1860, the *Recollections and Private Memoirs of Washington,* by George Washington Parke Custis, was published. The author seems to have used bits of information from Martin and Lossing, plus a few new details of his own.

In 1865, following the Civil War, Dr. James Thacher's *Military Journal...* was published, in which there also was an account of Captain Molly. It should be noted, however, that the first three editions of Thacher's journal, published in 1823, 1827, and 1854 did not mention her.

Dr. Thacher had died in 1844, ten years prior to the publication of the third edition of his journal. Thus, it would seem that it was the editors of Thacher's fourth edition who were responsible for including the Molly Pitcher account, which was sandwiched between previously published sections of Thacher's journal. Thacher's regiment, Colonel Henry Jackson's Additional Continental Regiment, was at the Battle of Monmouth, but Thacher himself was, at the time, doing hospital duty in the New York Highlands.

Where Thacher's editors found their information is not known, but they were the first in print to use the name "Molly Pitcher." By this late date, however, our heroine of Monmouth had been in her grave 33 years.

At her death in Carlisle, Pennsylvania, January 22, 1832, Molly Pitcher was legally known as Mrs. Mary McAuley or McCauly. Her funeral had been well attended by Carlisle friends and admirers. She was buried "with military honors," and several patriotic groups participated in the ceremonies. But no monument was placed upon her grave to spell out for future generations the details of her achievements at Monmouth.

The Carlisle Herald, in their issue of January 26, 1832, four days after her death, carried the following death notice:

"Died on Sunday last, Mrs. Mary McAuley, (better known by the name of Molly McAuley), aged about ninety years. The history of this woman is somewhat remarkable. Her first husband's name was Hays, who was a soldier in the war of the Revolution. It appears that she continued with him while in the army, and acted so much the part of a heroine, as to attract the notice of the officers. Some estimate may be formed of the value of the service rendered by her, when the fact is stated, that she drew a pension from the government, during the latter years of her life."

In the years following her death, Molly McAuley was fondly remembered by her Carlisle friends. Harriet Foulke, daughter of Dr. George M. Foulke, in whose home Molly McAuley was once employed, had vivid recollections of her, noting that, "She was homely in appearance, not refined in manner or language. But ready to do a kind act for anyone. She was of average height, muscular, strong, and heavy-set. She was a busy talker. She wore a short gown, white or calico, a linsey striped skirt, very short and full, woolen stockings, heavy brogans, and a broad white cap with wide flaring ruffles.

Mrs. Elizabeth White Dehuff said of Molly McAuley, "She died right across the street from us, near the corner of North and Bedford Streets. There were two apartments to the house. Mollie lived in the stone part right next to the corner."

Elizabeth Dehuff continued: "Yes, Mollie was a good kind-hearted woman. There was something good in her, for all she was do rough and coarse in her expression; she was as kind-hearted a woman as ever lived. The roughness was on the outside...she would always visit the sick and was always willing to sit up at night with the sick. I heard her say she carried water to the men on the battlefield. I remember hearing the neighbors calling her Mollie Pitcher. She was known pretty commonly as Mollie Pitcher; that was what we called her."

Mrs. Susan Hackendorn who came to live in Carlisle in 1828 as a teen-ager, said that she visited with Molly Pitcher on several occasions during the following few years when Molly would tell of her war experiences. Susan remembered particularly that Molly would say "You girls should have been with me at the battle of Monmouth and learned how to load a cannon."

One of those who knew Molly Pitcher best, in her later years was Wesley Miles, for Molly became Wesley's nursemaid in 1822. When Wesley's mother died that same year, Molly remained in the Miles household for some time afterwards, as Wesley's foster mother.

An 1883 newspaper article said that Wesley Miles eventually became a "prominent school teacher, an intelligent man who has been living for several years past in Williamsport, Pa." It was from Williamsport, in 1876, that Wesley Miles wrote his recollections of his boyhood with Molly Pitcher, which were published in the May 18, 1876 edition of The Carlisle Herald, as follows:

"I well remember there resided at the corner of Bedford and North Streets, or as the location was familiarly known as Lougheridge's corner, Carlisle, Pa., an aged Irish woman, then past sixty, healthy, active and strong, fleshy and short of stature, and remember her entire personal appearance, her peculiar dress of the period, manners, oddities, etc. She was very social, exceedingly talkative, and fond of walking about and visiting her neighbors and acquaintances of the town. The old lady was largely employed as a nurse, was careful of the sick, her delight to kindly administer to the afflicted of her own sex. Besides, too, she was passionately fond of children. The little ones on the street at play knew her well, and often would she interest them by stopping during her pedestrian rambles and having a pleasant talk with them.

"This Irish woman was employed by my father, early in 1822, to nurse my afflicted mother, bedfast for nearly a year, with a lingering disease, and to have a motherly care over myself, then scarcely seven years of age, and a younger brother. I well remember I had but little affection for her as a foster mother, indeed, for I then thought, she was too unreasonably strict in discipline. To go beyond her presence, and to the street to play, child-like, with other little boys, would excite her passion to profanity. Fleet as a deer, she was sure to catch her object of pursuit, in every attempt to escape, and loading it upon her shoulders, screaming with terror, she would hie off home, and now the rod was severely applied for disobedience to her stern commands. She remained with us until mother's death, September 22d, 1822, and for some time afterwards.

"I well remember when she died – a death greatly lamented by citizens of Carlisle. She was buried with military honors by volunteer companies, the 'Guards,' 'Artillery,' and 'Infantry,' either or all of them, for, at the time of her death, these organizations were in existence...

"The remains of this Irish woman rest in the 'Old Graveyard,' of Carlisle...Perhaps, not even a rude limestone marks her grave. No imposing monument has ever been erected to mark the spot where she lies, whose deeds of valor will be read so long as our Centennials are observed by the American people, deeds eminently worthy, even of the sterner sex.

"Reader, the subject of this reminiscence is a prototype of the 'Maid of Saragossa.'" The heroine of Monmouth, Molly Pitcher, otherwise known to us when a boy, as Molly McCauly, her real name; the other a burlesque or caricature, forsooth. She bore water in a pitcher for her husband on this memorable occasion."Discovery of the Wesley Miles recollections gave rise to the first suspicion that Molly Pitcher or Molly McCauly might not have been Mary Ludwig, a German girl, as has been generally accepted over the past nearly 100 years. Wesley Miles mentioned her three times as being Irish. First, he called her "an aged Irish woman;" second, "this Irish woman employed by my father;" and third, "the remains of this Irish woman." This provoked a reflection back to the statement of Harriet Foulke that Molly Pitcher wore "heavy brogans," which are described in Webster's Dictionary as "a stout coarse shoe wore in Ireland and the Scottish Highlands." The brogan reference was but a small matter, yet it helped feed a suspicion regarding Molly Pitcher's reputed identification as Mary Ludwig, a German girl.

The Wesley Miles recollections were very timely reported in The Carlisle Herald, being about six weeks prior to the centennial celebration of the Declaration of Independence. The article caught the attention of "Peter Spahr, a native of this place and a brickmaker, a man of strong sense and energy and enterprise, and who remembers Molly very well, resolved upon the work of erecting a monument to her grave, and of having the undertaking completed on the 4th day of July of that centennial year."

About $100 was raised by subscription to pay for the cutting and erection of the stone. The monument was completed, the correct unmarked grave was located, and on July 4th, as a part of the centennial celebration, there was a parade out to the cemetery for the unveiling. After the color guards etc., "Then, came carriages containing Mr. Peter Spahr, Miss Polly Malcaster, and others, who were to take part in the ceremonies of unveiling of the monument of Captain Mollie. This took place at half past twelve." Peter Spahr was the local Carlisle brickmaker who had spearheaded the monument drive. Polly Malcaster probably was Polly McCleaster, a descendant of Molly McCauly. The monument, as it was unveiled, read:

> Molly McCauly
> Renowned in History as
> Mollie Pitcher.
> The Heroine of Monmouth
> Died Jan. 1833
> Aged 79 years.
> Erected by the Citizens of
> Cumberland County
> July 4, 1876

The erection of the monument, and the publicity accruing from it, spawned another new generation of Molly Pitcher historians. The Carlisle newspapers were searched and, without much difficulty, Molly McCauly's death notice was found.

It was soon observed that the death notice said that she died in 1832, not in 1833 as stated on the monument. The 1832 date of the newspaper carrying the death notice was sufficient proof that the year of death was 1832. Thus, the town fathers hired a stonecutter to change the date to conform to the death notice.

The death notice was in disagreement with the monument as to the age at death. The death notice said aged "about 90 years," while the monument said "Aged 79 years." The reason why the age at death on the monument was not changed may have been the result of some local research. An 1830 Carlisle Census Record coupled with a local deed record, showed that, two years before her death, Molly McCauly was living with her son, John L. Hays, and his wife, Elizabeth, both age 40-50, together with their seven children. Molly McCauly was listed as "1 female 70-80," which age was consistent with the monument text.

The death notice provided other data for these new Molly Pitcher historians. The last sentence, which mentioned a pension, was one of the first avenues of attack. But not pension records was found for Molly McCauly in the National Archives at Washington, D.C.

Attention was then turned to Pennsylvania Records, where it was found that on January 29, 1822: "Mr. Mahon presented a petition from Molly McKolly, widow of an old soldier of the revolutionary war, praying for pecuniary aid." On February 11, 1822, there was introduced in the Senate "An act for the relief of Molly McKolly, widow of a soldier of the revolutionary war."

By February 20, 1822, the act read "for the relief of Molly McKolly for her services during the revolutionary war," implying that Molly McKolly was not being rewarded on the basis of her husband's service, but her own. The bill was passed and signed on February 21, 1822, granting Molly McKolly "the sum of forty dollars immediately and the same sum yearly during her life."

Unfortunately for historians, the bill gave neither her soldier husband's name nor her own maiden name. There were, however, some clues as to Molly McCauly's identity. Her death notice said that "Her first husband's name was Hays who was a soldier in the war of the Revolution."

A search of Pennsylvania marriage records soon revealed that a marriage bond had been issued July 24, 1769, to "Mary

Ludwick and Casper Hays." The first name of the bride and the last name of the groom fitted the death notice. From this, it was apparently concluded that Mary McCauly's maiden name was Ludwick or Ludwig and her husband's first name was Casper.

The next step for the researcher was to see if he or she could locate a Casper Hays who had been in Revolutionary War service, and whose regiment had been at the Battle of Monmouth. No Casper Hays could be found, but the search did uncover a "John Hayes" and a "John Hays." The first "Hayes," in 1775-76, was a gunner in Captain Thomas Proctor's company of Pennsylvania State Artillery, but John Hayes did not show up in subsequent Proctor returns. The second "Hays," in 1777, was a private in Captain John Alexander's company of Colonel William Irvine's 7th Regiment of Pennsylvania Infantry, but this man's service did not jibe with Pvt. Martin's statement that the man at Monmouth "belonged to the artillery."

Finding a John Hays in service, but no Casper Hays, the researcher apparently reasoned, in order to tie the marriage and service records together, that soldier John Hays must have used only his middle name in his marriage bond application, and that his real name was John Casper Hays.

Historians were not given the series of maneuvers, which were made in order to identify Molly Pitcher as Mary Ludwig, wife of John Casper Hays. They appear to have been given only the conclusion. Yet, everyone seemed satisfied because, at last, someone apparently had identified our heroine.

William S. Stryker was the first to provide the name of Molly Pitcher's parents. In 1899, he wrote his manuscript for *The Battle of Monmouth,* in which he gave their names.

Stryker died shortly after completing his manuscript, and his book was not published until many years later, in 1927. Yet, before he died, Stryker gave his findings to his friends and fellow historians. He said that Molly Pitcher was born "October 13, 1744," and that she was "Mary Ludwig, daughter of John George Ludwig, who came to this country with the Palatinates," referring to a region in Germany.

No one seems to have challenged Stryker on the basis that his date of birth did not fit the dates on the Molly Pitcher monument. Had the dates been compared, it would have been observed that, if Molly Pitcher died in 1832 "Aged 79 years," she would have been born in 1753, not 1744 as Stryker said, a matter of nine years out of time.

Five years after Stryker's manuscript was written John B. Landis published (about 1905), his book titled *Molly Pitcher.* Landis gave Molly's birthday as October 13, 1754. Where Landis found this date is not revealed in his book, nor was Stryker's in his. Yet, it is interesting to note that Stryker and Landis give the same month and day of birth, but Landis places his year of birth just 10 years later than Stryker. Then, Landis quotes the monument as reading that she died "Aged 78," when actually the monument reads "Aged 79." Whether this was done intentionally to make his date fit, is not known.

This was the uncertain state of Molly Pitcher research when, some 65 years after the Landis study, this paper was started. Upon a review of existing evidence, it appeared that much work lay ahead.

One of the first steps taken was to go to Carlisle, Pennsylvania, to consult primary source records in the Cumberland County Historical Society Library and in the Cumberland County Courthouse. Two trips were made there, plus a trip to the State Archives in Harrisburg before Molly Pitcher's identity began to appear.

The first break-through came from the Carlisle Tax Rate Books, which showed:

> 1783 Hays, William, Barber
> 1 house, 1 lot
> 1785Hays, William
> 1 house & lot rented
> 1 ditto his own
> 1 cow

Other sources revealed that before the Orphan's Court in1788 "Came...Mary Hays administrator of the estate of William Hays lately died intestate...leaving widow and one son, John, aged 5 years to survive him. Begs to sell ½ property to pay debts…"

The next year's tax rolls showed that the widow Hays had sold half of her property as requested of the court:

1789 Polly Hays
1 house, ½ lot

Mary or Polly Hays continued in this status for four years, when she married one John McCauly.

After her marriage, Mary's tax burden for her house and half of a lot was taken up by her new husband whose name the tax assessor recorded in several phonetic variations.

1793 John McCaley
½ lot, 1 cow
1795 John McCawley
1 house, ½ lot
2 cows, ½ dozen Tea Spoons
1802 John McCalla
1 house, ½ lot

Mary could not write as evidenced by the fact that she signed by her mark x on several legal documents. It is presumed that neither could John McCauly write, thus accounting for these spelling variations, commonly found in 18th century records under such circumstances.

About 1813, Mary McCauly again became a widow, and the following year the tax rolls read:

1814 Molly McCally
1 house, ½ lot
1817 Molly McCally, widow
1 house, ½ lot

Mary McCauly continued in this tax status for several years. By 1830 she appears in the Carlisle census records as a member of the household of her son, as previously noted. Two years later, Mary McCauly died.

Next, in the process of identification, was the task of finding a William Hays who could meet Pvt. Martin's description of a soldier belonging "to the artillery," and one whose regiment fought at the Battle of Monmouth. Several references soon were discovered placing a William Hays in the Pennsylvania State Regiment of Artillery, which regiment was authorized February 6, 1777, and became the 4th Continental Artillery regiment September 3, 1778. According to the history of this unit, the regiment served "notably at Monmouth and in Sullivan's Campaign of 1778," under the command of Colonel Thomas Proctor.

Further, in the National Archives and Records Service at Washington, D.C., it is recorded that William Hays enlisted at Bristol, Bucks County, Pennsylvania, on May 10, 1777, and was a gunner in Proctor's Artillery.

The next mention of William Hays was in a regimental return of Colonel Proctor's regiment, which listed him in Captain Francis Proctor Jr.'s 4th company as:

"Wm. Hays, Gunner."

The Hays service record was documented further in an April 3, 1779, return of Proctor's Artillery:

"Gunner: William Hays, Place of birth Ireland,
Date of Commission, May 10, 1777."

In the two volume work, *Pennsylvania in the War of the Revolution,* additional service information was revealed:

"Hayes, William, discharged January 24, 1781;
reenlisted July 27, 1781."

The three year enlistment of William Hays ordinarily would not have expired until May 10, 1781, a matter of an additional three months service, but there was an enlistment crisis in 1781. Most of the Pennsylvanians who had enlisted back in 1777, among them William Hays, had entered service upon receipt of a $20 bonus. Now, some states were paying as high as $1000 as an enlistment bonus, which made the old soldiers discontented. In fact, some troops refused to serve further under such circumstances.

The matter was finally resolved when governor of Pennsylvania, Joseph

Reed, authorized the following proposition to be presented to the angered Pennsylvania troops at Princeton, New Jersey: "His Excellency's proposals being communicated to the different regiments at troop beating this morning Jan. 8, 1781. They do voluntarily agree in conjunction that all soldiers that were enlisted for a bounty of twenty dollars ought to be discharged immediately with as little delay as circumstances will allow, except said soldiers who have been since voluntarily reenlisted."

On January 28, at Trenton, New Jersey, Brigadier General Anthony Wayne wrote to General George Washington informing him of a resolution of the dispute: "The Commissioners of Congress have nearly closed the settlement of the Inlistments of the Penna. Line. The 11th, which is the last regiment, will be finished this evening or tomorrow morning. We have now discharged out of the aggregate, 1220 men..." William Hays was one of those released, very likely at Trenton, January 24, three days before Wayne's letter to Washington.

William Hays took six months off, and reenlisted on July 27, 1781, at which time he presumably received a satisfactory enlistment bonus. His final discharge was probably about January 1, 1783. His company commander, Capt. Francis Proctor Jr., was discharged on that date. The war was over, and the independence of the United States had been acknowledged by Great Britain one month earlier, on November 30, 1782.

These events coincide with the William Hays appearance on the Carlisle tax rolls for the year 1783. Here, it is presumed he opened a barber shop, and later that year, William and Mary Hays had a son, John.

The above military records show that there was indeed a William Hays in the artillery and that his regiment was at Monmouth. But was this William Hays who was in Proctor's

Artillery, the husband of the woman, "Molly McCauly, renowned in History as Molly Pitcher" who is buried beneath
that monument at Carlisle, Pennsylvania? The following records clearly show that he was.

In the War Department Collection of Revolutionary War
Records, there is a document titled "Return of the Pennsylvania Line, entitled to Donation Lands, reported by the late
Comptroller General." This document lists Pvt. William Hays
of Col. Thomas Proctor's 4th Artillery, Continental Line, and
authorized Mary "McCalla widow of William Hays" to participate in Donations Lands.

Mary McCalla or McCauly acquired the land consisting
of 200 acres described as:

"Donation Lands #1717 Ret'd etc. 3rd Octr. 1806
to Mary McCalla of William Hays Private."

The following year Mary sold the 200 acres. The deed,
executed April 15, 1807, transmitted title to lands received
for services of William Hays, a soldier in the Army of the
United States. The deed was from John McCalla and his wife
Mary, formerly widow of William Hays, deceased, and John
Hays, son of William, all of Carlisle, Cumberland County,
Pennsylvania, to James Brady of Greensborough, Westmore-
land County, Pennsylvania.

Included in the Veterans Administration file for William
Hays is an affidavit of James Rowney or Roney of Carlisle,
dated October 27, 1807. It states "he has known Mary Hays
now Mary McCalla) late widow of William Hays a Gunner in
Coln. Proctor's Regiment of Artillerists during the Revolutionary War, and that the said Mary had one child named
John L. Hays about 27 years of age to the said William Hays
and none other to the best of his knowledge, that the said
Mary McCalla (late Mary Hays) and John L. Hays are now in
full life: the said Mary being intermarried to John McCalla."

In conclusion, having found that it was William and Mary
Hays who were at Monmouth, we should now set about the
task of finding the parents of both William and Mary. We
should make this our goal to be achieved before 1976, the bi-

centennial year, so that during that year the Molly Pitcher monument at Carlisle, Pennsylvania, may be rededicated in the true and full name of Molly Pitcher, one of America's foremost heroines.[19]

COMMENTARY

Samuel S. Smith was the author of a number of books on the Revolution, including *Sandy Hook and the Land of the Navesink* (1963), *The Battle of Monmouth* (1964), *The Battle of Trenton* (1965), *The Battle of Princeton* (1967), *Fight for the Delaware, 1777* (1970), *The Battle of Brandywine* (1976), and *Winter at Morristown* (1979) all of which were published in Monmouth Beach, New Jersey, by his own publishing house, Philip Frenau Press. He also authored a biography of Lewis Morris, published in 1983. He died in 1983.

This booklet is the text of a paper Smith delivered before the Battleground Historical Society in Freehold on the 194th anniversary of the battle of Monmouth in 1972. Its purpose is to show that Mary Hays McCauley of Carlisle, Pennsylvania, "is indeed the heroine of Monmouth, but she has been incorrectly identified as Mary Ludwig; and incorrectly identified as the wife of John Casper Hays."[20]

Smith begins by quoting or summarizing several key sources connected with the Molly Pitcher story: Joseph Plumb Martin (No. 1A), Rebecca Clendenen [sic] (No. 1C), Barber and Howe (No. 2G). Benson J. Lossing (Nos. 2J and 2K), George Washington Parke Custis (No. 2D), and Dr. James Thacher (No. 2O). He also cites quotations from Mary Hays McCauley's 1832 obituary (No. 7P) and from several of her neighbors in Carlisle: Harriet Foulke (No. 8I), Mrs. Elizabeth Dehuff (No. 8K), Mrs. Susan Hackendorn [sic] (No. 8H), and Wesley Miles (No. 8B).[21]

Smith uses the evidence from her neighbors, particularly Wesley Miles, to question that Mary Hays McCauley was German or the person known as Mary Ludwig. He then looks into the claim put forward to Wing (No. 3E), Egle (No. 3J), Stryker (No. 3L) and others that Mary Ludwig was married to John Casper Hays who as a soldier who fought in the artillery at Monmouth. Following arguments first proposed by Jeremiah Zeamer in 1907 (No. 4F), Smith shows that the Casper Hays whom Mary Ludwig married in 1769 was not the John Hays who fought at Monmouth.[22] He also shows that there is no evidence that Mary Ludwig married John Hays, but ample evidence that she married Casper Hays in 1769. "Finding a John Hays in service, but no Casper Hays, the researcher apparently reasoned, in order to tie the marriage and service records together, that soldier John Hays must have used only his middle name in his marriage bond application, and that his real name was John Casper Hays. Historians were not given this series of maneuvers, which were made in order to identify Molly Pitcher as Mary Ludwig, the wife of John Casper Hays. They appear to have been given only the conclusion."[23]

Smith then looked at the arguments of Stryker (No. 3L) and Landis (No. 4E) to investigate why they gave the same birth date, October 13, but differ ten years in citing Molly's birth year, 1754 vs. 1754. Here he sides with Landis, but depending more on the evidence of Mary Hays' McCauley's gravestone, which says she was 79 years old when she died in 1832, giving her a birth year of 1753 or 1754 (see No.9A).[24]

Smith next went to Carlisle to look up court and tax records on Mary Hays McCauley, and, following most of the sources cited by Zeamer in 1907, builds a very strong case that the name of Mary Hays McCawley's first husband was William Hays, who died in 1787 leaving her a five year old son named John.[25]

Smith then researched the Revolutionary War service of William Hays, and found that a soldier of this name served in the Pennsylvania artillery from 1777 to 1783 (see Chapter 12). Furthermore, this William Hays had a wife Mary who survived him and laid claim to his veteran's land grant in 1806 (No. 7C, 7D and 7E). The clincher came when Smith found an affidavit dated 1807 by a man named James Rowney (Roney) of Carlisle who swore that "he has known Mary Hays (now Mary McCalla [McCawley]) late widow of William Hays a gunner in Coln. Proctor's Regiment of Artillerists during the Revolutionary War" (No. 7F). This proves that Mary Hays McCauley was first married to William Hays, not John Hays or John Casper Hays, and that William Hays served in the Pennsylvania artillery during the Revolution.[26]

CONCLUSION

Smith's small booklet is significant for demonstrating that Mary Hays McCauley was married to William Hays, a soldier in Proctor's Pennsylvania artillery during the revolution. As such, she could not have been married to John Hays, who fought at Monmouth but was not in the artillery, or to John Casper Hays, a person who never existed. This in turn means that Mary Hays McCauley was not born under the name of Mary Ludwig, so rendering mute the lengthy debates concerning the birth date and birth place of Mary Ludwig.

Smith's booklet has not received wide acknowledgement. As a result, sources to this day still follow the disproven claim that Molly Pitcher was born as Mary Ludwig (see for example Nos. 6C, 6D and 6M).

Relief of Molly Pitcher at Monmouth, on monument erected in the Old Carlisle Cemetery by the State of Pennsylvania in 1916 (see No. 9D). Photo by the author.

6. SECONDARY SOURCES, 1974-1999

6A. Mollie Somerville, *Women and the American Revolution,* 1974.[1]

COMMENTARY

Somerville presents a balanced account of the different theories about Molly Pitcher, including Smith's booklet published in 1972 (No. 5G). She points out the similarities between the actions and names of Molly Corbin and Molly Pitcher, which are expanded upon in an accompanying essay on Margaret Corbin. She also points out the different theories on the name of her husband (John Hays or William Hays), the differing years for her birth (1744 or 1754), and the different possibilities for her national origin (German or Irish), without committing to one or the other. She does, though, accept that Molly was born near Trenton, New Jersey, and says that her husband was wounded, not killed, at Monmouth. She closes with a good summary of Molly's marriage post war life and marriage to John McCauley in Carlisle.

CONCLUSION

This is a balanced account, without being committal, that mentions without bias the different opinions current on some of the major controversies concerning Molly Pitcher.

6B. Walter H. Blumenthal, Women Camp Followers of the American Revolution, 1974.

Schoolbook annals still acclaim Mollie Pitcher (really Mary Ludwig), who followed her barber husband, John Hays (or Hayes). She fired the last gun-shot at Fort Clinton before it was captured by the foe, and when her husband was killed at Monmouth she manned the field-piece where he lay and fired round shot at the redcoats. She was twenty-four and an expectant mother, Washington next day made her a sergeant and had her put on the half-pay list for life—or, as another version has it, made her a sergeant and gave her a gold piece.[2]

COMMENTARY

Walter H. Blumenthal was born in 1883 and died in 1969. This brief account repeats a number of unsubstantiated statements and errors: that Mollie Pitcher (Mary Hays McCauley) was born under the name of Mary Ludwig; that she was married to John Hays; that John Hays was a barber; and that Molly Pitcher fought at the battle of Fort Clinton. Blumenthal does not give a source for his statement that Molly was pregnant at the time of the battle. This claim was picked up by later authors (for example, Teipe in No. 6O) but has no clear source. Landis says that Mary Hays McCauley's son John L. Hays "was said to have been born in a tent on the battlefield of Monmouth after the battle, but this he afterwards said was uncertain."[3] Court records from February 1788 state that John L. Hays was five years old at the time, which would place his birth year in 1782 or 1783, not 1778 (see No. 7B).

CONCLUSION

Blumenthal tells an abbreviated version of the story of Molly Pitcher, but his account contains a number of demonstrable inaccuracies.

6C. Mark M. Boatner, Encyclopedia of the American Revolution, 1976.

MOLLY PITCHER LEGEND... The name is generally associated with Mary Ludwig HAYS, who manned a gun at Monmouth, but is also applied to "Captain Molly" (Margaret) CORBIN of Ft. Washington fame.[4]

COMMENTARY

Lieutenant Colonel Mark M. Boatner was born in 1921. In addition to his *Encyclopedia of the American Revolution,* he is also well known for his similar book *The Civil War Dictionary.*[5]

Boatner correctly points out the confusion between the stories of Margaret Corbin and Molly Pitcher (Molly Hays), whom he discusses in separate entries. However, he subscribes to the theory disproved by Zeamer (No. 4P) and Smith (No. 5G) that Molly Hays' maiden name was Mary Ludwig.

6D. Mark M. Boatner, Encyclopedia of the Revolution, 1976.[6]

COMMENTARY

Boatner states that Mary Hays Ludwig was the "heroine of the Molly Pitcher legend." He gives her birth year as 1754 and describes her as "a stocky, ruddy-faced girl of Palatine German descent." She married a barber from Carlisle named John Caspar Hays. He enlisted in the 1st Pennsylvania artillery and she accompanied him to the war. At Monmouth he was serving in the infantry but "was ordered back to the guns," where he was wounded. Molly, who had been bringing water to the troops, "stepped up with a rammer staff to take his place in the crew and keep the gun in action." She later married George McCauley, whom she deserted because he was shiftless. She supported herself as best she could, "receiving some grants of money but apparently never being able to collect a military pension." She smoked a pipe, chewed tobacco, drank, and cussed "like a female trooper."

For background information on Mark Mayo Boatner III, see Commentary to No. 6C. Boatner apparently was not aware of Smith's 1972 work (No. 5G), which is not cited in his bibliography. For this reason he continues the discredited theory that Mary Hays McCauley was born under the maiden name Mary Ludwig and was married to John Casper Hays. Boatner accepts her birth year as 1754 and give the right year for her death, 1832. He states that Molly's husband was wounded at Monmouth, not killed, and does not make mention of meeting with Washington and receiving a battlefield commission the next day.

He incorrectly gives the name of Mary Hays McCauley's second husband as George McCauley instead of John McCauley.

CONCLUSION

Boatner accepts that Mary Hays McCauley was the historical Molly Pitcher, but continues the discredited theory that she was born under the name of Mary Ludwig in 1754 and was married to John Hays in 1769. He follows the general line of the developed legend, but modifies it to have her husband wounded at Monmouth, and does not deal with the issues of the location of her well or the alleged battlefield promotion given by Washington.

6E. John Todd White, "The Truth About Molly Pitcher," 1977.[7]

COMMENTARY

John Todd White argues in this essay that women camp followers played a more active role in the Revolutionary War than is usually believed. The standard interpretation of camp followers is that all they did was cook, wash and nurse (except for the prostitutes); this is what White calls the myth of "battlefield domesticity." White claims that they fought in the front lines more often than has been thought. He cites the Molly Pitcher story as important evidence for showing the role of women on cannon crews. Molly was not bringing water to the men, but to swab the cannons, which was a very important duty. Since cannons had a crew of only three men, it would be understandable if one of the women water bearers took the place of a fallen artillerymen, rather than see the cannon inactive or withdrawn from the field, a key motive attributed to Molly in some of the early accounts. That is why, White argues, Joseph Plumb Martin was not surprised to see Molly participate in combat; Martin tells his account (No. 1A) because of the interesting anecdote about the cannon ball sailing between her legs, and not because it was odd to see a woman helping to fire a cannon.

CONCLUSION

White argues that women commonly formed part of artillery crews during the Revolution. However, the only two examples he cites are Molly Pitcher and Margaret Corbin. He is incorrect to say that Revolutionary War gun crews consisted of only three men; they were supposed to have fifteen but usually functioned with around twelve. His theory that women were more actively involved in combat than is commonly thought was greatly expanded by Linda Grant De Pauw (see No. 6H).

6F. Elizabeth Evans, "Heroines All: The Plight of Women at War in America, 1776-1778," 1978.[8]

COMMENTARY

This paper was given at a symposium held in Freehold on April 8, 1978 to commemorate the two-hundredth anniversary of the battle of Monmouth.

Evans begins by pointing out that it was customary for British armies in the eighteenth century to be accompanied by women and children during their campaigns. In 1777 the British army in America had one woman to every eight men, and their German troops had about one to thirty. American armies also regularly had women camp followers, though their numbers were never proscribed or limited.[9] Camp followers had a rough life, particularly since they were issued rations at a reduced rate, but still followed the armies "out of concern for the welfare of their families." Besides doing the more familiar duties such as cooking, washing clothes and tending the wounded, camp followers even helped to plunder the enemy's dead and wounded. Evans cites one British source from the 1790s who noted how camp followers in that era not long removed form the Revolution helped by "fetching cartridges from the ammunition wagons and filling the pouches of the soldiers, at the hazard of their own lives, while others with a canteen filled with spirit and water, would hold it to the mouths of the soldiers, half choked with gunpowder and thirst, and when a man was wounded they would afford him all the assistance in their power to help him to the nearest house or wagon."[10]

Evans then briefly describes the fight at Monmouth and Molly Pitcher's role in it. She concludes by saying that "Mary Hays, or 'Molly Pitcher,' as she came to be called, and Margaret Corbin... should be remembered not for their courage alone, but for all the women who participated in campaigns."[11]

CONCLUSION

Evans discusses the role of camp followers in Washington's army, and some of the hardships they endured. She accepts that Molly Pitcher was Mary Hays, wife of William Hays, a gunner in Proctor's artillery, and that she knew how to load and fire both a musket and a cannon.

6G. James Kirby Martin, "Comments," 1978.[12]

COMMENTARY

This article consists of the comments that James Kirby Martin made to papers presented by Mark Lender and Elizabeth Evans (No. 6F) at a symposium held in Freehold, New Jersey on April 8, 1978 to commemorate the two-hundredth anniversary of the battle of Monmouth.

He criticizes Evans' paper for being a "descriptive compilation that does not do much to refine and deepen our knowledge of women in the revolutionary era."[13] He also criticizes Walter H. Blumenthal, author of *Women Camp Followers of the American Revolution,* for continuing the myth that American camp followers came from all classes of society. Instead, Martin argues, most of the camp followers were "young, single and poor, as were most of the men," a theory presented earlier by John Todd White (see No. 6E). Martin divides camp followers into three groups: those who followed their husbands in the traditional sense; prostitutes; and, the most important group, those who were "single and in desperate need of the bare necessities of life."[14] Martin concludes, "Perhaps the women of Washington's army were conveying the same sort of message: Let us fight for liberty, even stand in battle and fire the cannon so that we too may have the same freedom that a united people seeks through the act of political revolution."[15]

CONCLUSION

Martin's comments attack the traditional view of camp followers as being primarily composed of the soldiers' wives and womenfolk, and believes that most of the camp followers were poor, unattached women who followed the army because they needed to be fed and they wanted to fight for the ideal of liberty. This theory, at least in its latter elements, has not found widespread acceptance.

COMMENTARY

6H. Linda Grant de Pauw, "Women in Combat: The Revolutionary War Experience," 1981.[16]

COMMENTARY

Ms. De Pauw, who was a Professor of History at George Washington University, wrote this article in 1981 to prove her startling thesis that "During the American War for Independence tens of thousands of women were involved in active combat" (for further discussion, see Chapter 11). These included women who served as "women in the army" in both the medical corps and artillery units, as well as those who enlisted as regular troops and those who fought as irregulars either in the militia on the frontier.

Part of De Pauw's thesis is that women regularly served with artillery units as water bearers, and some at times even took the place of fallen artillerymen to help man the cannons (witness Margaret Corbin and the story of Molly Pitcher). However, DePauw claims, "there was no 'real' Molly Pitcher, for like G.I. Joe, the name describes a group not an individual."[17] In short, there was no historical Molly Pitcher, but instead a large number of women who served in the artillery in the war, whose memory has been combined into the legend of Molly Pitcher.

De Pauw claims that "At least two different women were observed at the battle of Monmouth alone," but the evidence she cites is Joseph Plumb Martin's account (No. 1A) and Mrs. Susan Heckendorn's statement about Mary Hays McCauley loading a cannon at Monmouth (No. 8H).[18]

CONCLUSION

De Pauw claims that the figure of Molly Pitcher was not one person, but was a collective memory of a number of artillery women who served in the war. Her theory was accepted by Teipe (No. 6O), but has been challenged in many of its broader aspects by Janice McKenney (No. 6I). She claims that Margaret Corbin was a transvestite.[19]

6I. Janice E. McKenney, "'Women in Combat': Comment," 1982.[20]

COMMENTARY

Ms. McKenney, who was with the Chief Organizational Branch of the U.S. Army Center of Military History, wrote this article in 1982 in response to Linda Grant DePauw's article "Women in Combat: The Revolutionary War Experience." She challenges De Pauw's interpretation of the role of women in the Revolutionary army, and specifically refutes De Pauw's claim that a large number of women served in support units for the artillery (see also below Chapter 11). She believes that the women with the army were all camp followers, and that female nurses should be classified separately.

McKenney accepts that the Molly Pitcher story refers to one person, the services of Mary Ludwig Hays McCauley.

CONCLUSION

McKenney challenges DePauw's assertion that "tens of thousands of women were engaged in combat" during the Revolution. She points out that the scattered evidence cited by De Pauw is not strong enough to support her claim that a large number of women were employed on the field in bringing water to artillery units. She may, however, go too far when she states that "to say that women made any significant impact during the American Revolution is to distort history."[21]

6J. D.W. Thompson and Merri Lou Schaumann, "Goodbye, Molly Pitcher," 1989.[22]

COMMENTARY

This article was written around 1976 by D.W. Thompson, who passed away before it was published. He earned a Bachelor's Degree from Dickinson College and a Master's Degree from Harvard, and was a past president of the Cumberland County Historical Society. Merri Lou Schaumann did the genealogical research for the article and edited it for publication. She has earned a Bachelor's Degree from Kent State University and is an author and professional genealogist who does volunteer work at the Hamilton Library, Cumberland County Historical Society.[23]

This article is significant for the way it summarizes the various stages in the development of the Molly Pitcher legend and evaluates many of the sources behind it, often in a critical manner. Its main points will be only summarized here.

The first section, "Molly Pitcher – The Problem," outlines the nature of the problem, specifically the difficulty of sorting out the conflation of the stories of the two women known as "Captain Molly," Margaret Corbin and Molly Pitcher.[24] In the second section, "Molly Pitcher," the authors claim that no one identified Mary Hays McCauley as Molly Pitcher until 1876, when most everyone jumped on a band wagon to claim her for the town of Carlisle. Her previously unmarked grave was located and a small monument to her was erected.[25]

The third section, "Growth of the Legend – The First Fifty Years" does an excellent job of summarizing the earliest sources that mention Molly Pitcher, including Waldo (No. 1B) and Plumb Martin (No. 1A).[26] The authors interpret that Waldo speaks of a woman firing a musket, not a cannon (see Commentary to No. 1B) and claim that Plumb Martin's account is generic with a touch of a bawdy tale (describing how the British cannon ball went between her legs). They then propose that "quite plainly the Margaret Corbin story may be the source of the Molly Pitcher story if, many years later, the locale was mistakenly supposed to be Monmouth instead of Fort Washington."[27] The section concludes with a discussion of how Benson Lossing confused the stories of heroic women who fired cannons at Fort Clinton, Fort Washington and Monmouth, and thought that they were one and the same person (see Commentary to Nos. 2I and 2K).

The fourth section, "Growth of the Legend – The Second Fifty Years" consists of two parts. The first part does an excellent job and summarizing the mid-nineteenth century accounts that popularized the legend of Molly Pitcher in an expanded format that came to contain several significant variations to the basic myth.[28] These include George Washington Parke Custis (Nos. 2D and 2E), Benson Lossing (Nos. 2J and 2K), and Nathaniel Currier (No. 2H). They also mention the story of Moll Pitcher, the soothsayer from Lynn, Massachusetts (Nos. 2A and 2C). The second part examines the source material specifically to Mary Hays McCaulcy.[29] Specific comments from Mary Hays McCauley's neighbors in Carlisle are cited, including those by Wesley Miles (No. 8B), Agnes Graham, and Polly McCleaster (No. 8E). The authors favor the interpretation that Mary Hays McCauley was of German descent and not Irish.[30] They concur that Mary Hays McCauley was never married to a Casper, John or John Casper Hays, and that "she was married to William Hays, as all court records clearly show."[31] These records, the authors point out, "were never seen, or else they were ignored" by such later writers as Wesley Miles (No. 8B), Agnes Graham, Dr. Conway Wing (No. 3E), Dr. Joseph Murray (No. 3G), John Landis (No. 4E), Mrs. Sarah W. Parkinson, and Judge Edward Biddle (see No. 8L). Only Jeremiah Zeamer (No. 4F) understood who her husband really was, "but his efforts were unsuccessful." The remainder of this part then discusses the primary evidence available concerning the life of William and Mary Hays after the revolution. The authors believe that William died in the summer of 1786.[32] Evidence is also given for the life of their son John L. Hays, whom they say was born in 1780, and for Mary's life with her second husband, John McCalla (McCauley). This section closes with a discussion of Mary Hays McCauley's pension and then her death in 1832.[33] An "Epilogue" gives the obituary of John L. Hays, son of William and Mary Hays, who died in March 1856 (No. 8A).[34]

CONCLUSION

This long and interesting article presents and evaluates a great amount of information concerning Molly Pitcher. Its basic thesis is that Mary Hays McCauley was NOT the historical Molly Pitcher, but that the figure of Molly Pitcher was a legend that grew out of a confused recollection of Margaret Corbin's heroism at the battle of Fort Washington. The appearance of this article reportedly caused a bit of an uproar in Carlisle. Constance McDonald wrote the next year, "The people of Carlisle reacted unfavorably to their tampering with a local legend. Television crews came to the Society to interview the author. The public of Carlisle resented the implications that what was literally engraved in stone was wrong."[35]

6K. Constance M. McDonald, "Molly Pitcher, Who Was She?" 1990.[36]

COMMENTARY

This is a summary of a longer research paper that Constance M. McDonald wrote while she was a student at Cameron University in Lawton, Oklahoma. It was written partly in response to the article "Goodbye, Molly Pitcher" published in 1989 by D.W. Thompson and Merri Lou Schaumann (No. 6J).

The purpose of this article is to show that the heroine Molly Pitcher was indeed Mary Hays McCauley. The author summarizes the legend of Molly Pitcher, and then cites testimony by Mary Hays McCauley's neighbors in Carlisle who knew her to be the real Molly Pitcher. McDonald relies strongly on the statements of Wesley Miles, who was "the first to put the real name of Molly Pitcher in print" (No. 8B).

McDonald cites a number of documents to show that Molly Pitcher was never married to John Hays. The necessary conclusion must follow that "If the man whom Molly Pitcher followed to war was not John Hays, then she was not Mary Ludwig Hays. Therefore the name Ludwig shouldn't be part of Molly Pitcher's fame." The author instead believes that Mary Hays McCauley was of Irish origin, citing the testimony of a number of her neighbors, including Harriet Foulke (No. 8I).

McDonald's conclusion states simply, "Mary Hays McCauly [McCauley] was not Just a figure of Folklore; she lived."

CONCLUSION

McDonald refutes the thesis put forward by Thompson and Schaumann that Molly Pitcher was only a legend, not a real person. She believes that Molly Pitcher was an actual historical figure and that this figure was the resident of Carlisle known as Mary Hays McCauley. She also points out how much Thompson's and Schaumann's thesis disturbed many residents of Carlisle.

6L. Carol Klaver, "An Introduction to the Legend of Molly Pitcher," 1994.[37]

COMMENTARY

This article is adapted from the Senior History Honors Thesis that the author wrote while attending Rutgers University.[38] It contains an excellent summary of the different theories and scholarship on the legend of Molly Pitcher.

Klaver begins by outlining the myth of Molly Pitcher and concluding that "Margaret Corbin probably contributed more to the myth than we realize."[39] She then discusses the nature and function of camp followers during the Revolution, whose function included bringing water to the troops and helping to remove the wounded.[40] The author then reviews Joseph Plumb Martin's account of a woman firing a cannon at Monmouth (No. 1A). Unlike some other authors, Klaver believes that Dr. Waldo's account refers to the same person as Martin, and not to a woman firing a musket.[41]

The author reviews the story of Molly Corbin and concludes that she was a different person than Molly Pitcher.[42] After discussing George Washington Parke Custis' version of the story (No. 2D),[43] she analyzes what she calls "The Patriotic Victorian View of the Myth" as put forward by John Landis in 1905 (No. 4E).[44] She points out that

Landis' belief in the historicity of Molly Pitcher was challenged by Jeremiah Zeamer (Nos. 4D and 4F), who may have had "an unwillingness to believe that a woman could significantly help troops in the Revolution." Landis, said Zeamer, wrote "more with a view to please prevailing morbid desire for sensational literature than to records an historical incident that actually happened." Klaver believes that "for the most part, Zeamer's evidence is either factual or quite sensible." His greatest contribution may have been to show that that there was no Mary Ludwig in Carlisle before the Revolution; the name of Mary Hays McCauley's first husband was William Hays, not John. Zeamer points out several problems with Landis' theory, says Klaver, but "he was not able to separate his Victorian sensibilities from his rebuttal of the Landis story." Klaver disagrees strongly with Zeamer's stance that women just did not fight on the battlefield, and certainly did not know how to fire a cannon.[45]

Klaver next discusses the modern twentieth century view of John Todd White (No. 6E) and Linda Grant De Pauw (No. 6H) that women were important members of artillery gun crews because they brought the water necessary for swabbing the cannon barrels between shots.[46] It was but an easy step, they say, for a woman who was bringing water to the troops or helping to remove a cannon, to step up and take the place of one of the men who had fallen on the firing line. She rejects their viewpoint that there were a large number of women on the front lines during the Revolution, stating "It is strange that we have no evidence that women were truly part of the army." Klaver then summarizes Janice McKenney's response to White and DePauw, but finds fault with her conclusion that women did not make any significant impact on the American revolution.[47]

The final author whom Klaver discusses is D.W. Thompson (No. 6J), who claims that the story of Molly Pitcher was a myth that became part of the national consciousness after 1840.[48]

In a well written section entitled "The Real Molly Pitcher," Klaver observes "It is certainly possible that Molly McCauly was the legendary Molly Pitcher, yet it is impossible to track the legend back to her...Molly McCauly was more than likely a camp follower, though less than likely the legendary Molly Pitcher."[49] It is her conclusion that "this generalized myth has been created to honor one mythical woman, while in reality many women were on battlefields during the American Revolution." What began as a legend was repeated so often that it became fact "in the eyes of the public."

The next section of the paper discusses the possible location of Molly Pitcher's well on Monmouth battlefield[50] and the monuments erected to her in Freehold and Carlisle.[51] An abridged section surveys the representation of Molly Pitcher in art and poetry.[52] The concluding section discusses the importance of Molly Pitcher to historic learning. "First of all, she is a patriotic symbol of the Revolution and the women who took part in the war. Secondly, the history of the myth is a vehicle to study the emergence of the myth." Molly Pitcher, Klaver suggests, is important as a cultural personification of liberty and the romantic universal "symbol of a woman refusing to give up in battle."[53]

CONCLUSION

Klaver gives a well thought out survey of the development and nature of the Molly Pitcher legend. She accepts that Mary Hays McCauley was a camp follower at Monmouth, but has difficulty equating her with the person of Molly Pitcher, who may indeed, she says, be a mythic legend. Klaver places the development of the Molly Pitcher legend within the framework of American intellectual history, and stresses her value both as a representative of the role of women in the Revolution and as a symbol of lady liberty on the battlefield.

6M. Carmela A. Karnoutsas, *New Jersey Women, A History*, 1997.

New Jersey's legendary "Molly Pitcher," like many other women, was a camp follower during the war. The daughter of a German immigrant, she was born Mary Ludwig on October 12, 1754, near Trenton. In 1769, at age fifteen, she married John Hays, a gunner in the Pennsylvania State Regiment of Artillery, and traveled with him. The presence of the woman at the battle of Monmouth on June 28, 1778, has confounded many historians. What was she doing at the battle and how did she obtain her nickname?

Mary Ludwig Hays had no children, and followed her husband to war. She earned her way by washing, cooking, mending, nursing, carrying powder and shot, and even swabbing out the cannons after they were fired. She also carried water to the soldiers on the battlefield on that hot day at

Monmouth Court House. Since "Molly" was a popular woman's name at the time, the soldiers would frequently shout "Molly Pitcher" or "Molly with the Pitcher" when in need of water. Hays became the "Molly Pitcher" immortalized in American history when she took over her wounded husband's cannon and fired it herself. Accounts differ as to whether she fired several rounds or just one. Reportedly, Washington thanked "Molly" for her valor when he reviewed the troops after the battle. Both sides claimed victory at the battle of Monmouth, but victory or no, New Jersey had a heroine and history a legend.[54]

COMMENTARY

Carmela A. Karnoutsas was born in 1942. She holds a doctorate from New York University (NYU) and teaches at New Jersey City University (NJCU).

Karnoutsas follows the general line of the legend of Molly at Monmouth, without committing herself to any details other than that Molly "reportedly" was introduced to General Washington after the battle. She accepts that Molly was born in 1754 near Trenton as Mary Ludwig, a mixture divergent sources. Most of the sources who claim that Molly was born as Mary Ludwig place her birth year as 1744 and birth place as Pennsylvania (for example, Egle, No. 3J; they also give the month and day as October 13). Most of the sources who claim that Molly was born in 1754 say she was born of Irish blood as Mary Hanna (for example, Salter, No. 3H). Molly was not married to John Hays at the time of the battle, as Karnoutsas states, but to William Hays (see No. 7F).

CONCLUSION

This account is representative of current scholarship on Molly Pitcher: an acceptance that she was at the battle, with an uncertainty about exactly what exactly happened there. Karnoutsas passes on the incorrect tradition that Molly's birth name was Mary Ludwig and that she was married to John Hays at the time of the battle. She does not make an attempt to identify Molly as Mary Hays McCauley.

6N. Donald F.X. Finn, Letter to New Jersey Historical Association, December 5, 1998

The Stryker-Rodda 'Revolutionary Census of New Jersey does not contain an entry for "Ludwig." A Mary Ludwig appears to have married a John Casper Hays, a Pennsylvania soldier but not an artilleryman. The best evidence available strongly suggests that Molly Pitcher was Mary Hanna, daughter of John and Susan Neau Hanna of Upper Freehold, Allentown, Monmouth County, New Jersey. She married William Hays, an Irishman and 'gunner' in Proctor's Artillery Brigade at the Battle of Monmouth (as did J.C. Hays). Molly, who was about 20-22 years of age at Monmouth, later had a daughter named "Polly" (and could not write, signed legal instruments with a cross, and lived in a phonetic language world). "Molly" was often used to described a "milkmaid" (Hanna's farm may have had cows), which gives us some food for further thought.

There is some evidence Molly visited her parents in the Spring of 1778 at Allentown and then joined her husband somewhere (Cranbury?) on his march to Englishtown/Monmouth Court House in June 1778. Her husband William certainly was not "killed" at Monmouth as several sources state...

If William Hays was wounded at Monmouth, he certainly survived and continued to serve as a "gunner" until January 1, 1783, when he was honorably discharged and returned home with Molly to Carlisle, Pennsylvania.

Molly was observed as taking the place of a "Matross" who was killed or wounded and serviced the front of the cannon (with a 'spunge' – ramrod), while "gunners" served at the rear of the cannon positioning, elevating and firing the gun.

It is interesting to note that there were at least two plays (one a comedy) about Molly Pitcher at Monmouth which drew popular attention c. 1900 in New York City. Photographs of the comedy are at the Library of Congress.[55]

COMMENTARY

Donald F.X. Finn was a historian and publisher, the owner of Twin Lights Press in Millington, New Jersey. He died in 2002.

Finn wrote this letter in critique of the book *New Jersey Women, A History,* by Carmela A. Karnoutsas (No. 6M). He accepts that Molly was born in Allentown, New Jersey, as the daughter of John Hanna, following the parentage first suggested by Sarah Smith Stafford around 1876 (No. 3A); Finn adds that her mother was Susan Neau Hanna. He is inclined to accept the account by McGeorge (No. 4A) that Molly was visiting her parents in New Jersey and then joined her husband while the army was marching to Monmouth. He rightly points out that Molly's husband was not killed at Monmouth, but returned with her to Carlisle after the war.

CONCLUSION

Finn's thoughts are mostly expressed as notes and suppositions. He believes that Molly was born as Mary Hanna in Allentown, but this cannot be proven.

6O. Emily J. Teipe, "Will the Real Molly Pitcher Please Stand Up?", 1999.[56]

COMMENTARY

Ms. Teipe builds theory first put forward by Linda De Pauw that Molly Pitcher was not one person but a personification of the collective tradition of a large number of women who served in the artillery during the Revolution (No. 6H). She rightly points out that the story of Molly Pitcher is confused with that of Margaret Corbin, since both were famous for fighting in the artillery. But she also says a third figure could figure in the Molly Pitcher myth, namely Deborah Sampson, a woman who fought and served in men's clothing until she was found out and forced to leave the army (see below No. 11F). This point is difficult to accept, particularly since Sampson fought in an infantry unit, not the artillery. It is also difficult to accept Teipe's claim that "The historical records presents other candidates too numerous to mention here." The simple fact is that there are only two women well attested to have served with the artillery in the Revolution, Molly Pitcher and Margaret Corbin.

Teipe's answer to the question, "Who was Molly Pitcher?" is simple and straightforward: "none of them and all of them." Teipe agrees fully with De Pauw that Molly Pitcher is "a legendary personality constructed from the tales of bravery and daring of Revolutionary women...The name Molly Pitcher is a collective generic term as much as G.I. Joe."

Teipe believes that Mary Hays McCauley was born under the name Mary Ludwig and that she married John Hays, a barber, in 1769. None of these point can be substantiated. She incorrectly states that Mary Hays McCauley is buried at "Old Graveyard (the name of the town) in Pennsylvania near Carlisle." This is a clear misreading of Landis' or some other early account (see No. 4E). Teipe also makes the unsubstantiated statement that Molly Pitcher was pregnant at the time of the battle of Monmouth (see Commentary to No. 6B).[57]

CONCLUSION

Teipe builds upon De Pauw's theory that Molly Pitcher was not one individual but a representation of the service of a large number of women in the Revolutionary War. She appears not to be aware of Janice E. McKenney's strong arguments against De Pauw (No. 6I).

Statue and monument to Mary Hays McCauley erected in the Old Carlisle Cemetery by the State of Pennsylvania in 1916 (see No. 9D). Photograph by the author.

7. SOURCES RELATING TO MARY HAYS MCCAULEY, 1787-1832

MARRIAGE OF WILLIAM HAYS AND MARY HAYS

7A. Cumberland County, Letters of Administration, October 3, 1787.

No. 193.Wm. Hays. Cumberland County, Pa. Be it re-membered that on the 3rd day of Oct. in the year of our Lord one thousand seven hundred and eighty-seven, Letters of Administration filed (?) in common form to Mary Hays widow of William Hays dec'd of all and singular goods and chattels rights and credits which were of the said William Hays dec'd. Inventory and account to be exhibited into the Register's office in the Borough of Carlisle in the time ap-pointed by law. Witness by my hand, Willm. Lyon, Reg.[1]

COMMENTARY

This document shows that Mary Hays filed and received Letters of Administration over the estate of her deceased husband William Hays in October 1787.

This means that he probably died in 1787, a date that has long been unclear. That this Mary Hays was the same woman who later married John McCauley, see Nos. 7C, 7D, 7E and 7F below. Unfor-tunately, we do not know the exact date and place where William Hays Mary Hays were married.

CONCLUSION

This document shows that Williams Hays, first husband of Mary Hays McCauley, probably died in 1787.

7B. Cumberland County Orphans' Court Records, February 12, 1788.

Came...Mary Hays administrator of the estate of William Hays lately died intestate...leaving widow and one son, John, aged five years to survive him. Begs to sell ½ property to pay debts...[2]

COMMENTARY

Williams Hay, husband of Mary (Molly) Hays at the time of the Revolution (see No. 7C), died in 1787 (see 7A). This court record indicates that he left behind his wife Mary and also a son, John. L. Hays (ca. 1783-1856; see No. 8A). It also states that William's estate had been inventoried on November 20, 1787 and had an adjusted value of eleven pounds, six shillings and four pence. Mary was destitute and appealed to the Orphans' Court that she be allowed to sell part of her husband's land in order "to maintain said orphan son agreeable to the acts of the assembly." The order was granted and she did so.[3]

CONCLUSION

This document establishes that William Hays and Mary Hays had a son named John who was born ca. 1783.

7C. Return of the Pennsylvania Line, entitled to Donation Lands.

Mary "McCalla widow of William Hays" of Col. Thomas Proctor's 4th Artillery, Continental Line, is authorized to participate in Donation Lands.[4]

COMMENTARY

After the Revolution, the Federal government belatedly gave land grants to Revolutionary War veterans, or their next of kin, who applied for them. In this document Mary Hays McCauley's (McCalla's) application as the widow of William Hays is granted.

CONCLUSION

This document shows that William Hays, first husband of Mary Hays McCauley, served in Proctor's 4th Pennsylvania artillery during the Revolution (see also Chapter 12 below). It also shows that she has remarried to a man named McCalla (McCauley) by 1806 (see also No. 7D below). The exact date of her second marriage is not known. It appears to have been some time between 1789 and 1793. Her second husband, John McCauley, died about 1813.[5]

7D. Records of Revolutionary War Donation Lands, October 3, 1806.

Donation Lands #1717 rec'd etc. 3rd Octr. 1806 to Mary McCalla of William Hays Private.[6]

COMMENTARY

This document shows that Mary Hays McCauley, widow of Revolutionary War soldier William Hays, received in 1806 the Donation Lands for which she had applied (No. 7C above). The grant was for 200 acres located in District No. 8 on the west side of the Allegheny River.[7]

CONCLUSION

Mary Hays McCauley applied for this land grant in No. 7C above and sold the land in No. 7E. below.

7E. Sale of property from Mary Hays McCalla (McCauley) to James Brady, April 15, 1807.

COMMENTARY

Mary Hays McCauley owned her first husband's Donation Land only six months before she sold it. This deed records that she "transmitted title to lands received for services of William Hays, a soldier in the Army of the United States." The grantors are listed as "John McCalla and his wife Mary, formerly the widow of William Hays, deceased, and John Hays, son of William, all of Carlisle, Cumberland County, Pennsylvania" and the grantee is listed as "James Brady of Greensborough, Westmoreland County, Pennsylvania."[8]

CONCLUSION

Mary Hays McCauley applied for this land in No. 7B above and received it in No. 7C.

7F. Affidavit by James Roney of Carlisle, October 27, 1807.

Cumberland County, Pa. to wit: Personally appeared before me the subscriber (John Cree) one of the associate judges of the court of Common Pleas...James Roney of the Borough of Carlisle, Cumberland Co., who, being duly sworn...saith that he has known Mary Hays (now Mary McCalla) late widow of William Hays, a Gunner in Col. Proctor's Regiment of Artillerists during the Revolutionary War, and that said Mary had one child named John L. Hays about 27 years ago to the said William Hays, and none other to the best of his knowledge, that the said Mary McCalla (late Mary Hays) and John L. Hays are now in full life...the said Mary being inter-married to John McCalla.[9]

COMMENTARY

Probably to satisfy James Brady as to her right to her first husband's Donation Lands, Mary Hays McCauley found it necessary to confirm that she was married at one time to William Hays, a soldier of the Revolution. James Roney, who gave this affidavit, was clearly a friend or neighbor who could swear to this.

CONCLUSION

This affidavit confirms beyond all doubt that Mary Hays McCauley was the widow of William Hays and mother of John L. Hays. Notice that there is no mention of her ever having been the wife of John Hays, Casper Hays, or John Casper Hays, as is claimed by those who would have her be the same woman as the Mary Ludwig who married Casper Hays in 1769.

MARY HAYS MCCAULEY'S PENSION, 1822

7G. Journal of the Senate of the Commonwealth of Pennsylvania, January 29, 1822.

Mr. Mahon presented a petition from Molly McKolly, widow of an old soldier of the revolutionary war, praying for pecuniary aid. And said petition was read, and referred to the committee on claims.[10]

COMMENTARY

By 1822 Mary Hays McCauley (McKolly) had spent the money she received from the sale of her first husband's Revolutionary War Donation Lands and was again in need of money, so she applied to the Pennsylvania legislature for relief, presumably a claim to part of the pension that he would have been due. Unfortunately, the name of her husband, William Hays, is not stated in this record.

The bill was presented by Mr. Mahon, state senator from Carlisle. It was reported favorably from the committee on claims on February 11, 1822, when it was read to the Senate and accepted without amendment. It was read a second time the same day, and was approved and ordered to be transcribed for a third reading.[11] It was approved on its third reading on February 14 and referred to the House of Representatives for their concurrence.[12]

CONCLUSION

In 1822 Mary Hays McCauley appealed to the state of Pennsylvania for financial aid based on the Revolutionary War service of her late husband, William Hays. The request was later altered to be made on her own behalf (No. 6H).

7H. Journal of the Thirty-second House of Representatives of the Commonwealth of Pennsylvania, February 16, 1822.

The House resolved itself into a committee of the whole. Mr. Kirk in the chair, on the bill from the Senate, No. 165, entitled, "An act for the relief of Molly McKolly, widow of a soldier of the revolutionary war."

And after some time, The Speaker resumed the chair, and the chairman reported the bill without amendment. And on motion, Said bill was read a second time, and agreed to, and *Ordered*, To be prepared for a third reading, The title being amended by striking therefrom these words, "widow of a soldier," and inserting in lieu thereof these words, "for services rendered in." On motion of Mr. Holgate and Mr. Sterigere, the rule which prohibits the reading of bills twice on the same day, being in this case dispensed with, said bill was read a third time and passed, and *Ordered*, That the Clerk return the same to the Senate and request their concurrence in the amendment thereto by this house.[13]

COMMENTARY

The act for the relief of Molly McKolly that was passed by the Senate and referred to the House of Representatives on February 14 was first introduced in the House on February 11, 1822.[14] It was presented on the floor as Senate Bill No. 265 on February 16 and accepted without amendment on its first and second readings.

However, before its third reading the bill was amended to read "An act for the relief of Molly McKolly, for her service during the revolutionary war." Most unfortunately, these services are not specified. Nor do we know who introduced the amendment and why. Nevertheless, the change is quite significant, that she be given relief in her own name for services during the war. These services could have been the acts of a common camp follower: washing, cooking, and caring for the wounded. This is what is suggested by one newspaper report of her receiving the pension (No. 7K). But the pension may have been given for deeds greater than these (see No. 7J and the newspaper accounts Nos. 7L, 7M and 7N).

The amended act was read and approved in the Senate on February 15.[15]

The amended act was then presented to Governor Joseph Hiester on February 19, and it was signed into law on February 21.[16]

CONCLUSION

It is most significant that Mary Hays McCauley's application for a pension based on the wartime service of her deceased first husband, William Hays, was amended by the Pennsylvania Legislature and was instead given "for her service during the revolutionary war." Unfortunately, her services are not specified. But it should be born in mind that only two other women known to have received a pension for their services in the Revolutionary War. These are Margaret Corbin, who was badly wounded while firing a cannon at the battle of Fort Washington (see No. 11A),[17] and Deborah Sampson, who served in the infantry disguised as a man (see No. 11F).

7I. "An Act for the relief of Molly McKolly, for her services during the revolutionary war," February 21, 1822.

Acts of the General Assembly of the Commonwealth of -
Pennsylvania,
1822, Chapter XXV.
An Act For the relief of Molly McKolly, for her services during the
Revolutionary war.

Sect. 1. BE it enacted by the Senate and House of Representatives of the Commonwealth of Pennsylvania in General

Assembly met, and it is hereby enacted by the authority of the same, That the State Treasurer be, and is hereby directed to pay to Molly McKolly, of Cumberland County, or her order, forty dollars immediately, and an annuity of forty dollars to commence on the first day of January, one thousand eight hundred and twenty-two, payable yearly during life.

    Joseph Lawrence, Speaker of the House of
        Representatives
    William Marks, Junior, Speaker of the Senate
    Approved, February the twenty-first, one thousand
        eight hundred and twenty-two.
    Joseph Hiester[18]

COMMENTARY

This is the full text of Mary Hays McCauley's pension received from the state of Pennsylvania in 1822. The amount received was the same as a widow's pension - $40, or a soldier's half pay.[19] J.A. Murray wrote in 1883 that he had it on the authority of the Hon. J.B. Linn, lately secretary of the Commonwealth, that "Molly drew a pension from the State for her services commencing Feb. 21st, 1822, and ending Jan. 1st, 1832; and as no application was made after that date, the presumption is that she died in 1832," which was the case.[20]

CONCLUSION

The fact that the pension Molly was awarded was the same as she would have received had she secured it in the name of her deceased husband, makes it all the more significant that the Pennsylvania Legislature voted to award it to her in her own name.

7J. Index to Journal of the Thirty-second House of Representatives of the Commonwealth of Pennsylvania, 1822.

McKolly, Molly, revolutionary heroine, relief bill...[21]

COMMENTARY

This short entry is most interesting for its impact and implications. It cites Molly McKolly as a "revolutionary heroine," language that is not used in any of the actual records of the discussion of her pension application or in the wording of the pension itself (No. 7I). Since the amendment to give her a pension in her own name rather than based on the service of her first husband originated in the

House of Representatives, this terminology that she was a "revolutionary heroine" may reflect some of the House's thinking when it made the change. To be sure, we cannot tell today what the indexer meant by the term "revolutionary heroine," but it is reasonable to assume that the phrase means more than the services of a regular camp follower.

CONCLUSION

This brief mention in the published journal of Pennsylvania's House of Representatives calls Mary Hays McCauley (Molly McKolly) a "revolutionary heroine," but does not specify what her heroic deed was.

7K. Carlisle, PA *American Volunteer,* February 21, 1822.

A bill has passed both houses of the Assembly, granting an annuity to Molly McAuley (of Carlisle) for services she rendered during the Revolutionary War. It appeared satisfactorily, that this heroine had braved the hardships of the camp and dangers of the field, with her husband, who was a soldier of the revolution, and the bill in her favor passed without a dissenting voice. *Chronicle.*[22]

COMMENTARY

This brief report in one of the newspapers from Mary Hays McCauley's home town, Carlisle, supports the awarding of her pension because she was a heroine who had endured the hardships of the war at the side of her husband. It does not, however, elaborate on what these hardships were.

CONCLUSION

It is not unexpected that Mary Hays McCauley's home town newspaper reported the awarding of her pension. What is unusual, though, is that notice of her pension was also reported in newspapers in New York, Philadelphia and Washington (see Nos. 7L, 7M and 7N).

7L. New York *National Advocate,* March 7, 1822.

Molly Macauly, who received a pension from the State of Pennsylvania for service rendered during the Revolutionary War, was well-known to the general officers as a brave and patriotic woman. She was called Sgt. McCauly, and was wounded at some battle, supposed to be the Brandywine, where her sex was discovered. It was a common practice for her to swing her saber over her head, and huzza for "Mad Anthony" as she termed General Wayne. It was an unusual circumstance to find women in the ranks disguised as men, such was their order [ardor?] for independence. Elizabeth Canning was at a gun at Fort Washington when her husband was killed and she took his place immediately, loaded, primed and fired the cannon with which he was entrusted. She was wounded in the breast by grapeshot.[23]

COMMENTARY

This is a strangely worded report of the background of Molly McCauley. Note that she is here called "Sergeant McCauley" and not "Captain Molly" or "Molly Pitcher." She was reported to have been wounded at "some battle," perhaps Brandywine. This report may have been a confusion for Margaret Corbin (here mistakenly cited as Elizabeth Canning), who was reported by at least one other source to have been wounded at Brandywine, though she was actually wounded at Fort Washington.[24]

CONCLUSION

It is significant that notice of the pension awarded to Molly Hays McCauley on February 22, 1822 was so promptly taken notice of in a New York City newspaper, even if the details of her accomplishment (and those of Margaret Corbin) are somewhat garbled.

7M. Washington, D.C. *National Intelligencer,* March 15, 1822.

Molly Macauly, who received a pension from the State of Pennsylvania for service rendered during the Revolutionary War, was well known to the general officers as a brave and patriotic woman. She was called Sergeant Macauly, and was wounded at some battle, supposed to be the Brandywine, where her sex was discovered. It was a common practice for her to swing her saber over her head, and huzza for "Mad Anthony," as she termed General Wayne. It was an unusual circumstance to find women in the ranks disguised as men, such was their ardor for independence. Elizabeth Canning was at a gun at Fort Washington when her husband was killed and she took his place immediately, loaded, primed and fired the cannon with which she was entrusted. She was wounded in the breast by grapeshot.—*Nat. Adv.*[25]

COMMENTARY

This is a notice of the pension received by Mary Hays McCauley in February 1822 (No. 7I). It is repeated with only a couple very minor changes from an article that appeared in the March 7, 1822 issue of the New York *National Advocate* (No. 7L). See Commentary to No.7L for a discussion of the article's content.

CONCLUSION

It is significant that notice of Molly Hays McCauley's pension was taken was far a field as Washington D.C., even if the details of her accomplishment are garbled and somewhat unclear.

7N. Philadelphia *Chronicle,* March 1822.

It appeared satisfactory that this heroine had braved the hardships of the Camp and dangers of the field with her husband who was a soldier of the Revolution, and the bill in her favor passed without a dissenting voice.[26]

COMMENTARY

This passage comes from a longer article that reported the granting of a pension to Mary Hays McCauley by the state of Pennsylvania in February 1822.

CONCLUSION

It is significant that notice of Mary Hays McCauley's pension was reported in Philadelphia, as well as in New York City (No. 7L) and Washington, D.C. (No. 7M).

OBITUARIES OF MRS. MARY MCCAULEY

7O. Obituary of Mary Hays McCauley, Carlisle *American Volunteer,* January 26, 1832.

Died on Sunday last, in this borough, at an advanced age, Mrs. Molly McCauley. She lived during the days of the American Revolution, shared its hardships, and witnessed many a scene of "Blood and carnage." To the sick and wounded she was an efficient aid, for which; and being the widow of an American hero, she received during the latter years of her life, an annuity from the government. For upwards of 40 years she resided in this borough, and was during that time recognized as an honest, obliging and industrious woman, She has left numerous relatives to regret her decease; who with many others of her acquaintance, have a hope that her reward in the world to which she has gone, will far exceed that which she received in this.[27]

COMMENTARY

Mary Hays McCauley died at January 22, 1832, not 1833 as initially carved on the grave stone erected in 1876 (see below Nos. 9A and 9B).

This obituary does not attempt to guess at Mary Hays McCauley's age. Nor does it mention any specific hardships she may have encountered during the revolution.

CONCLUSION

This obituary does not elaborate on the specific hardships endured by Mary Hays McCauley during the revolution.

7P. Obituary of Mary Hays McCauley, *Carlisle Herald,* January 26, 1832.

DIED on Sunday last, Mrs. MARY MCAULEY (better known by the name of Molly McAuley), aged about 90 years. The history of this woman is somewhat remarkable. Her first husband's name was Hays, who was a soldier in the war of the Revolution. It appears that she continued with him while in the army, and acted so much the part of the heroine, as to attract the notice of the officers. Some estimate may be found of the value of the service rendered by her, when the fact is stated, that she drew a pension from government [sic] during the latter years of her life.[28]

COMMENTARY

If Mary were indeed 79 years old, as her tombstone states, when she died in 1832 (her tombstone erroneously gives the year as 1733), she would have been born in 1753 and so would have been about 25 years old at the time of the battle of Monmouth in 1778; if she was about 90 years old, as this obituary states, she would have been born about 1742 and so would have been about 36 years at the time of the battle of Monmouth.

Census records suggest that she was born around 1755: she was listed as around 45 years old at the time of the 1800 census, and was between 70 and 80 years old at the time of the 1830 census.[29]

Evidence suggests that she could not write, since she signed her name with an "X" on several legal documents.[30] When she died she left behind only a few effects. Most were lost when the Confederates burned the house in which her grandson lived when they occupied Carlisle just before the battle of Gettysburg in 1863. Her few effects that survived were as of 1905 in the hands of John A. Hays and other relatives in Carlisle, and a Mrs. Martz of Ogden, Utah. [31]

CONCLUSION

This obituary does not elaborate on the specific hardships endured by Mary Hays McCauley during the revolution.

8. SOURCES RELATING TO MARY HAYS MCCAULEY, 1856-1926

8A. Obituary of John L. Hays, March 27, 1856.

Departed this life on Thursday last in this boro, Mr. John L. Hays, aged about 75 years, one of the few remaining who patriotically stepped forward in defense of our country and faithfully served 6 months tour on the Northern frontier in the War of 1812. The deceased was a sergeant in the Carlisle Infantry Co., now the oldest in the State of Pennsylvania and perhaps the union. His funeral took place on Saturday last, with military honors handsomely performed by the same Co. commanded by Capt. S. Crop, with the Brass Band, stationed at the Barrack under Col. C. May of the U.S. Army, at the head of the procession. The remains were followed to the grave by a large number of mourning relatives and a few of his associates in arms, who by their gray hairs, down cast looks and sorrowful eyes, showed plainly that it won't be long before it will be their turn.

The deceased was a son of the ever-to-be-remembered heroine, the celebrated "Molly Pitcher" whose deeds of daring are recorded in the annals of the Revolution and over whose remains a monument ought to be erected. The writer of this recollects well to have frequently seen her in the streets of Carlisle, pointed out by admiring friends thus: "There goes the woman who fired the cannon at the British when her husband was killed."...Signed: One Who Knows.[1]

COMMENTARY

This is the obituary of John L. Hays, only child of Mary Hays McCauley and her husband Williams Hays, who was born around 1783 (see No. 7B). Some sources claimed he was "born in a tent on the battlefield of Monmouth after he battle, but this he afterwards said was uncertain."[2] Court records from 1788 make it clear that John L. Hays was born in 1782 or 1783 (See No. 7B). His middle initial "L." is said by some to stand for "Ludwig" in honor of his maternal grandfather,[3] but this theory is not accurate due to the fact that his mother's maiden name was not Mary Ludwig, as shown above (see Commentary to Nos. 3E and 3L). Mary Hays McCauley lived with her son for a few years prior to her death in 1832, as the 1830 census of Carlisle shows.

This obituary is interesting for stating that John's mother was the famous "Molly Pitcher," a statement not made in her own obituaries just 24 years earlier. This shows the extent by which the Molly Pitcher legend had grown by 1856.

CONCLUSION

This obituary gives a good deal of information about the life of Mary Hays McCauley's only son, John L. Hays (ca.1783-1856). In it, Mary Hays McCauley is called "the celebrated 'Molly Pitcher.'"

8B. Recollections of Wesley Miles of Carlisle, 1876.

I well remember there resided at the corner of Bedford and North Streets, or as the location was familiarly known, Lougheridge's corner, Carlisle, Pa., an aged Irish woman. then past sixty, healthy active and strong, fleshy and short of stature, and remember her entire personal appearance, her peculiar dress of the period, manners, oddities, etc. She was very social, exceedingly talkative, and fond of walking about and visiting her neighbors and acquaintances of the town. The old lady was largely employed as a nurse, was careful of the sick, her delight to kindly administer to the afflicted of her own sex. Besides too, she was passionately fond of children. The little ones on the street at play knew here well, and often would she interest them by stopping during her pedestrian rambles and having a pleasant talk with them...This Irish woman was employed by my father, early in 1822, to nurse my afflicted mother, bedfast for nearly a year, with a lingering disease, and to have a motherly care over myself, then scarcely seven years of age, and a younger brother. I well remember I had but little affection for her, as a foster mother, indeed none, for then I thought, she was too unreasonably strict in discipline. To go beyond her presence, and to the street to play, childlike, with other little boys, would excite her passion to profanity. Fleet as a deer, she was sure to catch her object of pursuit, in every attempt to escape, and loading it upon her shoulders, screaming with terror, she would hie off home, and now the rod was severely applied for disobedience to her stern commands. She remained with us until mother's death, September 22d, 1822, and for some time afterwards...

I well remember when she died, a death greatly lamented by the citizens of Carlisle. She was buried with military honors by the volunteer companies...The remains of this Irish woman rest in the 'Old Graveyard' of Carlisle...Perhaps, not even a rude limestone marks her grave. No imposing monument has ever been erected to mark the spot where she lies, whose deeds of valor will be read so long as our Centennials are observed by the American people, deeds eminently worthy, even of the sterner sex.

Reader, the subject of this reminiscence is a prototype of the 'Maid of Saragossa.' The heroine of Monmouth, Molly Pitcher, otherwise known to us when a boy, as Molly McCauly, her real name; the other a burlesque or caricature, forsooth. She bore water in a pitcher for her husband on this memorable occasion.[4]

COMMENTARY

Wesley Miles was described in 1883 as "a prominent school teacher, an intelligent man who has been living for several years past in Williamsport, Pa."[5]

He knew Mary Hays McCauley well because she had served as housekeeper in the home of his father, Richard Miles, for a number of years. His statement that she was Irish aroused the ire of Mrs. McCauley's granddaughter, Polly McCleaster, who insisted that her grandmother was "as Dutch as Sauer Kraut, and her maiden name was Mary Ludwig" (No. 8E).[6] Mrs. McCleaster's opinion, however, is questionable because other evidence is clear that her grandmother's maiden name was not Ludwig (see Commentary to Nos. 3E and 3L).

This article was significant because it sparked Peter Spahr of Carlisle to start a drive to put a gravestone on Mary Hays McCauley's grave, which apparently had not been marked up until this time (see Nos.3G, 4E and 9A).[7]

CONCLUSION

This account gives interesting personal information about Mary Hays McCauley while she was serving as housekeeper to the family of Richard Miles in Carlisle in the early 1820s. She is described as being of Irish origin.

8C. Researches by J.A. Murray, 1883.

I gathered from these gentlemen [Peter Spahr and William Parks] the following additional items, some of which I have known or heard before. After her husband, John Hays, had entered the service of his country, he sent word to her to come and join him, which she promptly and cheerfully did, willing to render whatever aid and comfort she could, and she remained with him throughout the war, nursing the sick or wounded, and making herself generally useful. At the battle of Monmouth she rendered valuable services – cheering and encouraging the men, as well as carrying water to the excited and thirsty soldiers in the regiment to which her husband belonged, and hence received the familiar name of Molly Pitcher. Hays was not killed on that occasion, but knocked down and rendered insensible. She, however supposed he was killed, and instantly handled his weapon and did what she could to supply his place at the cannon. He afterwards revived, recovered and returned to duty. After the war ended they came to Carlisle, where Hays died. McCauley, who had been a fellow soldier with her husband and knew her well, subsequently married her. She survived her second husband and had issue only by her first husband.[8]

COMMENTARY

This passage comes from a long newspaper article written by Rev. Murray that appeared in the September 12, 1883 issue of the Carlisle *American Volunteer* (No. 3G).

This outline of Molly Pitcher's actions at Monmouth follows the general line of the legend as it was developed by 1837 (No. 2B). The significant exception is that he says that Molly's husband was not killed, only wounded, a fact that should have been well known to all citizens of Carlisle but was not. Note that Murray does not include any supplemental information relating to Molly's meeting with

Washington, her receipt of a battlefield commission, any parade after the battle, or money received form the French, all of which items appear in the Molly Pitcher story as spread by Custis and Lossing (Nos. 2D and 2K). Murray accepts that Molly was married to John Hays, but the real name of her first husband was William Hays (see No. 7C above).

CONCLUSION

This is a fair summary of the story of Molly Pitcher as understood by citizens of Carlisle in the 1880s.

8D. Peter Spahr, ca. 1883.

Mr. Spahr told me that she was a very masculine person, alike rough in appearance and character—small and heavy, with bristles in the end of her nose, and that she could both drink whiskey and swear.[9]

COMMENTARY

This passage come from a long newspaper article written by Rev. Murray that appeared in the September 12, 1883 issue of the Carlisle *American Volunteer* (No. 3G).

Peter Spahr was primarily responsible for the new grave stone erected on Mary Hays McCauley's grave in 1876 (see Nos. 3G, 4E and 9A).

CONCLUSION

This passage contains some interesting details on Mary Hays McCauley's appearance that are not recited elsewhere.

8E. Polly McCleaster, ca. 1883.

Mr. Parks, as did also Mrs. McCleaster, informed me that Molly had lived in the family of Dr. George D. Foulke, and other families, as well as faithfully served other persons in Carlisle, and though she generally wore a petticoat and short gown, and could drink grog and use language not the most polite, yet she was a kind-hearted woman, and helpful to the sick and needy. A woman—"for a' that..."

He [John Hays, grandson of Mary Hays McCauley] referred me to his widow sister, Polly M'Cleester, who is the oldest of the family. She is in her 81st year. I saw her, and though advanced in life, she is still somewhat vigorous, tall and slender like her father [John L. Hays]. After repeated and direct questions relative to the pension matter, she said that her grandmother had often tried unsuccessfully to get a pension, and had at last received one payment of $24 a short time before she died. It was the first she had received, and she was promised more if she lived. Polly, however, could not tell me whether it was form the State or general government. She was not then living with her grandmother, or in Carlisle, but with her husband in Papertown, several miles south of Carlisle, and hence she appeared to know the less about her...

While Polly did not remember the year in which her grandmother died, she was certain that it was in the month of January, adding, that her son, who is now about 54 years old, was then about 3 years old. She seemed to be indignant at Mr. Wesley Miles for stating that her grandmother came from Ireland, and said that "she was as Dutch as Sauer Kraut, and her maiden name was Mary Ludwig!" (Though her family name indicates her Teutonic origin, her married name certainly suggests a Celtic descent, and such a mistake could be easily made)....

Years ago I was most credibly informed by a venerable friend, Mr. James Loudon, that it was in Gen. Wm. Irvine's family that Mary Ludwig lived, in Carlisle, when she first saw and married John Hays, who was a barber by profession, as well as an enlisted soldier. Recently, too, I have been told the same thing by her aged namesake, Polly McCleaster, who detailed to me with manifest interest and pleasure that she distinctly recollected of hearing her grandmother say in regard to their short and amusing courtship, which commenced when she was sweeping in front of the Irvine home, dressed in her petticoat and short gown. Soon afterward they were married. And she was still working in the Irvine family when she was summoned to join her husband in the army. Polly cannot tell to which company or regiment her grandfather belonged. If she ever knew, she has forgotten.[10]

COMMENTARY

These passages come from a long newspaper article written by Rev. Murray that appeared in the September 12, 1883 issue of the Carlisle *American Volunteer* (No. 3G).

Polly McCleaster was the eldest daughter of John L. Hays, only son of Mary Hays McCauley and her first husband, William Hays. She was around 30 years old when her grandmother died, so certainly had the opportunity to get to know her well. She tells an interesting story of how her grandparents met that is not recited elsewhere.

The most significant element of this passage is Polly McClaester's statement that her grandmother was German and that her maiden name was Mary Ludwig; she also says that her grandfather's name was John Hays.[11] Polly insisted on this because she was angered by a claim by Wesley Miles that her grandmother was of Irish origin (No. 8B). Despite Polly's insistence, other evidence is very clear that the proper name of her grandfather was William Hays, and that her grandmother could not have been born with the name of Mary Ludwig. That Polly's memory could have been faulty is exemplified by the fact that she thought her grandmother never received any pension money until right before she died, whereas it is clear she received her pension for 10 years from 1822 to January 1832 (see No. 7I). This may be a case of Polly remembering the developed Molly Pitcher myth concerning Mary Hays McCauley's early years rather than more accurate information she may have known in her younger days.

CONCLUSION

These passages contain interesting quotations from Mary Hays' McCauley's oldest granddaughter, Mrs. Polly McCleaster. Polly strongly insists that her grandmother was married to John Hays and was born under the name Mary Ludwig, but both of these statements can be shown to be inaccurate.

8F. John Hays, ca. 1883.

John Hays, Molly's grandson, could not tell me just when his grandmother died, but after reflection said: I am now 84 years old, and was somewhere about 10 or 12 years old when she died and she died in the old stone house near Lockridge's corner, at the south east intersection of North and Bedford streets. He spoke of her as a short, thick, heavy woman, and often heard her say that, if it had not been for her the battle of Monmouth would have gone against us! He could not tell me positively that she ever received a pension but thought that towards the close of her life she had gotten something of the kind but referred me to his widow sister, Polly M'Cleester, who is the oldest of the family.[12]

COMMENTARY

This passage comes from a long newspaper article written by Rev. Murray that appeared in the September 12, 1883 issue of the Carlisle *American Volunteer* (No. 3G).

It contains a most interesting quotation by Molly about the battle of Monmouth as recalled by her grandson, John Hays.

CONCLUSION

In this passage Mary Hays McCauley's grandson, John Hays, recalls her as saying that "if it had not been for her the battle of Monmouth would have gone against us."

8G. Recollections of Mrs. Barbara Park, ca. 1890.

I will quote one more witness, Mrs. Barbara Park, who died in Carlisle, December 16th, 1896, where she had lived since she was nine years old. She knew Molly very well. She was a girl of about twelve years when the corner stone of the present Episcopal Church was laid on September 8th, 1826. A quarry on the Public Square, from which the stone for the foundation had been taken was still open at the time. She and a younger brother were on their way to see the ceremonies, and passing too near the quarry both fell in. She was some-what hurt. The first person to help them, notwithstanding her age, was Molly Pitcher, who first assisted her brother out and then herself. The occasion of the laying of the corner stone of the church was a public one. The military of the town, and numerous organizations were drawn up in parade. To the la-dies who were admiring the military demonstration, Molly said, "This is nothing but a flea bite to what I have seen." Mrs. Park was about nineteen years old at the time of Molly's death. Her appearance and dress she described the same as

Miss Foulke. She said Molly was a brave woman, and had a kind word for everyone. She was known as "Molly Pitcher" from her having carried water in a pitcher to the soldiers at the battle of Monmouth; and from her having assisted in firing the cannon, became known as "The heroine of the battle of Monmouth." She died at the home of her son, John L. Hays, in the stone house previously mentioned."[13]

COMMENTARY

This passage is quoted by John Landis in his 1905 booklet, "A Short History of Molly Pitcher" (No. 4E). This is a quotation from one of Molly's neighbors, Mrs. Barbara Park, who died in 1896. For the description referred to by Miss Foulke, see No. 8I.

In this passage, Mrs. Park claims to have heard Mary Hays McCauley speak of having seen a military engagement at some point. She unfortunately did not state the name of the battle.

CONCLUSION

This passage contains a recollection by one of Mary Hays McCauley's neighbors who heard her say that she had seen a military engagement at some point. She did not state the name of the battle.

8H. Summary of affidavit of given by Mrs. Susan Heckendorn, 1895.

Mrs. Susan Heckendorn, a very intelligent old lady residing in Carlisle, whose deposition was taken in 1895, when she was seventy-nine years of age stated that she had lived in Carlisle since 1828. She was a young lady of sixteen when Molly Pitcher died. She often saw her at the house of her son, John L. Hays, near the corner of Bedford and North Streets, and knew her very well. She said Molly was a rather large woman with a florid complexion, her hair mixed with gray. She attended the Lutheran Church. She often told this deponent and her girl friends the story of her army life, and her experience at the battle of Monmouth, and said to them, "You girls should have been with me at the Battle of Monmouth and learned how to load a cannon." Mrs. Heckendorn further stated that Molly died about 1832, and was buried in the public graveyard at Carlisle. She was present at the burial.[14]

COMMENTARY

This is a summary by John Landis of an affidavit given by one of Mary Hays' McCauley's neighbors, Mrs. Susan Heckendorn, in 1895 (see No. 4E). Mrs. Heckendorn's statement that Mrs. McCauley attended the Lutheran church might seem to support those who argue that she was of German origin. Her statement that she heard Mrs. McCauley say "You girls should have been with me at the Battle of Monmouth and learned how to load a cannon" is the strongest evidence we have that Mary Hays McCauley was the Molly Pitcher of Revolutionary War fame.

CONCLUSION

This passage contains the only preserved quotation of Mary Hays McCauley saying she fired a cannon at the Battle of Monmouth.

8I. Account of testimony of Harriet Foulke, 1896.

Miss Harriet M. Foulke, who a few years ago died in Lancaster, Ohio, a very intelligent and cultured old lady, testified in 1896, that she lived in Carlisle from 1809 to 1861. Her father, Dr. George M. Foulke, a prominent physician of Carlisle, attended Molly in her last illness. At that time Miss Foulke was nearly twenty-three years of age. Her description of Molly accords with that given before. She had a defective eye, which was also distinctly remembered by Mrs. Spangler, an aged lady of Carlisle, who recalled her appearance with great distinctness. Molly was often employed at Dr. Foulke's home in various kinds of house work, during a number of years. She was homely in appearance, not refined in manner or language, but ready to do a kind act for anyone. She was of average height, muscular, strong, and heavy-set. She was a busy talker. She wore a short gown, white or calico, a linsey striped skirt, very short and full, woolen stockings, heavy brogans, and a broad white cap with wide flaring ruffles. Miss Foulke further stated that she was so well known as the 'Molly Pitcher' of Monmouth, that no effort seems to have been made to perpetuate a fact which all seemed to recognize.[15]

COMMENTARY

This a summary by John Landis of "testimony" given by one of Mary Hays McCauley's neighbors, Harriet Foulke, in 1896 (see No. 4E). She describes Mrs. Hays' dress appearance, including the fact that she had a defective eye, as well as her unrefined manner and language.

CONCLUSION

This passage is significant for Miss Foulke's statement that Mary Hays McCauley "was so well known as the 'Molly Pitcher' of Monmouth, that no effort seems to have been made to perpetuate a fact which all seemed to recognize."

8J. Affidavit of Mrs. Mary E. Wilson, 1903

State of Pennsylvania, County of Cumberland.

Before me a Notary Public in and for said State and County, personally appeared Mary E. Wilson, who, after having been by me duly sworn according to law, doth depose and say that she is now forty-eight years old and resides in Carlisle, where she has lived all her life, that she is the daughter of Fred'k McCleaster, who was the son of John and Polly McCleaster, the said Polly McCleaster was the daughter of John Hays, who was the son of Molly McKolly, otherwise known as "Molly Pitcher" (whose maiden name was Mary Ludwig), and whose first husband was John Hays. She further says that she had had in her possession, since the death of her grandmother, Polly McLeaster, the pitcher, which was formerly the property of "Molly Pitcher," which was presented to her, the deponent, by her grandmother, Polly McLeaster, at the time of her death, with the strict admonition that she should be very careful to preserve it because it had been the property of her grandmother, Molly McKolly, alias "Molly Pitcher." She further says that her grandmother, Polly McCleaster, raised her the deponent, from her childhood up until the time of her marriage, and that she lived constantly

in her family, and that her grandmother told her frequently that the pitcher concerning which the affidavit was made, was presented to her personally by her grandmother, Molly McKolly, and that she had been charged by her to very careful of it as it was a favorite piece of ware, and as her grandmother stated frequently, that because her grandmother had given her such strict instructions about preserving the pitcher she often cautioned me about handling it, indeed forbade me from handling it at all. She, the deponent, further says that she frequently heard and saw her grandmother show this pitcher to her friends and neighbors and explain to them that it was the pitcher that belonged to her grandmother, "Molly Pitcher."

Deponent further says her grandmother died April 28th, 1884, at which time she, deponent, came into possession of the pitcher, which by reason of the admonitions given her by her grandmother, she has been very careful to preserve intact, until this date, when now she disposes of it to be cared for by the Cumberland County Historical Society and deposited with its collection. A description of the pitcher, which is the subject of this affidavit, is as follows, to wit: It is ewer shaped, wide mouth. Standing eight and one-fourth inches to the top of the handle and seven and seven-sixteenth inches high to the centre of the mouth and four inches in diameter at the base; the figures on the outside of it are brown in color on a white base, and are made up for the most part of Chinese or Japanese pagodas, and something resembling fortifications with the figures of two men on these fortifications, one holding in his right hand something in the shape of a three-leafed clover and the other man apparently suspended in the air and pointing upward, around the handle and top of the pitcher it is edged with blue.

My grandmother often told me about her grandmother Molly McKolly alias "Molly Pitcher" telling her about being in the army and carrying water to the wounded and dying.

Witness my hand this 13th Aug., 1903. Mrs. Mary E. Wilson.

Sworn and subscribed before me this 13th of August 1903.

John R. Miller, Notary Public, Carlisle, Pa.

My commission expires April 18, 1907.[16]

COMMENTARY

This is an affidavit by Marty Hays McCauley's great-great-granddaughter, Mrs. Mary E. Wilson, concerning the authenticity of an oriental pitcher once owned by her great-great-grandmother, Mary Hays McCauley. Yes, this was Molly Pitcher's pitcher. It was a Chinese ewer, clearly not anything that was ever carried on a battlefield. Still, it is interesting as a family heirloom. It was donated to the Cumberland County Historical Society in Carlisle in 1903, where it can still be seen today.[17]

Mrs. Wilson states that she often heard her grandmother say that she had heard Mary Hays McCauley talk about being in the army and bring water to the troops. She makes no mention, however, of hearing any stories about Molly Hays McCauley ever firing a cannon.

CONCLUSION

This affidavit concerns the authenticity of a pitcher once owned by Mary Hays McCauley. It was given by her great-great-granddaughter, Mrs. Mary E. Wilson, who often heard family stories about Mary Hays McCauley talking about "being in the army and carrying water to the wounded and dying."

8K. Affidavit of Elizabeth Dehuff of Carlisle, July, 1908.

AGED WOMAN SWEARS TO THE REALITY
OF HEROINE OF BATTLE OF MONMOUTH

Carlisle, Pa. July 23. Through the efforts of Duncan M. Graham and John R. Miller. Local attorneys, a sworn statement from Mrs. Elizabeth Dehuff of Carlisle, who is ninety-one years old and who is the only living being who knew the redoubtable heroine of American History, "Molly Pitcher," who lies buried in Carlisle's ancient graveyard, going to refute the attack of several historians who have questioned the identity of the woman buried and honored here.

"Mollie Pitcher" was the name that history gave to Mollie Ludwig Hays McCauley, the heroine of the Battle of Monmouth, who while serving water to the embattled soldiers, served in her husband's place at the cannon's mouth after her spouse had been killed.

Mrs. Dehuff's affidavit follows:

Elizabeth Dehuff being duly sworn deposes and says: I was born on February 18, 1818 and am now in my ninety-first year. I was born Elizabeth White. I remember distinctly about my father requiring the ages of us all to be put down in the family bible. My mind is clear and my recollection is vivid and especially with relation to the occurrences of my childhood. Mollie McCauley lived right across the street from us. She died right across the street from us, near the corner of North and Bedford Streets, there was two apartments to the house. Mollie lived in the stone part right next to the corner. She died there at the home of her son, John L. Hays. I lived right across the street from where Mollie died. She was of low stature, short, stout, heavily built woman, and wore a petticoat and short gown; they did not wear dresses at that time; and it seems that there was a little something the matter with her eye, I just can't remember that. She wore a white cap and her hair was white with the cap. But, oh my! She was at our house so much. She was rough and uncouth in her ex-pressions when she would tell of the battlefield and I remem-ber of my mother telling her, "Oh Mollie, Mollie! I won't have that kind of talk or swearing before these children." Poor old Mollie! She would tell of the battlefield and how she used to carry water to the soldiers. She used to tell a lot of things that happened at the battle, but I can't remember all what she said, and when her first husband was killed she took his place at the cannon's mouth. Yes, she did that; I remem-ber her telling that she did, I Remember it distinctly. Old Mollie McCauley, she lived with her son, John L. Hays, a tall fine looking man, and he taught school. I went to school to him. He taught right on the corner of North and Bedford where Mollie Pitcher died. He taught the school on the corner next to her house... Mollie would often tell of incidents of the battle, I often heard her speak of it myself... Yes, Mollie was a good kind-hearted woman. There was something good in her, for all she was rough and coarse in her expression; she was as kind-hearted a woman as ever lived. The roughness was on the outside. It seems to me that she kept a little cake shop over on Louther Street. Some pretty hard people lived in the vicinity of her home, but she would always visit the sick and was always willing to sit up at night with the sick. I heard her say she carried water to the men on the battlefield. I remember hearing the neighbors calling her Mollie Pitcher. She was known pretty commonly as Mollie Pitcher, that was what we called her. She used to tell of the many, many acts she did on the battlefield. She died on the corner of North and Bedford Streets at her son's and she was buried form that place, as I said before. I have made this statement without anyone dictating or suggesting anything to me about it, and from my own knowledge, and the text of this statement was read to me before I swore to it, and everything herein contained is true, as I clearly recollect it, in the presence of the notary public, John R. Miller, D.M. Graham and Viola Ziegler as stenographer. Elizabeth Dehuff.[18]

COMMENTARY

Mrs. Dehuff was 91 years old when she gave this affidavit. She was said to be "the only living being who knew the redoubtable heroine of American history, 'Molly Pitcher,' who lies buried in Carlisle's ancient graveyard." Her sworn statement was taken by two attorneys, Duncan M. Graham and John R. Miller, for the purpose "to refute the attack of several historians who have questioned the identity of the woman buried and honored here." One of the historians referred to may be Jeremiah Zeamer (see Nos. 4F).

Mrs. Dehuff gives a physical description of Mary Hays McCauley and her dress, and confirms the statement of Harriet Foulke that she has "a little something the matter with her eye" (No. 8I). John Landis says that "She had a defective eye, the left, having met with an accident which finally caused its blindness. This was later in life, and was said to have been caused by a particle of lime entering the eye."[19] Mrs. Dehuff states that Mrs. McCauley used to speak often of the battlefield, and that she said she took the place of her husband when he was killed at the cannon's mouth. Either Mrs. Dehuff's memory was inaccurate, or Mrs. McCauley told the story to please her audience, since we know that her first husband William Hays was not killed at Monmouth, but survived the battle and the war.

CONCLUSION

This affidavit was given in 1908 by 91-year-old Mrs. Elizabeth Dehuff. She remembered Mary Hays McCauley speaking often of her actions on the battlefield, and often heard her neighbors refer to Mary Hays McCauley as Mollie Pitcher.

8L. Judge Edward Biddle, June 28, 1916.

COMMENTARY

Judge Edward Biddle gave the main address at the unveiling of the Molly Pitcher statue at her grave in Carlisle on June 28, 1916. During the address he cited the record of two payments in the County Commissioners' "payment book" of April 1811 Made to Molly McCauley for performing manual labor. One was in the amount of $15.00 for "washing and scrubbing the court house" and the second was for $1.03. Another payment of $22.36 was made to Molly McCawley among others for "cleaning and whitewashing the public buildings."[20]

CONCLUSION

This information shows that Mary Hays McCauley did occasional jobs at manual labor for the town of Carlisle in the period from 1811-1813.

8M. Recollection by William S. Myers of a conversation with Miss Caroline Ege of Carlisle, 1926.

For a number of years I spent a part of each summer in Carlisle. In 1905 I met there Miss Caroline Ege, a life-long resident, who died in 1909 at the advanced age of eighty-seven. As a child she had known Molly McCauley, remembered her well, and told me interesting facts in regard to her. In response to a letter of inquiry to a member of Miss Ege's family I received the following reply (August 1926): "Yes, you are correct in quoting-'Molly was a rough, common woman who swore like a trooper." She smoked and chewed tobacco, and had no education whatsoever. She was hired to do the most menial work, such as scrubbing etc. I think there are some of her descendents still living in Carlisle.[21]

COMMENTARY

William Starr Myers was a professor of politics at Princeton University. In 1926 he was the editor of William S. Stryker's unpublished study, *The Battle of Monmouth*, which was published by Princeton University Press in 1927. This account tells the recollections of an aged neighbor of Mary Hays McCauley, Caroline Ege, concerning Mrs. McCauley's manner and appearance.

CONCLUSION

This passage is another testimony by one of Mary Hays McCauley's neighbors commenting on how rough and uncouth she was.

Mary Hays McCauley's Corrected Grave Stone (see No. 9B).

9. MARKERS AND MONUMENTS

AT THE GRAVE OF MARY HAYS MCCAULEY IN THE OLD CEMETERY, CARLISLE, PENNSYLVANIA

9A. Mary Hays McCauley's Gravestone, 1876.

Molly McCauley
Renowned in History as
Mollie Pitcher.
The Heroine of Monmouth
Died Jan. 1833
Aged 79 years.
Erected by the Citizens of
Cumberland County
July 4, 1876

COMMENTARY

Mary McCauley's grave was apparently not marked when she was buried after her funeral in January 1832. In the spring of 1876 Wesley Miles wrote a newspaper article decrying the fact that her grave was not honored (see Nos. 3G and 3H), and Agnes Graham wrote a letter to the same effect to the editor of the Carlisle *American Volunteer* (see No. 4E). These inspired Peter Spahr to start a movement to set up a monument for her in time to be dedicated on the centennial of the Declaration of Independence on July 4, 1876. Over $100 was raised, and the monument was prepared. The location of Molly's previously unmarked grave was confirmed, and the monument was set up there (see Nos. 3G and 4E). The gravesite was confirmed in 1892 Frederick Hays, Molly's grandson, gave permission for a Mrs. Patton to gig up the grave; Mrs. Patton was looking for the unmarked graves of her infant brother and sister, which she believed to be in the area. Frederick Hays and Mrs. Patton's attorney were witnesses when the grave marked as that of Mary McCauley was dug up and the body of an adult woman exhumed.[1]

On the day of the dedication there was a procession to the cemetery led by a color guard. "Then came carriages containing Mr. Peter Spahr, Miss Polly Malcaster, and others, who were to take part in the ceremonies of unveiling of the monument of Captain Mollie.

This took place at half past twelve."[2] The ceremony drew the largest crowd of people seen in Carlisle in some time. "It was a military funeral in all its details—pall bearers, soldiers, muffled drums, arms reversed and the usual salute fired at the grave."[3] Troops were provided by the volunteer companies of Carlisle—the Guards, Artillery and Infantry.

Wesley Miles described the ceremony as follows: "I was present. An immense crowd thronged the old graveyard, patiently waiting for two hours in the terrible heat, for the arrival of the immense procession of friends, societies, etc. It was headed by the speakers and Carlisle band. Of the number in our carriage, one was a granddaughter of Mollie's aged 75 years, named Polly McLaister, who unveiled the monument. Captain Vale delivered an excellent oration, recounting the scenes of Monmouth, the army movements, Mollie's devotion to her husband, his death and she taking his place at the cannon, her subsequent history, death, and burial."[4]

This monument cites the year of her death as 1833, but her obituary notice is clearly dated 1832 (Nos. 7O and 7P above). The monument gives her age as "Aged 79 years," while the obituary says she was "about 90 years." The 79 figure may be the more accurate, since she is listed in the 1830 census as being between 70 and 80 years old at that time, two years before she died.[5]

CONCLUSION

When Mary Hays McCauley died, her grave was originally unmarked or had only a simple monument. It remained in this condition until 1876, when Peter Spahr, prompted by Wesley Miles, arranged that a large upright marker be placed on the grave.

9B. Mary Hays McCauley's corrected gravestone, ca. 1885.

Molly McCauley
Renowned in History as
Mollie Pitcher.
The Heroine of Monmouth
Died Jan. 1832
Aged 79 years.
Erected by the Citizens of
Cumberland County
July 4, 1876

COMMENTARY

The marker erected over Mary Hays McCauley's grave originally had the incorrect year of her death, 1833 (No. 9A). Rev. J.A. Murray wrote in 1883 that the date did not look right to him, so he checked the local newspapers and found that the correct date should be January 1832. As he noted, this is "one of those grave(stone) mistakes that will sometimes occur."[6] The monument was corrected at some later date, reportedly by the Civic Club of Carlisle.[7] It is today difficult to read in its entirety due to weathering over the years.

The monument gives Mrs. McCauley's age when she died as 79 years, which would place her birth in the year 1753. One of her obituaries, however, says that she was "about 90" when she died, which would place her birth in the year 1743. The 1753 date suggested by this grave marker would seem to be preferable since census records show that she was between 70 and 80 years old in 1830 (born between 1750 and 1760).[8]

In 1896 the Daughters of the American Revolution proposed that Mary Hays McCauley's body be exhumed and removed from Carlisle to the National Cemetery at Gettysburg. Their "delirious scheme" never was carried out.[9]

Another plan to move Mary Hays McCauley's body surfaced in New Jersey in the 1960s. A group called "The Friendly Sons of Molly Pitcher" was formed for the purpose of bringing her body to Freehold to be reburied at the foot of the Monmouth Battle Monument on Court Street (Nos. 9G and 9H). News of their plans reached the authorities in Carlisle, who for a time placed a police guard on Mary's grave. The mayor of Carlisle was reported as saying that The Friendly Sons of Molly Pitcher "wouldn't dare march on Carlisle," and as of yet they have not.[10]

CONCLUSION

Mary Hays McCauley's grave stone erected in 1876 incorrectly gave the year of her death as 1833. It was afterwards corrected to read 1832. She was probably born around 1753, as the gravestone suggests, rather than in 1744, as some sources declare.

9C. Cannon dedicated at the grave of Mary Hays McCauley, 1905.

Erected in memory of
Mollie McKolly
Renowned in history as
Mollie Pitcher
by the P.O.S. of A of Cumberland
County, 1905[11]

COMMENTARY

On October 9, 1904 the Carlisle Camp No. 171 of the Patriotic Order Sons of America voted to look into the placing of a cannon at the grave of Mary Hays McCauley, better known as "Mollie Pitcher." They requested an appropriation of $5000 from the State Legislature to obtain the cannon, but only $2000 was appropriated, and that amount was vetoed by the Governor, Samuel W. Pennypacker. Apparently the organization had to incur the expense itself.[12] Among those objecting to the expenditure of public moneys on such a project was Jeremiah Zeamer of Carlisle (see No. 4D).

The cannon was dedicated on June 28, 1905 after a lengthy parade and with suitable ceremonies. The cannon itself was unveiled by Miss Nellie Kramer, great-great-granddaughter of Mary Hays McCauley. The full ceremony and its speeches were printed up in a booklet published by John B. Landis, historian for the P.O.S.of A. (see No. 4E).[13]

CONCLUSION

The Patriotic Sons Order of America dedicated a cannon at the grave of Mary Hays McCauley on June 28, 1905.

9D. Statue erected by the State of Pennsylvania, 1916.

MOLLY
PITCHER
MARY MCKOLLY
MCAULEY
MARY HAYS
NEE
MARY LUDWIG

BORN OCTOBER 13, 1744
DIED JANUARY 22, 1832

COMMENTARY

This monument, dedicated by the state of Pennsylvania on June 16, 1916, is surmounted by a life-size bronze statue of Molly Pitcher and is flanked by a bronze relief on each side. The relief on the left depicts her given water to a fallen soldier, and the relief on the right depicts her helping to fire a cannon. The face on the statue was based on a composite of the faces of five of her great-grandchildren. The Patriotic Order of the Sons of America added the cannon, flagstaff and bronze relief.[14]

Local legend says that, "If a little girl stands in front of Molly's buxom statue and looks up into her face, makes a wish, closes her eyes, then walks around the statue three times and looks up at Molly's face again, the wish will come true."[15]

The text of this monument claims Molly to be the daughter of John Ludwig, and gives her birth date as 1744. As discussed above, Mary Hays McCauley could not have been born as Mary Ludwig (see Commentary to Nos. 3E and 3L), and her birth year was more likely 1753 than 1744 (see Nos. 9A and 9B).

CONCLUSION

In 1916 the state of Pennsylvania a large bronze statue depicting a young, noble and determined Molly Pitcher holding a rammer. The inscription below the statue says that she was born as Mary Ludwig on October 13, 1744. Neither fact can be substantiated.

9E. BRONZE PLAQUES ERECTED IN 1916.

MARY LUDWIG ("Molly Pitcher"). Daughter of John Ludwig. Born October 13, 1744 – Died January 22, 1832. Married John Hays 1769. John Hays enlisted December 1, 1775 in Procter's First Pennsylvania Artillery. Re-enlisted January 1, 1777. Sergeant John Hays was wounded at the Battle of Monmouth June 28, 1778. Mary Ludwig Hays ("Molly Pitcher") returned to Carlisle, Pa. with her wounded husband and after his death she married Sergeant George McKolly (or McCauley). She died January 22, 1832 and was buried with military honors. The Pennsylvania assembly

1821-1822 granted a pension to Molly McKolly (or McCauley) for services rendered. This monument is erected by the Commonwealth of Pennsylvania June 28, 1916. Commissioners. Roy L. Schuyler, Chairman. Herman A. Miller, Vice Chairman. William S. Wacker, Treasurer. William A. Rupp, Secretary.

Mary Ludwig Hays ("Molly Pitcher") accompanied her husband during his service in the Continental Army and rendered valuable service in the capacity of an army nurse and by reason of her many acts of kindness became known throughout the army, from the oft-repeated expression "here comes Molly and her pitcher," as "Molly Pitcher." At the Battle of Monmouth, June 28, 1778, Sergeant John Hays was severely wounded and as he fell to the ground Molly sprang to the cannon he had been serving, which had been ordered to the rear. But before the gun could be withdrawn she had taken her husband's place and rendered such valiant service that General George Washington after the battle thanked her personally for her bravery and heroic action.

"Molly Pitcher"
(Mary Hays)
O'er Monmouth's field of carnage drear
With cooling drink and words of cheer
A woman passed who knew no fear,
    The wife of Hays the gunner.
With ramrod from her husband's hand,
    Beside his gun she took her stand.
And helped to wrest our well-loved land
    From England's tyrant king.
From the ranks this woman came,
    By the cannon won her fame.
'Tis true she could not write her name
    But freedom's hand hath carved it.
Shall we then criticize her ways?
Nay, rather give her well-earned praise.
Then doff our caps and voices raise
    In cheers for Molly Pitcher.
                    —Gordon Woods Parkinson

COMMENTARY

These plaques was erected by the state of Pennsylvania and were unveiled on June 28, 1916, the 138th anniversary of the battle of Monmouth, at the same time as the monument No. 3J above. The plaques state that Mary Hays was born under the name of Mary Ludwig and was married to John Hays at the time of the battle of Monmouth. As shown above, she was not born as Mary Ludwig (see Commentary to Nos. 3E and 3L) and her husband at the time of the battle was named William Hays (see No. 7F). The account given of Molly Pitcher at the battle of Monmouth says that her husband was wounded and she was presented to General Washington after the battle.

For some of the comments made by Judge Edward Biddle at the dedication of this monument, see No. 8L.

CONCLUSION

Some of the information on these plaques (that Molly's maiden name was Mary Ludwig and she was married to John Hays in 1778) was corrected in newer plaques erected nearby by the United States Field Artillery Association in 2000 (No. 9F).

9F. New Bronze Plaques

Mary Hays McCauley. Renowned in history as "Molly Pitcher, The Heroine of Monmouth" and wife of William Hays, the gunner. Note: The name "Ludwig" is not associated with Molly Pitcher.
History corrected in the year 2000 during the 250th anniversary celebration of
Cumberland County.
Sponsored by the United States Field Artillery Association.

This site maintained by the Borough of Carlisle, the United States Field Artillery Association, and the 'Redlegs' of Carlisle Barracks.

COMMENTARY

These two plaques were set up in 2000 to correct the information stated on the monument erected by the state of Pennsylvania in 1916 that Mary Hays McCauley was born as Mary Ludwig (No. 9E).

MARKERS AND MONUMENTS IN NEW JERSEY

9G. Background of the Monmouth Battle Monument, Freehold, New Jersey

As the centennial anniversary of the battle of Monmouth approached, Governor Joel Parker, then a resident of Freehold, realized that if no effort was made at that time to lay the corner stone of a monument to commemorate the event, it would never in any future time be accomplished. At commencement exercises of the Freehold Institute held a year preceding the anniversary, Governor Parker was invited to address the students. In the course of his remarks, he referred to the approaching centennial and suggested that a monument be erected and dedicated on the centennial anniversary of the battle. At his suggestion, editors of the newspapers, in connection with the clergymen and judges of the county, were appointed a committee to raise funds to erect a monument. To this committee was added Governors Joel Parker and William A. Newell. The former was chosen president of the organization which became known as the Monmouth Battle Monument Association. The other officers chosen were Major James S. Yard, secretary, and John B. Conover, treasurer. Numerous meetings of the Association were held in the fall and spring of 1877-1878, but it soon became evident that sufficient funds could not be raised to erect a suitable monument on the centennial anniversary day. A site had been donated by Mrs. Mary A. Schanck, containing three and one-quarter acres, in the shape of a triangle, with roads on three sides. Early in the spring of 1878 a committee of one from each township was appointed, to act in conjunction with a committee of citizens of Freehold, to make arrangements for the celebration of the centennial anniversary of the battle. It also became apparent that in order to hold real estate the Association should be incorporated, therefore an act was framed by Governor Parker and passed by the Legislature, March 19, 1878, and a certificate of incorporation was filed in the clerk's office of the county of Monmouth, May 28, 1878. Provision was made by the Association for procuring a corner-stone, and placing it in the proper position on the one hundredth anniversary of the battle. The amount deemed necessary for the erection of the monument was ten thousand dollars, of which less than three thousand had been collected. To increase this amount, five thousand medals of white metal and one hundred of bronze were manufactured, to be sold on the day of the celebration. The corner stone was laid on the day appointed with appropriate ceremonies. Freehold presented a gala appearance: on every side floated the Stars and Stripes, the houses of both rich and poor being adorned with the national colors. The crowd was swelled by visitors from towns within a radius of fifty miles, numbering over twenty thousand of happy sight-seers. A military parade marched through the streets of the little village, headed by the Second Brigade, National Guard of New Jersey. After the military contingent came Masonic societies in their full regalia, followed by a long line of carriages containing prominent citizens of New Jersey. Next in order was Company A, Washington Centennial Guards of Princeton, in the uniform worn in the days of the Revolution. Then followed the Joel Parker Association of Newark, presenting a creditable appearance, one hundred strong, clad in dark clothing and wearing high white felt hats. The rear of the line was brought up by the Delaware Hose Company of Bordentown; dragging their machine were thirty men in white shirts and wearing black helmet hats. The procession after moving over the prescribed route reached Monument Park, where a stand had been erected, and the ceremonies of laying the corner-stone took place a little after one o'clock. The stone was laid in accordance with Masonic form and usage, after conclusion of which ceremonies addresses were made by Governor Parker and other prominent citizens, the troops then reformed and were reviewed by Governor George B. McClellan. This concluded the festivities of the day, which in every way had been brilliant, successful, and creditable in the highest degree.

The first meeting of the Monument Association after the centennial celebration was February 22, 1879. The treasurer reported there was on hand $3624.78 towards the erection of a monument by the following June 28; the receipts had increased over $1200. The Association was now in a position to receive the deed for the site, as one of the stipulations of the gift was that $5000 would be raised for the building of the monument before a deed would be executed. The fund continued to increase gradually but slowly, and on July 10, 1880, the treasurer reported the amount was nearly $7000. It now became apparent that $10,000 would soon be reached. This was finally accomplished through the exertions of Governor Parker, Major James S. Yard and James T. Burtis. The active promoters of the project began to think that a monument of sufficient dimensions worthy of so memorable event could not be erected for the amount subscribed, and application was made to the Legislature of the State for an appropriation equal to the amount already obtained. This was granted, and $20,000 was appropriated by the national government; thus the fund had increased from less than $3000 when the cornerstone was laid to over $40,000. The contract for the monument was awarded to Maurice J. Power of the National Fine Art Foundry of New York City, for the sum of $36,000. The design was executed by Emelin T. Litttell and Douglas Smythe, and J.E. Kelly was the sculptor.

The work of construction was delayed so that it became impossible to unveil the monument on the anniversary of the battle, and November 13, 1884 was fixed upon as the day of its dedication. The base of the monument is in the form of an equilateral triangle, with a cannon at each angle. Three spurs of granite form the base of the shaft, surmounted at the point of contact by a large drum-shaped block on which are five bronze reliefs illustrative of the battle. Above the tablets and around the shaft are the coats-of-arms of the thirteen original States, in bronze, festooned with laurel wreaths. Rising above is the shaft proper, consisting of three sections joined by rings of bay leaves. The shaft is surmounted by a composite capital on which is the statue of Columbia Triumphant. The monument is of New England granite, ninety-four feet in height. The tablets, five feet high and six feet in width, represent five scenes in the Monmouth battle - Ramsey "defending his guns;

Washington rallying the troops; Molly Pitcher; Council of War at Hopewell; and Wayne's charge.

The day of the dedication was duly celebrated, the sky was cloudless, the weather temperate, the atmosphere clear and invigorating, and the breeze unfolded the thousand flags that floated over Monument Park and Freehold. The military parade, while there were not as many troops present as at the former celebrations, was impressive in character: it consisted of the First, Fourth and Seventh regiments of the National Guard under the command of Brevet Major-General William J. Sewell. As soon as the procession reached Monument Park, the ceremonies of unveiling were opened with an invocation of the Divine blessing by Right Reverend Bishop Scarborough. Then followed the formal delivery of the monument to the State of New Jersey, the presentation being responded to by Governor Leon Abbett. The orator of the day was Judge Parker, and on the finish of his oration the ceremonies were concluded by a benediction by Rev. George C. Maddock, and the firing of a national salute by the artillery. The throng of people was estimated between fifteen and twenty thousand. The ceremonies and parades which had been held in this commemoration of the battle of Monmouth must ever remain as the most memorable.[16]

COMMENTARY

This selection describes the background and construction of the Monmouth Battle Monument dedicated in Freehold on November 13, 1884.

9H. Description of the Monmouth Battle Monument, Freehold, 1884.

The monument in commemoration of the battle of Monmouth erected this week at Freehold, New Jersey, is a notable work of art. The first movement toward the erection of this monument was made in response to an address delivered by ex-Governor Joel Parker at Freehold on the ninety-ninth anniversary of the battle, June 28, 1877. A preliminary meeting for this purpose was held September 17, and the Battle Monument Association was organized October 2, 1877. The people of the State, and especially for Monmouth County, during the years 1878, 1879 and 1880, contributed nearly $10,000 to this object. The State of New Jersey, by an act of March 14, 1881, appropriated $10,000 and placed the work under the charge of a Commission instructed to select a design, contract for, erect and finish a monument in the Park at Freehold, where the battle commenced June 28, 1778. The Congress of the United States passed a law, approved July 6, 1882, granting an appropriation of $20,000 for this purpose.

At a meeting of the Commission, held March 2, 1883, the design executed by Emelin T. Littell and Douglas Smith, architects, and J.E. Kelly, sculptor, and exhibited by Maurice J. Power, of New York city, was accepted, and a contract was awarded to Mr. Power, of the Power Bronze Foundry, for the erection of the monument for the sum of $35.000.

The base of the monument is in the form of an equilateral triangle, with cannon at each angle. Three spurs of granite form the base of the shaft, surmounted at the point of contact by a large drum-shaped block, on which five bronze reliefs descriptive of the battle will be placed. Above the tablets and around the shaft are the coats of arms of the thirteen original States, festooned with laurel leaves. Rising above this is the shaft proper, consisting of three sections, which are joined by rings of bay leaves. The shaft is surmounted by a composite capital, on which is a statue of Columbia Triumphant. This monument is constructed of New England granite, polished, and is about one hundred feet high.

The tablets, five feet high and six feet wide, merit special mention. The models thereof were designed by Mr. J.E. Kelly, of New York city, and the bass-reliefs were cast at the Power Bronze Foundry. They represent with graphic "exactness five scenes in the Monmouth battle. Three of them are already finished and in position on the monument. A brief description will be of interest to the public.

1. *Ramsey Defending his Guns.* This represents Lieutenant-Colonel Nathaniel Ramsey, of Maryland, in the closing effort to hold his position until the main army could be rallied. General Washington had told him he depended on his exertions, and he had promised to check the enemy. He tried

with his gallant regiment to defend the guns of Lieutenant-Colonel Oswald, until, having become dismounted, he was overwhelmed by the superior numbers of the British dragoons. In the foreground he is represented with historical accuracy in a hand-to-hand conflict with a detachment of the Seventeenth British Regiment Light dragoons. Colonel Ramsey's portrait is from a miniature and a silhouette, taken from life, and furnished by his family. His sword is modeled form the short-bladed weapon which he actually carried and used with great effect that day, and which is still preserved. The uniform, horse furniture, and all the equipments of the dragoons are taken from the official records of the regiment. So particular has the artist been that the "death's head" may be seen on the hat of the troopers of the Seventeenth Dragoons—the organization allowed to wear the same by the orders of the King, with the motto, "Death or glory." In the background Oswald is directing the men in their attempt to carry off the guns. It will be remembered that Ramsey, badly wounded in this personal combat, was taken prisoner by the British. Sir Henry Clinton, in soldierly admiration of so brave a man, ordered his"release on parole the following day.

2. *Washington Rallying the Troops.* The Commander-in-chief is here depicted riding down the American lines on the spirited horse which had just been presented to him by New Jersey's war Governor, William Livingston, and rallying the troops after General Lee's unaccountable retreat. He is placing the regiments of Stewart and Ramsey and Livingston in position to check the advance party of the British. General Washington's head and figure are modeled from Houdon's life cast, now in possession of Mr. Power. The model is worked on a scale, and is entirely accurate in all its properties, from Houdon's measurements. The styles of the uniform and horse equipments of the chieftain are all from authentic sources.

3. *Molly Pitcher.* The head and figure of the heroine of Monmouth is an ideal woman of great muscular power. Her dead husband is at her feet, and General Knox is seen in the background directing his artillery line. A wounded soldier uses his right hand instead of his left in thumbing the vent.

This, it is readily seen, improves the composition of the picture. The old Tennent Church, still standing as a memorial of the battle, is seen on the extreme left of the relief.

4. *Council of War at Hopewell.* This tablet is unfinished. It will represent Generals Washington, Lee, Greene, Stirling, Lafayette, Steuben, Knox, Poor, Wayne, Woodford, Patterson, Scott, and Duportail as they appeared in the important council held at Hopewell, Old Hunterdon County, New Jersey, June 24, 1778. General Washington is listening attentively as General Lafayette, standing by the table, is urging the council to decide on making a strong demonstration against the British column, even if it brought on a battle. The position and general expression of other officers clearly indicate their opinion of Lafayette's appeal. General Lee, who preferred to let the British force parade unmolested across the State, looks anxious and indignant that the military experience and judgment do not entirely control the board. It is easy to see that the foreign officers Steuben and Duportail want to make a strong attack, and not simply feel out the enemy. General Patterson agrees with them, and so does the truehearted Greene. General Wayne, always ready for fight, can hardly wait until Lafayette is finished, that he may speak a few words of ardent patriotism. Colonel Scammell, Washington's Adjutant-General, who afterward gave his life for liberty on Yorktown's ramparts, is here engaged in noting the opinions of the general officers for the guidance of his chief.

5. *Wayne's Charge.* The other unfinished relief depicts Mad Anthony Wayne leading his troops, in the final charge of the day, through a trampled corn field, and the battalions of British grenadiers falling back, and trying in vain to carry away the body of their dead commander, Lieutenant-Colonel Henry Monckton. The parsonage of Tennent Church is seen in the background.

All lovers of American art will be charmed with the wonderful beauty of these reliefs; all students of the Revolutionary epoch will be struck with the zealous care displayed by the skillful artist to have every detail historically correct. The great delicacy with which these bronze panels have come from the sculptor's hand will be seen in the fact that all the

picturesque qualities of the original mould have been reproduced in the successful cast without the usual chasing.
William S. Stryker, Adjutant-General of New Jersey[17]

9I. Plaque in Monmouth Battlefield State Park, 1978.

In honor of
the battle of Monmouth Heroine
Molly Pitcher, June 28, 1778.
Gift of the historical societies of
Monmouth County D.A.R.
Monmouth County Heritage Committee
and friends
Dedicated October 28, 1978.

COMMENTARY

This plaque was set up on a boulder on Combs' Hill, immediately northeast of the Monmouth Battlefield State Park Visitor Center, in the fall of 1978. When first erected, it had the date of the battle listed incorrectly as July 28, 1778. This was corrected in March of 1979.[18]

Battle of Monmouth Monument at Freehold, New Jersey, 1884.

10. MARY HAYS MCCAULEY'S MAIDEN NAME

THE MARY LUDWIG THEORY

10A. Rev. C.P. Wing, 1878

The original name before marriage was Mary Ludwig (so recorded in the family bible). She herself probably came from Germany. The first we discover of her was at Trenton, N.J., where she had quarters with Gen. Irvine. Her husband was John Hays, a barber, a sergeant in a company of artillery.[1]

10B. Dr. William H. Egle, 1893.

Mary Ludwig, the daughter of John George Ludwig, was born in Lancaster county, Pennsylvania, October 13th, 1744. Her parents were emigrants from the Palatinate, Germany. Mary's early years were spent in the family of afterwards Gen. William Irvine, then residing at Carlisle. Here she became acquainted with John Hays, to whom she was married July 24th, 1769.[2]

10C. C. Malcolm B. Gilman, 1964.

Mary Ludwig, daughter of John George Ludwig, a dairy farmer from near Trenton, New Jersey, was born on October 13, 1754. She was christened at The Lawrenceville Presbyterian Church, then the Church of Christ. (Records of the Church of Christ and Mon. Co. Historical Assoc.).[3]

10D. Isabella Crater McGeorge, 1900.

On a small dairy farm that lay between Princeton and Trenton, in Mercer County, New Jersey, there was born in 1754, of German parentage, Mary Ludwig. As is the manner in German households, Mary was taught first obedience without question; to utilize what was at hand, and to make the most of circumstances; when times bettered out—to thank God they were not worse.

It is said that she was not pretty, but had Titian eyes, small features and was rather short in stature—but was so strong that with ease she could carry a three-bushel bag of wheat across her shoulder and deposit the same in the upper room of the granary. As was the custom of the times, she wore the "short gown and petticoat." This consisted of a sack like upper garment, and her preference was for a blue and white cotton skirt.[4]

COMMENTARY

The first written claim that Mary Hays McCauley was born under the name Mary Ludwig appears in a letter that Rev. C.P. Wing of Carlisle wrote to the editor of the *Pennsylvania Magazine of History and Biography* in 1878 (No. 3E). The evidence he offers is the family bible, which apparently no longer exists. Notice that he does not offer a birth date or the names of her parents, just a speculation that she was born in Germany.

The second written claim that Mary Hays McCauley was born under the name Mary Ludwig appears in 1893 in a an entry in Dr. William H. Egle's massive genealogical study strangely entitled *Notes and Queries* (No. 3J). Here he gives not only a birth date, but also a place and the name of her father. Egle does not, however, state his source for this information.

C. Malcolm Gilman in his 1964 book *Monmouth, Road to Glory* (No. 5F) is the only author to offer a source for the Mary Ludwig's birth date and place and the name of her father. However, this record is not able to be located at either of the places Gilman cites. The published records for the Lawrenceville Presbyterian Church list no christenings before 1821,[5] and no records relating to the christening of Mary Ludwig could be located at the library of the Princeton Theological Seminary or the Monmouth County Historical Association.[6] Also note that Gilman's date is exactly ten years later than Egle's, perhaps to agree better with Mary Hays McCauley's grave stone erected in 1876, which says that she was 79 years old when she died in January 1832 (Nos. 9A and 9B). Egle also claims a different birth place, Lancaster county, Pennsylvania, not near Trenton, New Jersey. The claim that her father was a dairy farmer from near Trenton sounds very much like the background claimed for Mary Hanna's father (see No. 4A).

Isabella Crater McGeorge in the fourth passage offers an expansive interpretation of Mary Ludwig's background and appearance

(No. 4A). She offers no new evidence for her statements, but only extrapolates and makes ethnic generalizations form the sources previously cited.

All four sources quoted above are in agreement that Mary came to Carlisle through her association with the Irvine family. This connection is also accepted by those who say that Mary was born under the name Mary Hanna in Allentown (see Nos. 10E and 10F below). This association, at least in Carlisle, is supported by her granddaughter's anecdote of how Mary met her future husband John Hays while she was sweeping in front of the Irvine home.[7]

All three sources quoted above are also in agreement that Mary married John Hays in Carlisle. The only source with direct evidence of this marriage is C. Malcolm Gilman, who cites the following marriage record from the Church of Christ in Carlisle: "married this day Mary Ludwig to John Hays. Mary is a simple kindly child of good faith."[8] This is the only primary source record that shows a Mary as married to John Hays. William S. Stryker cites as evidence of this marriage a marriage bond that was issued on July 24, 1769 between Casper Hays and Mary Ludwig, and then claims without evidence that this Casper Hays was actually John Hays or John Casper Hays; he needed to make this assumption because he could not find any record of a Casper Hays serving in the artillery during the Revolution.[9] This marriage bond as recorded in the *Pennsylvania Archives* records does not give their town, nor does it say that John Hays was a barber, as Stryker claims.[10] Curiously, there is a another marriage record from a later volume of the *Pennsylvania Archives* series which shows that a John Hays (Haas) was married to Mary Ludowick (Ludwig) at St. Michael's and Zion Church in Philadelphia on July 25, 1769, the day after the marriage bond just cited was taken out. This looks too coincidental, and would make it seem that John Hays and Mary Ludwig were married in Philadelphia on July 25, not Carlisle on July 24 as Gilman claims. It would just be too coincidental for two couples with exactly the same names to be married in Pennsylvania just two days apart in July of 1768. Interestingly, this Mary Ludwig is listed as a widow.[11]

Numerous records cited above make it clear that Mary Hays McCauley's first husband was named William Hays, not John Hays (see No. 7F), and that this William Hays was a gunner in Proctor's artillery during the Revolution (see Chapter 12). This makes it difficult to explain why numerous sources, and even Mary Hays McCauley's own granddaughter, Polly McCleaster, insist that she was married to a John Hays.[12]

There are two reasonable explanations for this. One is the possibility that Mary Ludwig actually married a man named John Hays in 1769, but then was remarried to William Hays right before or during the Revolution. Certainly stranger events have occurred. For example, numerous cases are known where a man lost his young wife due to difficulties at child birth or some other accident, and then married one of her sisters.

There is no reason why Mary Ludwig could not have married a man named John Hays and then married a William Hays for her second husband (or third husband, since the Philadelphia marriage records says she was a widow when she married John Hays).

The second possibility is that Egle, Gilman and their followers were mistaken about Mary Hays McCauley ever being married to a John Hays. There is a strong possibility that Mary Hays McCauley's neighbors may have gotten the first name of her first husband (William Hays) mixed up with the first name of her second husband (John McCauley) and so come up with the name of John Hays. It is also possible that Wing's and Egle's sources were not remembering actual information told to them by Mary Hays McCauley concerning the identity of her first husband, and that their memory was influenced by the a developed tradition that his name was John Hays. These are the same neighbors who repeated the story that Mary Hays McCauley's first husband was killed at Monmouth, even though they should have been aware that William Hays survived the war and lived in Carlisle until 1787. By the time many of these neighbors were giving their testimony in the late 1800s, one hundred years after William Hays' death, many seem to have lost track of his true name and death date.

OTHER LUDWIG DATA

Landis relates that some people believe that Mary Hays McCauley's son John L. Hays was born in a tent on the battlefield of Monmouth right after the battle, but Hays did not believe that was so.[13] Other evidence is clear that he was born in 1782 or 1783 (see No. 7B). Wing says that the son was born in Trenton.(No. 3E), and McGeorge says he was born on Mary's father's dairy farm between Trenton and Princeton (No. 4A). Neither source states their evidence.

A few sources claim that the middle initial of Mary Hays McCauley's son John L. Hays stands for "Ludwig," and cite this as evidence that Mary's maiden name was Mary Ludwig.[14] However, there is no direct proof that John L. Hays' middle name was Ludwig.

A great deal of research has been done into Mary Ludwig's actual background. The name of her father is said to be John George Ludwig, though the source is not given, presumably the baptismal records cited by Gilman.[15] A John George Ludwig is known to have emigrated to New York around 1710.[16] There is also a John Ludwig, a butcher from Philadelphia, who died in early 1769. He left behind a wife Anna Mary, a son Martin, and a daughter Mary.[17] Orphans Court records from July 1770 show that John's son Martin Ludowick [sic] was over fourteen years of age, and his sister Mary was under fourteen.[18] Revolutionary War muster rolls records show that a J.M. Ludwick enlisted in Proctor's regiment of artillery on April 24, 1777; this was the same unit that William Hays joined on May 10, 1777 (see No. 12A). In September 1784 John Martin Ludwig testified in Philadelphia that he had served in the army and was discharged as unfit for duty on January 21, 1783.[19] At least one source poses the possibility that William Hays may have married Mary Ludwig, the sister of the John Martin Ludwig with whom he served in Proctor's Artillery.[20]

CONCLUSION

A number of sources have claimed that Mary Hays McCauley was born under the name Mary Ludwig, but they claim a variety of birth dates and places for her. Gilman's claim to have seen her 1754 baptismal record at the Presbyterian Church in Lawrenceville cannot be corroborated. Gilman's claim to have seen a marriage record of John Hays and Mary Ludwig in Carlisle in 1769 is questionable because the marriage bond record gives the groom's name as Casper Hays. Another marriage record shows that the marriage between John Hays and Mary Ludwig may have taken place in Philadelphia and not in Carlisle.

Evidence is firm that Mary Hays McCauley was married to William Hays and that William Hays was the father of her son John L. Hays. Though it is conceivable that she was married to a John Hays before she married William Hays, it is more likely that the marriage to John Hays was first claimed by genealogists who needed

Mary to be married to him because he was a soldier who could have served at the battle of Monmouth.

Rejection of Mary Ludwig as her likely maiden name also brings into play the question of Mary Hays McCauley's ethnic background. If she was born as Mary Ludwig, she would have been of German origin. If she was born under another game, her ethnic origin would be undetermined. In short, the evidence is inconclusive, even doubtful, that Mary Hays McCauley was born of German origin under the name Mary Ludwig.

THE MARY HANNA THEORY

10E. Sarah Smith Stafford, 1876.

Molly Pitcher was a daughter of John Hanna of Allentown; he was an Irish Presbyterian, and had another daughter named Betty, who married Hugh Ager. Ager was a servant of Samuel Rogers, who was reputed to be of noble Descent, and Betty was brought up by him. Molly lived as a servant with Mr. Bruere, father of Captain Bruere, of the Monmouth Militia. Her father (Hanna) and Ager were said to have been Irish redemptionists, that is, were sold for a time to pay for their passage. The name Pitcher was a nickname given by the soldiers because she often carried a huge pitcher around to water them. Some said she also followed the soldiers as the wife of John Maban.[21]

10F. Reverend George Swain, 1876.

From among us it is said was the famous Molly Pitcher; she who, at the battle of Monmouth, acted the role of cannoneer in the place of her husband or some other brave who had fallen beside his gun. She is reputed to have been the daughter of one Jno. Hanna, of Allentown, was of North Ireland extraction, and had been for a time a servant in the family of Captain James Bruere. She was, perhaps, the wife of a soldier named Jno. Maban.[22]

10G. Donald F.X. Finn, 1998.

The best evidence available strongly suggests that Molly Pitcher was Mary Hanna, daughter of John and Susan Neau of Upper Freehold, Allentown, Monmouth County, New Jersey. She married Williams Hays, an Irishmen and gunner in Proctor's artillery at the Battle of Monmouth.[23]

COMMENTARY

The claim that Mary Hays McCauley was born under the name of Mary Hanna originates with Sally Smith Stafford (1802-1880), a school teacher who was born in Allentown. She unfortunately does not give any sources for her assertions. Nor does she claim to know Mary's birth date. Rev. Swain's statement is not an independent source, but is derived directly from Miss Stafford, as he admits in a footnote.[24]

Advocates of this theory cite the following evidence. Tax records form Allentown show a Hannah family living on High Street across from the town's Presbyterian Church.

John Hannah's will makes reference to a daughter named Mary. Mary Hannah is known to have married a soldier named John Cavana (Cavanaugh), who was a casualty at the battle of Monmouth.[25] This information is all interesting, but still does not provide any evidence to support Miss Stafford's claim that Mary Hanna was the maiden name of Mary Hays McCauley.

CONCLUSION

The theory that Mary Hays McCauley was born under the name Mary Hanna was first put forth by Sally Smith Stafford in 1876. There is no primary source material whatever to support this claim.

SUMMARY

We do not know Mary Hays McCauley's maiden name, nor are we likely to learn it. Claims were put forth starting in the 1870s that she was either German (Mary Ludwig) or Irish (Mary Hanna), but the Ludwig claims are based on questionable or unsubstantiated primary sources, and the Hanna claims have no primary sources at all. If anyone knew her maiden name for certain after she died, this information surely would have been stated in her obituary or sometime sooner than forty odd years after her death.

Nor can we determine Mary Hays McCauley's ethnic background for certain. Her granddaughter Mrs. Polly McLeaster claimed that her grandmother was "as German as Sauer Kraut,"[26] and Susan Heckendorn says that she attended the predominantly German First

Lutheran Church in Carlisle.[27] On the other hand, a number of her former neighbors believed she was of Irish origin.[27] She clearly cannot have been both. The preponderance of evidence would suggest that she may have been Irish. Her husband William Hays was Irish, and her second husband John McCauley may well have been so also; it was more common in those days to marry into common ethnic background than outside it.

11. CAMP FOLLOWERS AND WOMEN WARRIORS

CAMP FOLLOWERS

At various times it has been argued that there were no women at all fighting with Washington's army or that most women with the army were "camp followers" in the strictest sense, that is, prostitutes. Recent scholarly work has shown that women did indeed have a legitimate role in the army, but debate has raged as to the nature of this role. In addition, more names keep surfacing of women who actually did take part in the fighting at various times.

Evidence is clear that eighteenth century armies, particularly Britain's force in America, were regularly accompanied by women and their children.[1] For example, the British army stationed at New York City was computed on August 22, 1781 to consist of 23,489 men, 3615 women and 2173 children. Women received rations at half the rate of a man and children at one-quarter rate.[2] Not all of these woman would in fact have been married to soldiers; some were doubtless prostitutes and many were probably living in common law marriage. But their presence with the army was legitimate enough that they would be fed by the King in return for the important services they performed—cooking, washing, mending, caring for the sick.[3] Their presence helped keep the troops happy as well as healthy.

Camp followers, or "women of the army" as George Washington called them, also accompanied the American army on all its campaigns. Their services were the same as in the British army—cooking, washing, mending and nursing.[4] Walter Blumenthal stated in 1974 that "the number of women attached to American forces varied considerably at different times and locations,"[5] and this fact has been more empirically demonstrated by John U. Rees in a series of articles he wrote in the 1990s.[6] Reese's research, for example, has shown that 400 women were with Washington's army in December 1777 at Valley Forge, a ratio of about one woman to every forty-four men.[7]

At the end of the encampment at Middlebrook, New Jersey in April and May 1779, the number of women varied from one to three per company, and varied from week to week from one to every thirteen men to one for every fifteen men.[8] The troops stationed at and around West Point, New York on January 24, 1783 consisted of 19,443 men, accompanied by 405 women and 302 children, a ratio on one woman for every twenty-six men.[9]

Women and children traveling with the American army were regularly given rations at a reduced rate from that of the men. It was not until 1802 that women with the army were granted full rations "not exceeding the proportion of four to a company;" matrons and nurses stationed at hospitals were also to receive full rations.[10]

It is difficult to estimate the number of "women of the army" who served with the army during the Revolution. Linda Grant de Pauw in a provocative article published in 1981 (No. 6H) challenges the traditional view of the function of the camp followers and claims that "tens of thousands of women were involved in active combat."[11] She says that women were not brought along just to sew and cook, a viewpoint she calls the "myth of battlefield domesticity." Instead, "their primary duties were performed as support units attached to the medical corps and the artillery." [12]

De Pauw includes among her "women of the army" the nurses and matrons who were employed in the hospitals. Regulations in 1777 required that one matron and 10 female nurses be employed for every 100 wounded. There was always a shortage of women willing to serve in this capacity, says De Pauw, but "there was sometimes an excess with the marching army."[13] She goes on to show how large numbers of women served in four different areas: with artillery units; as regular soldiers; in militia units; and on the frontier.

De Pauw specifically cites the story of Molly Pitcher as an example of how women were employed in artillery units to bring water to the cannons, not the men. A large quantity of water was essential to artillery units in order to swab, clean and cool the cannons between rounds. Having women bring up the water used for these purposes freed up the male cannonneers (gunners and matrosses) to do their required jobs. Besides, says De Pauw, it does not make sense for women to bring water for the men to drink; this would have caused them to suffer from "an almost inevitable fatal condition known as 'cold water disease'" (now known as heat stroke). Occasionally, these women assistant artillerymen would take the place of men who fell as casualties and would actually help to fire cannons, as the examples of Molly Pitcher and Margaret Corbin attest.

De Pauw's theory has been followed and expanded by Emily Teipe (No. 60), but was severely challenged by Janice McKenney in a short rebuttal article published in 1982 (No. 61). McKenney rightly points out that "her isolated examples do not adequately support her conclusions that 'tens of thousands of women were involved in active combat.'"[14] De Pauw cites only three cases, Margaret Corbin, Joseph Plumb Martin's account of the woman known as Molly Pitcher and Mrs. Susan Heckendorn's statement about Mary Hays McCauley's presence at Monmouth, and then extrapolates that a great number of women were serving on artillery crews during the war. Likewise she extrapolates from a few known cases of women serving in the ranks, most notably Deborah Sampson and Samuel Gay, that there was a huge number of women who did likewise. McKenney does not doubt that more women served in the ranks disguised as men, but points out that those whose identities were found out (Sampson and Gay) were speedily sent home; there is simply no evidence that thousand upon thousands fought on the front lines. Lastly, McKenney questions De Pauw's citation of one New Jersey militia muster roll that has some women's names listed as evidence that thousand of women were regular members of the militia; this muster roll is instead an anomaly that is still not fully understood.[15]

McKenney also specifically challenges De Pauw's interpretation of "cold water disease" and cites the necessity to keep the troops supplied with drinking water in order to prevent heat exhaustion, especially on such a hot and humid day as occurred during the battle of Monmouth. She specifically notes that water was brought to the cannons in buckets and not pitchers; pitchers were used to distribute drinking water to the men.[16] Since Molly Pitcher was not known as "Molly Bucket," she was obviously engaged at bringing drinking water, not water for the cannons.[17] A full gun crew consisted of from 12-15 men, and it was the job of the matrosses to assist the gunners in loading, firing and sponging the cannon; the matrosses were also responsible for bringing up the water to the cannons, and for dragging the cannons into position. McKenney concludes, "Women, although they may have risen to the occasion at times, were never relied upon as artillerists."[18] It should here be pointed out that Mary Hays McCauley's husband William Hays was clearly a gunner, not a matross as some of the early sources on Molly Pitcher claim, such as Custis in 1840 (No. 2D).

CONCLUSION

There is an abundance of evidence that woman camp followers, also known as "women of the army," accompanied the American armies during the Revolution. They were a recognized part of the army, and were allowed to draw rations for themselves and their children in return for their services as cooks and laundresses. Records show that there were usually around three to six women per company, depending on the year and theater. General Washington was constantly concerned about the number of women and children accompanying his army, since they often slowed him down or got in the way and had constantly to be fed. In August 1777 he noted that, "the multitude of women in particular, especially those that are pregnant, or have children, are a drag upon every movement."[19] But he was well aware that many of his soldiers might not stay in the ranks if their dependents were not cared for, particularly since so many of his men were young and did not own a home or property, and there were no regulations in those days for what is now known as "dependents' allowances." [20] Not all camp followers were prostitutes. Most performed more practical services such as nursing, cooking and washing, but the camp followers were never considered an official branch of the army, nor did they fight in the front lines in the tens of thousands as De Pauw claims.

WOMEN WARRIORS

There are only a handful of documented cases naming women who fought in battle during the Revolution. They are listed below. There may certainly have been more, but certainly not the 20,000 estimated by Linda Grant De Pauw.[21] A little comparative mathematics with the Civil War provides some interest on this point, though we must bear in mind that the two ages were socially quite different. If around 400 women served in the fighting ranks disguised as men during the Civil War out of over 3,000,000 enlistments in that conflict, as is commonly accepted, the proportionate number of women in the ranks for the approximately 200,000 men serving in the Revolution would be a grand total of 27.[22]

Only three women are known to have received pensions for their military service during the Revolutionary War: Margaret Corbin (from the federal government in 1779 and from the state of Pennsylvania); Mary Hays McCauley (from the state of Pennsylvania in

1822), and Deborah Sampson/Robert Shurtleff (from the federal government in 1805 and from the state of Massachusetts).

11A. Margaret Corbin

Margaret Corbin was born in Franklin County, Pennsylvania on November 12, 1751. In 1772 she married John Corbin of Virginia, who enlisted in the 1st Company of Pennsylvania Artillery when the Revolutionary War broke out. Corbin's unit was heavily engaged on November 16, 1776 at the battle of Fort Washington, New York. When he was mortally wounded, Margaret took his place as a matross (assistant artillerist) and was severely wounded herself by a grapeshot that struck her in the arm and breast. After recovering she was assigned to the Corps of Invalids (wounded soldiers who could not service on active duty but could still do garrison duty). On July 6, 1779 Congress voted her the following pension: "Resolved, That Margaret Corbin, who was wounded and disabled in the attack on Fort Washington, whilst she heroically filled the post of her husband who was killed by her side serving a piece of artillery, do receive, during her natural life, or the continuance of said disability, the one-half of the monthly pay drawn by a soldier in the service of these states; and that she now receive out of the public stores one complete set of cloaths, or, the value thereof in money." She was mustered out of the army in April 1783 and settled in Highland Falls (also known as Buttermilk Falls) near West Point, New York. There she died, broken down and poor, in 1800. In 1926 her body was reburied at West Point.[23]

11B. Samuel Gay

Samuel Gay served as a corporal in the 1st Massachusetts until she was found out. Her army records state that she was "Discharged, being a woman, dressed in mens cloths. Augt. 1777."[24]

11C. Mary Hays McCauley

Mrs. Susan Heckendorn, a neighbor of Mary Hays McCauley, heard her say that "You girls should have been with me at the battle of Monmouth, and learned how to load a cannon."[25] For this reason, and other evidence cited in Chapter 8, Mary Hays McCauley is believed to be the historical Molly Pitcher who fought at the battle of Monmouth on June 28, 1778.

11D. Molly Pitcher

Even if Mary Hays McCauley is not to be identified as Molly Pitcher, Joseph Plumb Martin gives evidence that he saw a woman helping to fire a cannon during the battle (see No. 1A).

11E. Sally St. Clair

Sally St. Clair was killed at the battle of Savannah. She is "believed to have kept her sex a secret until her death."[26]

11F. Deborah Sampson

Deborah Sampson is the most well known case of a woman masquerading as a man in order to serve on the firing line during the Revolution. She was born in Plymouth, Massachusetts on December 17, 1760 and had an awkward childhood, being raised by friends and then serving as an indentured servant until she was eighteen. She was reported to be five feet eight inches tall and "rather horse-faced."[27] This enabled her to enlist in the army in early 1782 by masquerading as a man. However, her identity was revealed when she went drinking with her messmates at a tavern. But this did not deter her. In May 1782 she enlisted under the name of Robert Shurtleff in Captain George Webb's Company of the 4th Massachusetts regiment. Her comrades were suspicious of her because she had such a smooth face, and called her "Smock Face" and "Molly," but otherwise accepted her as a fellow.

Sampson fought honorably and even served for a time as an orderly to General Samuel Patterson. In one skirmish at Tappan Zee she received a saber wound on the left side of her head. In another engagement at East Chester she received a bad wound from a musket ball in the thigh. She managed to conceal her sex through these two hospital visits, but when she came down with brain fever during the Yorktown campaign and her doctor found out her secret. He agreed to protect her, but the doctor's nephew fell for her and her true identity became revealed to all. General Washington found out, and "Robert Shurtleff" was honorably discharged.

After the war she married a farmer from Massachusetts named Benjamin Gannett and between 1786 and 1790 bore three children to him, Earl, Gilbert and Patience. In 1792 she petitioned the state of Massachusetts for her back pay, furnishing affidavits as to her service by two of her commanding officers. In 1797 she published a narrative of her wartime experiences entitled *The Female Review,* and by 1802 she was earning money by giving lectures on her life as a female warrior; at the conclusion of her presentation she would usually go through the manual of arms. In 1805 Congress voted her a pension of $4.00 a month as an invalid soldier, an amount that was doubled in 1818. Among the advocates who supported her pension claims was none other than the famous Paul Revere of Boston, who wrote, "When I heard her spoken of as a soldier, I formed the idea of a tall, masculine female, who had a small share of understanding, without education, and one of the meanest of her sex. When I saw and discoursed with her I was agreeably surprised to find a small, effeminate and conversible woman, whose education entitled her to a better situation in life." Deborah Sampson/Robert Shurtleff died in Sharon. Massachusetts on April 29, 1827.[28]

11G. Unknown woman at Monmouth

Dr. Albigence Waldo reported that he heard an unidentified wounded officer say that he saw a woman from his platoon pick up the gun of her fallen "gallant" and fire it "like a Spartan heroine" during the battle of Monmouth (see No. 1B).

WOMEN IN PROCTOR'S ARTILLERY

11H. Jane Norton

Jane Norton stated in a declaration dated December 13, 1836 that she accompanied her late husband, William Norton, when he was a soldier in Proctor's Artillery during the Revolution. She also submitted a statement dated February 19, 1825 from Lieutenant Colonel Thomas Forrest of Proctor's Regiment attesting that Mary Norton accompanied her husband on several campaigns, including Brandywine and Germantown, and that she assisted in relieving wounded soldiers.[29]

CONCLUSION

This passage is evidence of a woman named Mary Norton who accompanied her husband, a soldier in Proctor's Artillery, during the battles around Philadelphia in the fall of 1777. She assisted at caring for the wounded and perhaps helped carry them form the battlefield.

11I. Jacob Nagle's experience at the battle of Brandywine

Marching through Wilmington, Mr. Bittle took me to my father who was then lieutenant colonel of the Ninth Pennsylvania Rigment, and shortly after full cornel of the Tenth Pennsylvania Rigment. I was then not quite sixteen. When the army encamped my father took me to Cor'l Prokter who commanded the grand park of artillery. I laid in his markee that night that night, and the next day I messed with Adjudent Hosner who had the charge of me, being a young soldier.

We then marched and the army encamped on the Brandewine on the right of Shads ford on the hier ground. Our artillery was ranged in front of an orchard…Mr Hosner brought some potatoes and butter the evening before the British arrived, and we concluded to have a glorious mess for breakfast. Mr. Hosner gave it to one of the soldiers wives that remained with the army to cook for us in the morning. Early in the morning, she had the camp kittle on a small fier about 100 yards in the rear of the Grand Artilery, with all our delicious meal, which we expected to enjoy (on the 11 of September 1777). The Brittish at this time hoisted the red flag on the top of the farm house on the rige of the hill a breast of us, and their artillery advancing towards us down the ploughed field, we then began a cannonading. The armies at this time had not completely formed. Unfortunately one of the enemies shot dismounted the poor camp kettle with the fier and all its contents away with it. The woman informed Mr. Folkner. He replied, "Never mind, we have no time to eat now." Therefore we made another fast day.[30]

COMMENTARY

This passage, written by a civilian son of a Pennsylvania officer, tells how an unnamed woman from Proctor's Artillery was cooking breakfast for her command on the morning of the battle of Brandywine, when a shot from a British cannon struck the camp kettle and scattered its contents before they could be eaten.

CONCLUSION

This passage shows is an example of a unnamed woman who did cooking for the men of Proctor's Artillery in September 1777.

ANOTHER WOMAN WHO BROUGHT WATER TO THE TROOPS AT MONMOUTH

11J. The story of Amy Bayles Potts

COMMENTARY

Samuel Potts was born about 1750 and was residing in Cranbury when he married Amy Bayles on April 23, 1776. He served in the Revolution as a wagon master, but at the battle of Monmouth is said to have fought in the ranks. Reportedly "his brave young wife carried water to the soldiers during and after the battle." Mr. Potts died in 1821 or 1822, having amassed considerable holdings in real estate. Nothing more is known of his wife beyond the fact that she was the mother of at least six children, three boys and three girls.[31]

CONCLUSION

This account is evidence of another woman besides Molly Pitcher who brought water to the troops at the battle of Monmouth on June 28, 1778.

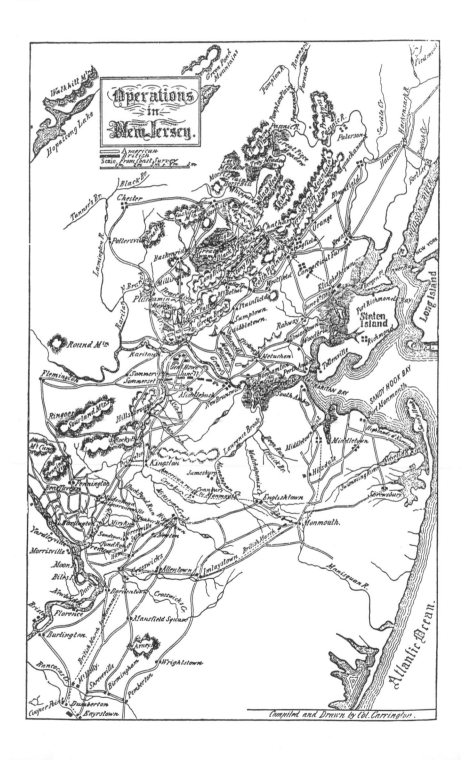

12. DOCUMENTS RELATING TO WILLIAM HAYS' MILITARY SERVICE

12A. Enlistment in Captain Proctor's artillery battery, May 10, 1777.

H [?] 4 Artillery Continental Troops

Wm Hays Appears with the rank of Gunner on a General Return of the Pennsylvania State Regiment of Artillery, Commanded by Colonel Thomas Procter, Esq.

> REVOLUTIONARY WAR
>> Return dated April 3d, 1779.
>> Where born: Ireland
>> State belonging to: Penn.
>> Where Inlisted: Bristol
>> Where resided before Inlisted:
>> State: Penna.
>> County: Bucks
>> Town: Bristol
>> Company belonging to: Capt. Proctor
>> Term of Inlistment: During the war
>> Date of Inlistment: 10th May 1777[1]

COMMENTARY

This document shows that William Hays enlisted in Capt. Thomas Proctor's company of artillery on May 10, 1777 to serve for the length of the war (his commander's name is also commonly spelled as "Procter"). For a summary history of this command, see No. 12F below).

Note that William's place of residence is stated to be Bristol, Pennsylvania, not Carlisle as one would expect from many secondary sources (for example, Custis in No. 2D). His birthplace is listed as Ireland. Unfortunately, his age and marital status are not recorded.

Also note that he is listed as a Gunner, not a Mattross as some of the accounts state (see for example No. 2D). The record seems to indicated that Hays belonged to what is now called Company "H," which was commanded by Captain Amos Wilkinson.[2]

CONCLUSION

This document establishes that William Hays was born in Ireland and was residing in Bristol, Pennsylvania, when he enlisted on May 10, 1777 in Proctor's Pennsylvania artillery company for service "during the war."

12B. Furlough, March 19, 1779.

A GENERAL RETURN OF THE PENNSYLV. STATE REGT. OF ARTILLERY COMMANDED BY COLN. THOS. PROCTOR, MAR 19TH, 1779.

On Furlough:
1 Serjt., Adams
1 Serjt., Wilks
1 Corp'l, Toy
1 Gunner, Hays at Carlisle
1 Gunner, McNeesley
2 Matrossses, Lodge & McCracken[3]

COMMENTARY

This document shows that a Gunner names Hays was on furlough from Proctor's artillery regiment in March 1779. Surviving roster records for Proctor's regiment list only one Gunner named Hays: the William Hays who enlisted in Bristol on May 10, 1777 (No. 9A). It is significant that he went to Carlisle during this furlough in 1779, since that is where he would settle when the war was over in 1783 (No. 12D).

CONCLUSION

This document shows that William Hays was on furlough from Proctor's artillery regiment on March 19, 1779, and that he spent this furlough in Carlisle, where he would settled after the war ended in 1783.

12C. Discharged January 1781 and re-enlisted July 1781

CONTINENTAL LINE.
[4TH] PENNSYLVANIA ARTILLERY

Privates
Hawkins, Francis
Hayes, William, discharged January 24, 1781;
    re-enlisted July 27, 1781.
Heavins, Thomas [4]

COMMENTARY

This record shows that William Hays was discharged in January 1781 and then re-enlisted in the same command in July 1781.

The reason for this happening is probably as follows. In 1781 many troops in the Pennsylvania line were unhappy because they had received an enlistment bonus of only $20 when they had first enrolled in 1777 or thereabouts. By 1781 enlistment bonuses were running as high as $1000 in some states. As a result, some Pennsylvania troops refused to serve any longer. This caused the governor of Pennsylvania, Joseph Reed, to intervene. On January 8, 1781 the troops of the Pennsylvania line were informed that "all soldiers that were enlisted for a bounty of twenty dollars ought to be discharged immediately with as little delay as circumstances will allow, except said soldiers who have been since voluntarily re-enlisted."[5]

William Hays was clearly one of the soldiers discharged under this arrangement, since his records show he was discharged on January 24, 1781. Four days later, Brigadier General Anthony Wayne wrote to George Washington from Trenton, "The Commissioners of Congress have nearly closed the settlement of the Inlistments of the Pennsa. Line. The 11th, which is the last regiment, will be finished this evening or tomorrow morning. We have discharged out of the aggregate, 1220 men."[6]

William Hays went home for six months and then reenlisted in his old command, Proctor's 4th Pennsylvania Artillery, presumably with a nice bonus. Unfortunately, the amount (or even existence) of this bonus is not recorded.

It is interesting to note William Hays was home on furlough during the spring and summer of 1781, and nine months later his son William L. Hays was born (see Commentary to No. 7B).

CONCLUSION

This record shows that William Hays served in Proctor's Pennsylvania Artillery until January 1781, when he was discharged;

he re-enlisted in the same unit in July 1781. This means that he was enrolled in this command at the time of the battle of Monmouth on June 28, 1778.

12D. Date of muster out

COMMENTARY

The exact date that William Hays was mustered out of the army is not recorded. It may have been on January 1, 1783, since on that date his regiment was reduced to four companies and his company commander, Captain Francis Proctor Jr., was discharged on that date. The last members of the command were mustered out on November 15, 1783.[7]

William Hays must have moved immediately to Carlisle after his muster out, since he is listed in the Carlisle Tax Records Books for 1783 as: Hays, William, Barber. 1 house, 1 lot.[8]

William Hays' property expanded by 1785, when the Carlisle Tax Records Book for 1785 has this entry: Hays, William. 1 house & lot rented. 1 ditto his own. 1 cow.[9]

He probably died in 1787 (see No. 7A).

CONCLUSION

This record shows that William Hays served in Proctor's artillery until the close of the war in 1783. Upon discharge he moved to Carlisle, Pennsylvania, and was employed as a barber.

12E. Marriage to Mary Hays

COMMENTARY

We unfortunately do not know when and where William and Mary Hays were married. Orphans' Court records show that their son John L. Hays was five years old in February 1788 (No. 7B), so it is not likely that the couple were married after William's discharge from the army in 1783. Any doubt that William and Mary Hays were married is dispelled by court records in 1787-1788 (Nos. 7A and 7B), and the affidavit in 1807 by James Roney that he knew well "Mary Hays (now Mary McCalla) late widow of William Hays a Gunner in Col. Proctor's Regiment of Artillerists during the Revolutionary War." (No. 7F). Mary Hays, widow of William Hays, married John McCauley between 1789 and 1793 (No 7C).

CONCLUSION

We do not know when and where William and Mary Hays were married.

12F. Summary history of Proctor's Artillery

COMMENTARY

Proctor's artillery took its name from its commander, Captain (later Colonel) Thomas Proctor (his name is also commonly spelled Procter). He had been born in County Langford, Ireland, in 1739 and was working as a carpenter in Philadelphia when the war began.[10]

Proctor's artillery began as a single company authorized by the Pennsylvania Council of Safety on October 16, 1775. Its purpose was to man Fort Island (now Mud Island, the site of Fort Mifflin), located in the Delaware River near the mouth of the Schuylkill. Thomas Proctor was appointed captain of the new command on October 27. 1775. The unit was expanded to two companies in August 1776, and to eight companies in February 1777. At that point General Washington wanted the command to be transferred to the Continental Army, but Pennsylvania refused to release its control over the regiment. Eventually, however, Pennsylvania agreed to let the regiment serve outside the state. For this reason the regiment was known thereafter as the 4th Continental Artillery Regiment, though its technical name was still the Pennsylvania State Artillery Regiment.[11]

The regiment's main purpose was to defend Philadelphia, which is where it was stationed for much of the war. A detachment of Proctor's original company served at the battle of Fort Washington, New York, on November 11, 1776. One member of this detachment was John Corbin, who was killed in action; his wife Margaret then took his place at the gun and was badly wounded, winning immortality as "Captain Molly" (see 2I).[12]

Another member of the regiment at this time was John Hays, who enlisted on December 1, 1775 for one year's service.[13] John Hays is the reputed husband of Mary Ludwig, who was thought for a long time to be the Molly Pitcher of Monmouth fame.[14] However, evidence is now clear that Mary Hays McCauley, the best candidate to be the historical Molly Pitcher, was married to William Hays at the time of the battle, not John Hays (see No. 7F).

On February 28, 1777 the Pennsylvania Council of Safety authorized the payment of a twenty dollar enlistment bonus for new recruits in Proctor's artillery.[15] William Hays would have received this bonus when he enlisted in the command on May 10, 1777.

The first battles the regiment fought in after William Hays enlisted were during the Philadelphia campaign that fall, when portions of the command were engaged at Brandywine and Germantown. The regiment lost so many men during the winter at Valley Forge (1777-1778) that it was left behind to garrison Philadelphia while the bulk of Washington's army marched off to the battle of Monmouth (see No. 12H below).[16]

By August 4, 1778, the regiment's strength was down to 220, and a report on March 19, 1779 shows only 142 men available for duty. Part of the command participated in General Sullivan's expedition to central New York in 1779. Detachments were made to Fort Pitt, Carlisle, and New Jersey in 1780. Those members of the regiment who were with Washington's main army participated in the mutiny of the Pennsylvania Line that broke out on January 1, 1781 (see Commentary to No. 12C). After the mutiny was resolved and the troops sent home on furlough, those who re-enlisted gathered at York beginning in late May. There another mutiny broke out because the men wanted to be paid in specie (hard coinage) rather than devaluated paper money. General Wayne resolved this revolt by executing six of the mutineers, including two artillerymen.[17]

On May 26, 1781 one company of the regiment started for Virginia with six cannons. When they attempted to cross the Potomac River at Georgetown, their boat capsized and all six guns were lost. William Hays was lucky to miss this accident, since he did not reenlist until July 27. He probably served at the siege of Yorktown, which surrendered on October 19, 1781.

After Yorktown, three companies of Proctor's artillery were sent south to join Nathanael Greene's army in South Carolina. The regiment's March 21, 1782 report shows how scattered the command was at the time: 70 men were in Philadelphia, 34 were at Fort Pitt, and 131 were with Greene. We do not know which detachment Hays was serving with. As previously noted, the regiment was reduced to four companies on January 1, 1783, and the last men of the unit were discharged on November 15, 1783.[18]

Thomas Proctor, who had organized the regiment and been promoted its colonel on

February 7, 1777, did not serve until the end of the war, resigning on April 18, 1781. He died on March 16, 1806.[19]

Historian John B.B. Trussell Jr. did a study of the regiment's records. He found that only 87 of 205 men for whom there are records were native born Americans. Of 96 men who were born abroad, 60 were Irish and 23 German. Fifteen of the 18 men listed as gunners were foreign born, including William Hays. Trussell concluded that a disproportionate number of foreign born men held technical positions such as gunner, while the native born Americans held a higher proportion of the less skilled jobs like matross and musician.[20]

The original uniform of Proctor's artillery was a short blue coat faced with white or buff, white breeches, and a round hat bounded with worsted. After October 2, 1779, all artillerymen were supposed to wear a blue coat faced and lined with scarlet, with yellow buttons bearing the raised letters U.S.A. Many of Proctor's officers, however, continued to wear their Pennsylvania uniforms after 1779 instead of the prescribed Continental uniform.[21]

CONCLUSION

We do not know what battles William Hays participated in besides Monmouth.

12G. William Hays' battery assignment

COMMENTARY

Unfortunately, it is not clear to which company in the regiment William Hays belonged. His enlistment records in the National Archives seem to indicate that he belonged to what was later called Company H. Trussell's history of the Pennsylvania line says that Company H was commanded by Captain Amos Wilkinson until he resigned on June 7, 1779. After that the company ceased to exist, with its personnel apparently dispersed among the other companies of the regiment.[22]

Samuel S. Smith says that Hays belonged to Captain Francis Proctor Jr.'s company, which was known as Company F.[23] His source was probably the copy of a return for "The Pennsylvania State Regiment of Artillery Commanded by Colonel Thomas Procter, Esqr.

Taken April 3d 1779" that is on file at the National Archives. Parts of this are difficult to read, but the layout of names, and order of the companies listed, make it clear that Hays was in Captain Francis Proctor's company.[24] Francis Proctor Jr. was the brother of the regimental commander, Thomas Proctor; their father, Francis Proctor Sr., was the commander of Company C until he was dismissed from the service on May 14, 1778.[25] Francis Jr. was promoted to Major in 1782 and retired on January 1, 1783.[26]

CONCLUSION

Surviving evidence does not make enable us to tell which company of the 4th Continental Artillery William Hays was serving at the time of the battle of Monmouth.

12H. Assignment of Proctor's artillery during the Monmouth campaign

Colonel Thomas Procter's Fourth regiment, Continental artillery, and the Invalids sent from the hospitals at Valley Forge, with some small parties of Pennsylvania militia, replaced the above detachments in guarding the City of Philadelphia and in preserving order there.[27]

COMMENTARY

In this passage battle historian William S. Stryker states that Thomas Proctor's artillery was assigned the task of garrisoning Philadelphia when Washington entered New Jersey on June 22, 1778. Unfortunately, he does name cite his source for the information. It may have been a letter that Benedict Arnold, commander of the garrison of Philadelphia, sent to General Washington on June 22. In this letter Arnold states that he has sent Colonel Henry Jackson's regiment of 400 men to move against the enemy's rear. Arnold adds that "Their places are supplied by Colonel Proctors Regiment who will do Garrison duty."[28]

Stryker's statement is supported by the surviving monthly statistical strength reports for Washington's army. The return for May 1778 shows that Proctor's 4th Continental Artillery was stationed at Valley Forge with a strength of 159 officers and men fit and ready for duty.[29] Returns for Washington's command for June 1778 do not include Proctor's unit, so we must assume that it was not with Washington's army as of the date of that report, which was July 5, 1778.[30] In fact, Proctor's regiment is not listed with Washington's army until it appears again on the October 1779 monthly report.[31]

This evidence from Stryker and the monthly statistical reports for Washington's army is significant for the following reason: if Proctor's artillery was not at Monmouth, then William Hays could not have been there, and if William Hays was not there, then his wife Mary Hays (Molly Pitcher) could not have been there, either.

However, the presence at Monmouth of at least a detachment of Proctor's Artillery is supported by a variety of evidence.

The most comprehensive collection of documents relating to Proctor's Artillery was published in the *Pennsylvania Archives* series in 1906.[32] The editor of this collection noted as follows: "No regimental returns have been found prior to September 3, 1778, when by resolution of Congress, Procter's regiment was made part of the quota of troops to be furnished by the State of Pennsylvania, which was to be credited for the men now in the regiment, and also for any that should be recruited therein. From its necessarily detached service very little of the history of the regiment has survived; but detachments from it were engaged in nearly all of the operations of the main army, subsequently notably at Monmouth and in Sullivan's campaign of 1779."[33] The presence of a portion of Proctor's artillery at the battle of Monmouth is also accepted by Robert K. Wright, Jr., author of the reference study, *The Continental Army.*[34]

These two sources unfortunately do not cite the evidence for their conclusion that a portion of Proctor's Artillery was at Monmouth. The follow pieces of evidence, however, can be marshaled to support this conclusion.

First, the statement by Dr. William Read (No. 12I) that he heard General Washington speak of Proctor's role in fighting the British right wing during the afternoon portion of the battle (see Commentary to No. 12I).

Second, the pension claim of Margaret S. Morris, widow of Jonathan Ford Morris, a Lieutenant in Proctor's Artillery, who states that her husband was present at Monmouth.[35] Unfortunately, we do not know which company he served in. Morris resigned from the army on November 28, 1778 to become a surgeon's mate.[36]

Third, a statement by Neville Craig that his father, Captain Isaac Craig, was at Monmouth.[37] Neville Craig had a large quantity of military papers belonging to his father, who served as a Captain in Company E from March 3, 1777 until he was named regimental major on October 7, 1781. The elder Craig resigned on June 17, 1783 and died on June 14, 1826.[38]

Fourth, is the evidence that Jacob Heiney, a private in Col. Thomas Proctor's regiment of Pennsylvania Continental Artillery, served in the battles of Bound Brook, Brandywine, Germantown, Monmouth and Sullivan's expedition in 1779. He was born in Darmstadt, Germany, around 1730 and died in Lancaster, Pennsylvania.[39]

Fifth, the presence of gunner William Hays at the battle. Had Hays been a member of a unit that was definitely not at Monmouth, or had he not a member of an artillery unit, there would be a much stronger case against his being at Monmouth.

This combined evidence suggests that a detachment of Proctor's Artillery was indeed present at the battle of Monmouth. What may have happened was that a portion of Proctor's command was brought along with Washington's army because Washington needed all the guns and experienced gunners he could muster for his intended battle. Then, once the battle was over on June 28, this detachment could have returned to Philadelphia to rejoin its regiment. As a result it would not have been present when the rest of the artillery with Washington's army was mustered for its monthly report on July 5, 1778.[40]

We are not, however, able to establish what companies or how many of Proctor's men were at the battle. No regimental returns survive earlier than September 3, 1778, ten weeks after the battle of Monmouth,[41] and the muster rolls for Proctor's regiment are so fragmentary that it is "impossible to determine with any assurance the composition of any given company."[42] As a result, it is impossible to reconstruct the assignment and composition of the companies of Proctor's artillery regiment in the summer of 1778.

CONCLUSION

Proctor's artillery was left behind to garrison Philadelphia while most of Washington's army crossed over to New Jersey on its way to the battle of Monmouth.

However, Dr. William Read's narrative (No. 9G) and records concerning Lt. Jonathan Ford Morris, Captain Isaac Craig and Private

Jacob Heiney seem to indicate that Colonel Proctor and some detachment of his command were indeed at the battle.

12I. Dr. William Read's account of Proctor's artillery at Monmouth

Dr. Read saw Gen. Washington riding to and fro along the line, sometimes at full speed, looking nobly, excited, and calling loudly to the troops by the appellation of brave boys. He saw Washington standing to the right of the line, with a number of officers near him, and saw a cannon ball strike a wet hole in the side of the hill, and the dirt fly on him. Two officers then rode up, and seemed to reason with him, and lay hold of the bridle of his horse. The General, coolly standing in his stirrups, was said to say to the officers who urged that that was no place for him, he being observed by the enemy, "that he was admiring the manner in which Proctor was handling their right." Dr. Read was near enough to hear the word Proctor, and was told what the General said. He then moved off at full   speed, all the throng following and Read among the rest.[43]

COMMENTARY

Dr. William Read was born in England on April 12, 1754, and came to Georgia with his parents at the age of five. In 1774 he went to study medicine with Dr. Benjamin Rush in Philadelphia. In early June 1778 he returned home to visit his family following the death of his father near Savannah. He then headed north to offer his services to the army, hoping to obtain command of a company of horse or foot, or maybe to serve in the line. Accompanied by his servant, he rode 70 or 80 miles on the day of the battle of Monmouth and reached Freehold just as the fighting was at its height.[44]

During the afternoon's fighting Dr. Read was on the army's main position along Perrine Hill when he witnessed the incident described above. He saw a British cannon ball almost strike General Washington, who was riding up and down the battle lines, and was impressed how coolly the General behaved in the face of enemy fire. He heard Washington say the name "Proctor" and was told that the General had said he "was admiring the manner in which Proctor was handling their right."

After the battle Dr. Read could not avoid helping the wounded. Before long he had a commission as a medical officer and was placed in charge of the hospital set up in Princeton to take care of casualties from the battle of Monmouth.[45]

This passage is important evidence that Colonel Proctor and at least part of his command were at the battle. It is also evidence for the location of this command on Perrine Hill.

CONCLUSION

Dr. Read's statement that he heard Washington speak of the role of Proctor's artillery in the battle, is important evidence for establishing the presence of Proctor and part of his command on the battlefield. It also helps to locate their position on Perrine Hill (see Conclusion to Chapter 13 below).

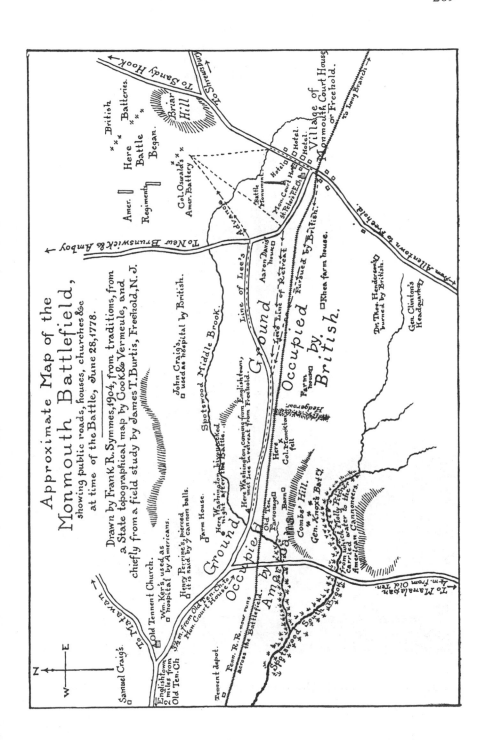

Approximate Map of the Monmouth Battlefield, showing public roads, houses, churches &c at time of the Battle, June 28, 1778.

Drawn by Frank R. Symmes, 1904, from traditions, from a State topographical map by Cook & Vermeule, and chiefly from a field study by James T. Burtis, Freehold, N. J.

270

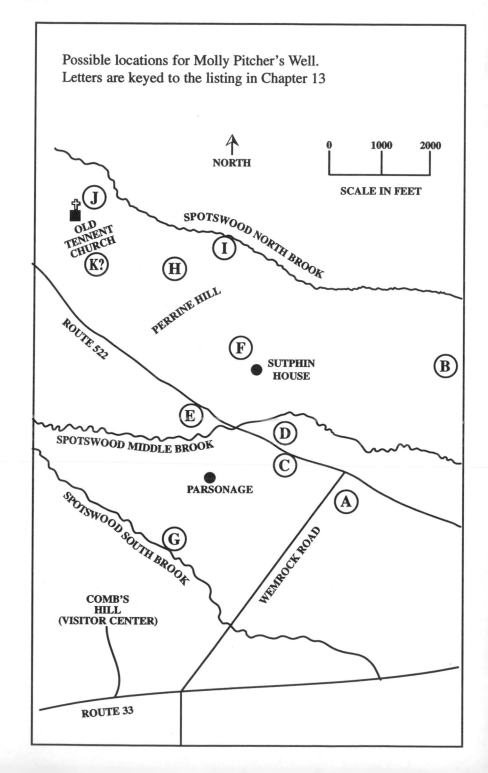

13. THE LOCATION OF
MOLLY PITCHER'S WELL

COMMENTARY

If Molly Pitcher drew water for the men of her husband's battery, then the source for this water must be near the position held by this command. There are three sources suggesting the location of Proctor's guns during the battle.

First, Dr. William Read's narrative (No. 12I). Dr. Read had reached the battlefield at mid-day, just as Lee's advance wing was withdrawing from Freehold. Later in the day he was near the main American position when he saw General Washington riding up and down the line encouraging the troops. At one point he saw Washington "standing to the right of the line" when a British cannon hit nearby and splattered dirt on him. His officers urged him to move to a safer position, but Washington refused to, because he was "admiring the manner in which Proctor was handling their right."[1] This narrative is significant because it places Proctor's guns on the main American line drawn up by Stirling on Perrine Hill during the afternoon portion of the battle. More specifically, it places Proctor's guns at a position from which they were able to shoot at the right wing of the British line, which was stationed during the afternoon in or behind the orchard to the northeast of the Sutphin house.[2]

Second, Joseph Plumb Martin's narrative (No. 1A). Martin relates that he personally saw a woman attending a cannon "the whole time" with her husband "during the heat of the cannonade."[3] This cannonade took place from about 1:00 to 3:00 P.M., and was carried out by a force of about 16 guns that Lord Stirling had posted along Perrine Hill.[4] At this time Martin was stationed with a large detachment of picked men who formed a covering force to the cannons on Perrine Hill. Martin relates: "When we had secured our retreat, the artillery formed a line of pieces upon a long piece if elevated ground [Perrine Hill]. Our detachment formed directly in front of the artillery, as a covering party, so far below on the declivity of the hill that the pieces could play over our heads...As soon as the troops had left this ground [the Hedgerow area] the British planted their cannon upon the place and began a violent attack upon the artillery and our detachment, but neither could be routed."[5]

Third, Rebecca Clendenin in her pension application states that her husband, Sergeant John Clendenin, described a woman named Captain Molly who brought water to the thirsty men during the battle (No. 1C). Clendenin was a member of Colonel Thomas Craig's 3rd Pennsylvania Continental Regiment of the 3rd Pennsylvania Brigade (see Commentary to No. 1C). The 3rd Pennsylvania Brigade was posted on the right wing of Stirling's position on Perrine Hill during the afternoon's artillery bombardment, and then around 4:00 was one of three regiments to move forward with Wayne to cross the West Morass and engage the 1st British Grenadiers.[6] It is most likely that Clendenin saw or heard of "Captain Molly" bringing water to the troops while he was in position along Perrine Hill, rather than during his regiment's sharp and fast moving fight on the other side of the West Morass at 4:00 P.M.[7]

It is most significant that all three of these sources relate to Stirling's position on Perrine Hill: Dr. Read heard Washington say that Proctor's guns were striking the British position from somewhere on the ridge; Joseph Plumb Martin was stationed at the base of the ridge when he witnessed a woman helping to fire a cannon on top of the hill; and John Clendenin saw or heard of a woman bringing water to the troops from his position on the southwestern end of the hill. These three sources collectively, then, place Proctor's command somewhere on Perrine Hill during the afternoon's fighting. More specifically, Read's account would place Proctor at a position from which he could strike the right of the British line. Presumably this would have been from the left, or northeastern, end of Perrine Hill. This would be the location for Proctor's position as best we can interpret from the sources. It follows that Molly Pitcher's "well" would need to be near by.

SUGGESTED LOCATIONS FOR MOLLY'S WELL

13A. Spring in north meadow on the Jasko farm, marked with a stone lettered "Molly Pitcher's Spring."[8]

This spring was "rediscovered" in the April of 1937 by Alexander Jasko, who found an old 50 gallon barrel buried in the ground as a well-head. Mr. Jasko, who had purchased the farm from John R. Parker, had been told at the time the it was the site of Molly Pitcher's spring, but he did not get around to investigating the area near Wemrock Road until 1937.[9] Later an old axle and two coins, one from the late 1700s, were found at this well site.[10]

William Davison Perrine of Princeton Junction, who was born in Manalapan, recalled in early 1937:

Molly Pitcher's spring was in the edge of the bank, and is not where Molly Pitcher's well [13C below] is pointed out. My grandfather, Ezekial Davison, born 1807, and who died in 1899 in his 92nd year, made frequent trips over the battle ground, and took notes on it. Often he mentioned of stopping at Molly Pitcher's spring and getting a good, clear, cold drink of water from this spring, of which was a half barrel sunk in the edge of the bank about 100 feet east of the Pennsylvania railroad tunnel and Wemrock cut off on the south side of the railroad from which Molly Pitcher carried water to the thirsty soldiers.[11]

It was later discovered that the spring had been covered over during repairs to the railroad line in 1923. The inscribed stone was set up by Jasko and Perrine in 1938 and was repainted by William Perrine sometime before 1956.[12] The current spring is caused by a tile drain constructed in the Civil War era. Another nearby spring between the railroad and Englishtown Road is fed by the same source.[13] This may be the spring that was remembered by local historian Samuel C. Cowart, who related that he was told that the spring was in this area, but on the east side of the railroad tracks.[14]

The only American artillery that were in this area were some batteries attached to Lee's advanced wing during their withdrawal from Monmouth Courthouse early in the afternoon. This area was behind British lines for all the afternoon's fight.[15] It is not a likely source for Molly Pitcher's well, though it is presently marked as such and even has its own designated parking area off of Wemrock Road near Route 522.

13B. Spring on the property of Charles Willoughby in Freehold Township.

This spring, which lies east of the St. Rose of Lima Cemetery and adjoins the "Craig House" farm, was thought to be Molly's well in the 1930s by local historian Samuel Craig Cowart. In 1937 Cowart wrote, "The real location of this historic spring, I am satisfied, is at the foot of a hill, on what is now the Willoughby property, a small tract of land on the south side of Spotswood brook, which brook forms the southerly line of my Cowart farms, formerly known as 'The John Craig farm.'"[16] Cowart preferred the site because it was on the location of what was called "the third skirmish line of the battle of Monmouth near a point where the American artillery probably was set up." He noted, "Molly wouldn't have used a spring a half mile away with this one so near by. She probably would have been shot by the British if she walked that far." Mr. Willoughby, however, was less confident that this was the proper well site. "It's just as uncertain as Cain's wife whether or not this is the spring. It may be and it may not be but one thing is certain, the British and the Americans must have done some heavy battling around here for I've found numerous cannon balls, small shot, spurs and stirrups laying around the ground." Willoughby's spring for a long time was boxed in by boards, giving it the appearance of a well.[17]

It can now be shown that there were no American artillery units posted in this area during the battle.[18] The relics Mr. Willoughby found are probably related to Lee's withdrawal and Wayne's fight in the Point of Woods.

13C. The "Railroad Well."

Located on the south side of Route 522 near the Hedgerow.[19] This well was popularly pointed out because of its proximity to the railroad line and the Englishtown Road. One source even suggests that the well "was constructed by railroad men who feared lawsuits from persons crossing railroad property to look for the real well."[20] It was marked by two oval signs lettered "Mollie Pitcher's Well." After the original signs faded, new ones were erected by the railroad around 1940, lettered in the railroad's colors of red and gold.[21]

No American artillery units are known to have fought in this immediate area at any time during the battle.[22] This site was in advance of the American artillery position formed along the Hedgerow before 1:00 P.M. (Knox's line), so it is unlikely anyone would have come to this spot to get water. It should also be noted that there is evidence that this well may not have existed until after the time of the battle.

In 1926 Samuel Craig Cowart told William S. Stryker that Dr. Joseph C. Thompson (1804-1890) told him that he (Thompson) dug this well in the 1850s.[23] This report is confirmed by the following 1926 newspaper article:

The well located along the Pennsylvania Railroad tracks on the Tennent Road, known as Molly Pitcher's Well and is supposed to date back to Revolutionary times, was not dug until several decades after the war was over, according to Mrs. William Augustus Thompson Jr., East Main Street, Freehold, daughter-in-law of the late Dr. Joseph C. Thompson, who dug this well about the middle of the 19th century. In revealing some of the facts relating to this well and its origin, Mrs. Thompson said last week that the doctor purchased the farm about the year 1832 from a man by the name of Rhea, if her memory had not failed her, and at the time there was an old farm house located quite a long way from the road in which Dr. Thompson lived until he built a new home nearer the road. The ground surrounding the new home was filled with marl which affected the water on the place and made it undesirable for drinking purposes so Dr. Thompson dug the present "Molly Pitcher's" well and laid pipe from the well to the residence. This well was the means of furnishing the household with water during all the years until but a few years ago, when the pipes, it is thought, gave away, and stopped the flow of water. During World War I tourists visited the well and many of them took bricks from the inside for historic souvenirs and by the time any mention was made of the missing bricks several had been taken. The Pennsylvania Railroad Company rebricked the well and built the present covering around the place to preserve it for future "historic reference," Mrs. Thompson said.[24]

The *Freehold Transcript* summarized the status of this well of this well in the following article:

Molly Picher's Well. A number of years ago a Pennsylvania railroad section boss, or somebody with less knowledge, discovered an old well along the track between

Freehold and Tennent and forthwith erected two large signs
bearing the legend "Molly Pitcher's Well." Since then some
patriotic society, with more zeal than knowledge, has erected
a neat stone curb around the well, and almost any nice day in
summer pilgrims may be seen examining the alleged scene of
Molly's exploits. The *Transcript* has more than once referred
to this fake memorial, but to no purpose so far as getting the
untrue signs removed. The *New York Times* of Sunday
printed a dispatch from Asbury Park stating that the Asbury
Park Post of the American Legion who had intended to take a
stone from the well to be placed at the tomb of the Unknown
Soldier in Arlington, had decided not to do so because of the
fact that Molly got the water from a spring or a brook on the
day of the battle. This well was not dug until along in the
early fifties and naturally Monmouth's heroine could not
have carried water from it to the thirst soldiers. In the interest
of historic accuracy the fake signs should be removed, and
the Pennsylvania railroad company cease to make itself ri-
diculous.[25]

A bronze plaque, now missing, was erected here in September 1948 by the Francis Hopkinson Chapter, D.A.R. stating: "Molly
Pitcher's Well. This well has for many years been known as Molly
Pitcher's Well. The real source of water which Molly carried to the
soldiers during the battle of Monmouth is believed to be about 200
yards east of this location, under the R.R. cut [referring to 13A
above]."[26]

A possible source for the mistaken identity of this well was
told in 1937 by William C. Richardson of Haddonfield, formerly a
resident of Freehold:

My story, which may meet with some criticism and con-
tradiction from better informed historians, was handed down
to me by my father, Charles F. Richardson, long resident of
Freehold. He was a small boy when the railroad was built
from Jamesburg to Freehold and he told me that the water
boy of the construction crew was an Irish lad known as
Mollie Doolin. I think there must be some persons still in
Freehold who can remember Doolin in his later years when

he was crossing watchman for the railroad at Monmouth Avenue.

According to my father, Mollie Doolin carried water from the well on Dr. Thompson's farm and it was known by the railroad builders as Mollie's well. It was so called by railroad men for several years until somebody conceived the idea that it was Molly Pitcher's well and not Mollie Doolin's and erected a sign to that effect, which sign later was replaced by the structure now marking the well. From what I was taught about the battlefield in my early years I feel sure that Mr. Samuel C. Cowart is correct in saying that Molly Pitcher obtained the water she used from a spring that has now disappeared.[27]

13D. Spring in the barnyard of the Thompson-Taylor farm.

The presence of this spring induced the Taylors to call their farm "Molly Pitcher Farm."[28]

Several American guns were posted on the Hedgerow line south of this spring from about noon to 1:00 P.M., but none were from Proctor's Artillery. This spring was behind British lines for the rest of the afternoon.[29]

13E. Herbert's Spring, located south of Route 522 and west of the West Morass.[30]

Donald Craig Butcher of Freehold heard the story of this spring from H.M. Herbert of Seaside Heights, who died in the late1930's at age 94. Herbert grew up here and said that there was a spring in front of his house, between the house and the railroad, that was remembered as Molly's well by his father and grandfather, who marked it with a sign. The spring was low and marshy, with a large tree nearby. During the 1860s the sign was stolen a couple times and was each time replaced by Mr. Herbert with a sign hand painted by his father. The tree near the spring was felled by lightning in the late 1800s. The Herberts at one time dug a channel so that the spring would drain to nearby Spotswood Brook.[31]

This spring was behind American lines while the fighting was going on along the Hedgerow in the early afternoon. However, no cannons were posted in the immediate area, nor did Proctor's guns fight on this side of the West Morass.[32]

13F. Well on the Sutphin farm.[33]

This well site was favored in the 1970s by historian Samuel S. Smith, who wrote, "Within 400 yards of Stirling's position is an 18th century farmhouse. And within a few steps of the house is a superb well that still furnishes the household with an abundant supply of cool drinking water. It is a very old well, and it must be concluded that it was in existence during the Battle of Monmouth, and that Molly Pitcher had access to it." [34]

This well site is the subject of the following sign erected in the late 1970s by Robert Farrell on the north side of Route 522, one-half mile east of the Cobb House:

> Molly Pitcher. America's First Heroine. During the Revolutionary War on June 28, 1778. A blistering hot day at the battle of Monmouth. A woman who was with her husband, John Casper Hays, who served in the Pennsylvania Regiment carried water to the thirsty American soldiers who shouted "Molly, Molly Pitcher" when they needed water. Through heavy bombardment Molly carried the water to the parched soldiers during the artillery dual [sic]. Her husband was wounded and she immediately helped load and fire the cannon continuing the barrage against the British. Legend has it that General George Washington commended Molly Pitcher after the battle and commissioned her a sergeant on the battlefield. This seems to be substantiated by the fact that she was given an army pension and buried in her home town with full military honors in 1832. The home where she drew the water is to your Northeast. Robert H. Ferrell.

It is unlikely that American troops posted on Stirling's Ridge, one-half mile to the west of this well, would have drawn water here during the fighting because it was located between the two armies' battle lines. In fact, the 42nd British Infantry occupied the orchard nearby for a good portion of the afternoon.[35]

13G. Spotswood South Brook.[36]

This could have been a source of water for the cannoneers posted on Comb's Hill, but Proctor's Artillery was not among them.[37]

13H. Spring in the big ravine on the Perrine Farm.[38]

This spring, whose location is shown on a 1778 map of the battlefield drawn by Colonel Richard Butler, is about 1000 feet behind the position held by Proctor's Artillery.[39]

13I. Spotswood North Brook.

This stream, located north of Perrine Ridge, could also have served as a source of water for Proctor's Artillery posted nearby.

13J. Well near the Ker house.

Ancestral tales and traditions are still told that relate to the church [Old Tennent Church] and its people in connection with the Battle, and with a good degree of authenticity. It is said that the house of Wm. Ker, now long since taken down, that stood about a quarter mile from the church, was one of the places used as a hospital at the time of the Battle. Also it is a current story in the present Bills' family, descendants of the George and Tone families, that their great-grandmother and her mother nursed the wounded soldiers at the church; and their great-grandfather George and his brother carried water all day to the wounded soldiers on the battle-field from Molly Pitcher's spring; and also that their great-grandmother, aided by her mother, entered the British lines, having the pass-word from her father   an American soldier of the most loyal type, and by means of a few biscuits and two or three chickens, bought silk for a gown and broadcloth for a cloak, bringing them home secretly, and keeping them without her father's knowledge, for her wedding apparel, some five years after.[40]

This passage unfortunately does not state specifically where the spring referred to was located. It would have been somewhere near Old Tennent Church, as indicated in the passage.

13K. Well used by Joseph Plumb Martin late in the battle.

During the afternoon's action Private Joseph Plumb Martin of the 8th Connecticut was detailed to a large force that covered the front of Stirling's position on Perrine Hill (see Nos. 1A and Commentary at beginning of Chapter 13). At one point this force moved forward to drive the British troops back from the area of the Sutphin orchard. Plumb Martin recalled, "After the action in our part of the army had ceased, I went to a well, a few rods off, to get some water." Here he found an infantry captain whom he had seen wounded in the thigh early in the action by a British cannon shot. Plumb Martin took pity on the captain, and carried him "to a meetinghouse a short distance off, where the rest of the wounded and the surgeons were."[41]

We cannot tell from Plumb Martin's description which well he refers to in this passage. All we know that it was on the north side of Spotswood Middle Brook, and not too far from Old Tennent Church, which was the location of the field hospital he refers to. It should be noted that every farm in the area would have had a well, a fact that makes determining the location of Molly Pitcher's well (if it was indeed a well and not a spring) all the more difficult.

CONCLUSION

The information provided by Dr. Read, Joseph Plumb Martin and Mrs. Clendenin (see introduction at the beginning of this Chapter) shows that the well or spring from which Molly Pitcher allegedly drew her water has to be located near the position held by Proctor's guns on Perrine Hill. It was too dangerous to get water from the Sutphin well (No. 10 F) because it was too close to the British position. The water source had to be behind the American artillery line on Perrine Hill. The most likely locations would be the spring in the ravine on the Perrine farm (No. 13H) or Spotswood North Brook (No. 13I). It is interesting that some of the early sources mention her getting water from a spring, not a well or stream (including No. 2B). This would make the spring in the ravine on the Perrine farm (No. 13H) the better alternative; this spring is also closer to Proctor's presumed position than the North Brook is. This is the interpretation favored by Dr. Garry Wheeler Stone, Historian at Monmouth Battlefield State Park, who has verified through archaeological research the location of some of the cannons on the north end of Stirling's line.[42] An overlook with an interpretive exhibit are being constructed in early 2003 on Perrine Hill just above the site of this spring.

14. DID MOLLY PITCHER REALLY EXIST?

THE CASE FOR MOLLY PITCHER

The existence of Molly Pitcher, the heroine of the battle of Monmouth, can be demonstrated by three unrelated but interconnected groups of evidence: the primary sources, which show in their original form what she did at the battle; the pension awarded to Mary Hays McCauley in 1822, which shows that she indeed acted bravely and notably in the war; and the testimony of Mary Hays McCauley's neighbors, which confirm what it was that she did.

Each of the three primary sources cited in Section I give a slightly different view of what Molly did at Monmouth. Joseph Plumb Martin says that he saw a woman helping to man a cannon during the engagement (No. 1A). Dr. Albigence Waldo says that he saw a woman fighting after her husband was shot down (No. 1B). Rebecca Clendenin says that her husband told her he saw a woman carrying water to the troops (No. 1C). Two of these three statements relate to the action on the same part of the field (Martin and Clendenin); the scene for Waldo's statement cannot be specified. This location is Perrine Hill, a position where about half of the American guns were engaged during the afternoon part of the battle.

Molly Pitcher was famous for doing two brave deeds during the battle: bringing water to the troops and helping to fire a cannon. Unfortunately, her heroism at Monmouth has been confused with that of another brave woman with a similar name, Captain Molly Corbin, who was wounded while helping to fire a cannon after her husband was killed at the battle of Fort Washington on November 16, 1776. Due to their similar names and the fact that both helped to fire cannons, their careers were later confused and intertwined. Specifically, Mrs. Alexander Hamilton (No. 2I), Benson Lossing (No. 2K) and others thought that the "Captain Molly" who resided near West Point, New York, was the same woman as the "Molly Pitcher" of Monmouth fame. This confusion lasted for years and was not straightened out for good until the earlier twentieth century: Molly Corbin fought at Fort Washington and is buried at West Point, New York; Molly Pitcher fought at Monmouth and is buried in Carlisle, Pennsylvania. Due to the intertwining of the two stories, certain elements of Molly

Corbin's saga crossed over to that of Molly Pitcher, specifically, the death of her husband and probably the nickname "Captain Molly."

The facts about Molly Pitcher became further obscured when a full scale legend about her developed in the 1830s in New Jersey. During this era of hero building, the nation began idolizing the heroes of the Revolution, and figures such as Ben Franklin, Betsy Ross, and even George Washington himself began to take on heroic proportions, During this time additional details were added to the Molly Pitcher story: that she volunteered to man the cannon after her husband fell so that it would not be withdrawn from the field; that she was presented to General Washington personally after the battle; that Washington gave her a battlefield commission and a pension; and that French officers gave her money. None of these accretions can be proven beyond doubt by primary sources, yet they too became part of the legend that was being spread on a national scale, first by George Washington Parke Custis in 1840s (Nos. 2D, 2E and 2F), and then by Benson Lossing in the 1850s Nos. 2J and 2K). Other authors followed suit, and by 1860 the story of Molly Pitcher, with its later accretions, was part of the national fabric.

These expanded mythic presentations of the story of Molly Pitcher, however, should not cloud our vision of what actually happened: she brought water to the troops and helped fire a cannon. This is just what her neighbors recalled in later years. Mrs. Susan Heckendorn heard her say, "You girls should have been with me at the Battle of Monmouth and learned how to load a cannon." (No. 8H). Mrs. Elizabeth Dehuff heard her speak of taking water to the troops (No. 8K). Harriet Foulke (No. 8I) and Mrs. Barbara Park (No. 8G) knew her as Molly Pitcher. Her own grandson, John Hays, heard her say "If it had not been for her the battle of Monmouth would have gone against us!" (No. 8F).

Mary Hays McCauley's neighbors were not the only ones aware of her brave service during the war. In 1822 the state of Pennsylvania awarded her a veteran's pension, not in the name of her deceased husband, but in her own name "for service rendered in the revolutionary war." These services are not spelled out, but in papers related to the pension she is called a "heroine (No. 7J). The fact that she was awarded a pension is quite significant, since only two other women are known to have been awarded pensions for their service in the war – Molly Corbin, who was wounded while firing a cannon at

Fort Washington (No. 11A), and Deborah Sampson, who was also wounded in the war (No. 11F). The significance of Mary Hays McCauley's pension can also be seen in the fact that it was reported soon afterward in newspapers in New York, Philadelphia and Washington. This would not have been done had she been but a simple camp follower.

It is also significant that Mary Hays McCauley has been the only candidate proposed over the years to be the actual historical Molly Pitcher. Linda de Pauw's argument that "Molly Pitcher" was a generic name for camp followers who brought water to the troops loses force because there is not evidence of the term being applied to other women. In addition, evidence shown above is clear that Mary was married to William Hays, a gunner in Proctor's artillery during the war, and therefore could readily have been present with him at Monmouth.

The facts of Molly Pitcher's heroism should not be lost sight of in the ongoing arguments about her date and place of birth, her maiden name (Ludwig, Hanna or otherwise), and her nationality, points that we may never be able to establish for certain.

THE CASE AGAINST MOLLY PITCHER

The case for Mary Hays McCauley being the real Molly Pitcher is built on a deck of cards. Each piece of evidence cited to support Mary Hays McCauley's identity as Molly Pitcher has a weakness or loophole, and there is no clear-cut "smoking gun" to confirm her case.

The primary sources cited are particularly weak. There is no proof that Joseph Plumb Martin, Dr. Albigence Waldo and Rebecca Clendenin are speaking of the same woman. In addition, none of these three sources relate the she was carrying out both key elements of the story, bringing water to the troops and also firing a cannon. Plumb Martin tells of a woman firing a cannon; Clendenin speaks only of a woman bringing water to the troops; and Dr. Waldo speaks of a woman who may have been firing an infantryman's musket. These three sources could just as well be speaking of three different women. Each of these three sources also has questions about their authenticity. Dr. Waldo's account is cited by William S. Stryker, but no one today can locate Waldo's original manuscript (see Commentary to No. 1B). Plumb Martin's account did not appear in print until 1830, about the time that the Molly Pitcher legend was being created. There is some question if he could actually have seen a woman working a cannon at the top of Perrine Hill from his position at the base of the hill; he might just have been repeating a story he heard at the battlefield or long afterwards. Clendenin's story appears even later, in 1840. It is possible she padded her pension application by repeating the then popular of Molly Pitcher. Or possibly a professional pension agent may have added the story for her in order to make her claim seem more authentic.

Likewise Mary Hays McCauley's neighbors may well have exaggerated their recollection of Mary Hays McCauley in order to make her and their town seem more important. It is interesting to note that neither of her obituaries makes mention of her having been Molly Pitcher. However, when her son John L. Hays died in 1856, after the Molly Pitcher legend had been fully developed and spread nationally by Custis, Lossing and others, his obituary does mention his mother as being the famous Molly Pitcher (No. 8A). Also, it should be noted that when Mary Hays McCauley died in 1832, she was not honored with a fancy gravestone or plaque commemorating her deeds as Molly Pitcher; she may in fact not have received any gravestone at all. She was not honored with a fancy stone acknowledging her as Molly pitcher until 1876, when one was erected in the flurry of patriotism, surrounding the nation's centennial (No. 9A). Even then, probes had to be made to find where Mary Hays McCauley's grave was actually located.

The main telling point is that the wording of the actual pension received by Mary Hays McCauley in 1822 makes no mention of her being "Molly Pitcher." Nor does it mention her firing a cannon, bringing water to the troops, or even being at Monmouth. Added to this is the fact that the newspaper accounts of her pension would surely have mentioned her bravery at Monmouth if such had indeed been the case. Instead, the Carlisle papers mention only her "services rendered" and the fact that she was a heroine who "braved the hardships of the camp and dangers of the field, with her husband" (No. 7K). The New York and Washington papers, in fact, were totally confused about what distinguished service Mary Hays McCauley was supposed to have performed, and state that "she was wounded at some battle, supposed to be Brandywine, where her sex was discovered." (Nos. 7L and 7M).

The legend of Molly Pitcher clearly grew up a generation after the war, when writers and painters like George Washington Park Custis and Dennis Malone Carter were eager to capitalize on the nation's growing thirst for Revolutionary war heroes and heroines. Benson Lossing and the partnership of Currier and Ives especially profited by popularizing stories like Molly Pitcher's, creating a standardized myth that still survives today. Along the way the legend was embellished with additional details, many through a conflation with the story of Molly Corbin.

It should also be pointed out that we cannot be sure whom Mary Hays McCauley was married to at the time of the battle of Monmouth. She was clearly married to William Hays at some point prior to his death in 1787, but we do not know when, since no record survives of their marriage certificate. Arguments about her birth place, birth date, nationality and possible maiden name only cloud the basic question. Lastly, there is no solid evidence that Mary was with her husband William Hays at Monmouth, nor can it even be conclusively proved that William's command was at the battle (see Chapter 12).

This is not to question that Mary Hays McCauley was a heroic woman who was with the army in the field and fully deserved the recognition and pension given her by the state of Pennsylvania in 1822. That she was the legendary figure of Molly Pitcher is another case all together. It is more likely that, as De Pauw (No. 6H), Teipe (No. 6O) and others have argued, the figure now known to history as Molly Pitcher was a combination of Margaret Corbin and many other brave women who accompanied the Continental armies in the Revolution and sometimes even fought shoulder to shoulder with their men.

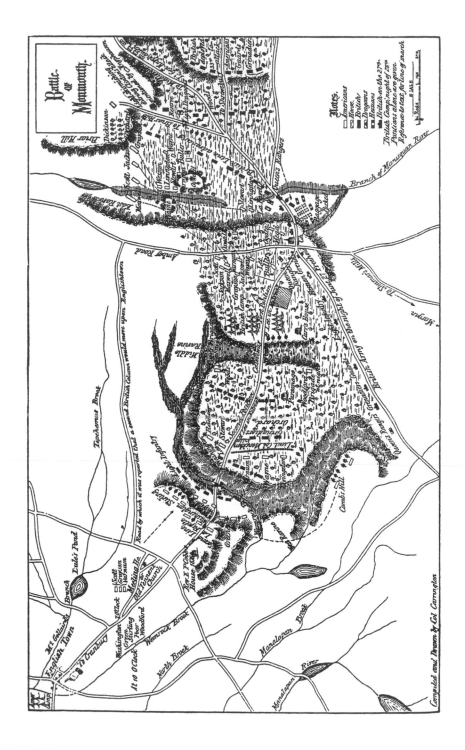

NOTES

CHAPTER 1

1. Joseph Plumb Martin, *Private Yankee Doodle* (N.P.: Eastern Acorn Press, 1962), 132-133. Excerpt quoted with the permission of Little, Brown and Company.
2. Martin, *Private Yankee Doodle*, vi-xvi.
3. Martin, *Private Yankee Doodle*, 128, 132.
4. As quoted in William S. Stryker, *The Battle of Monmouth* (Princeton, NJ: Princeton University Press, 1927), 189.
5. John Rhodehamel, Editor, *The American Revolution: Writings from the War of Independence* (New York: Literary Classics of the United States, Inc., 2001), 827.
6. Carol Klaver, "An Introduction to the Legend of Molly Pitcher," *Minerva: Quarterly Report on Women and the Military*, Vol. 12, No. 2 (Summer 1994), 38, and D.W. Thompson and Mary Lou Schaumann, "Goodbye, Molly Pitcher," *Cumberland County History*, Vol. VI, No. 1 (Summer 1989), 7, 17.
7. Records Ser. W 3223, Pension file of John and Rebecca Clendenin, National Archives.
8. *Ibid.*
9. Garry Wheeler Stone, "Battle of Monmouth Maps," 1999.

CHAPTER 2

1. J.T. and E. Buckingham, "Moll Pitcher, A Poem," *The New-England Magazine*, Vol. 2, Issue 5 (May 1832), 442.
2. Thomas Franklin Currier, *A Bibliography of John Greenleaf Whittier* (Cambridge, Mass.: Harvard University Press, 1937), 30, 44.
3. Currier, *Life and Letters of John Greenleaf Whittier*, 31, and Samuel T. Pickard, *Life and Times of John Greenleaf Whittier* (Boston: Riverside Press, 1894), 104.
4. Pickard, *Life and Letters of John Greenleaf Whittier*, 104.
5. Currier, *Life and Letters of John Greenleaf Whittier*, 21.
6. *New-Jersey State Gazette*, December 1, 1837.

7. Stanley J. Kunitz and Howard Haycraft, Editors, *American Authors, 1600-1900* (New York: H.W. Wilson Company, 1938), 425.

8. Alonzo Lewis and James Newhall, *History of Lynn, Essex County, Mass., 1619-1893* (Lynn, Mass.: George C. Herbert, 1890), 1: 374.

9. *National Intelligencer* (Washington, D.C.), Feb. 22, 1840. This section appears word for word the same in Custis' 1859 books *Recollections and Private Memoirs of Washington, by G.W. Parke Custis of Arlington* (Washington, D.C.: William H. Moore, 1859), 47-48, and *Memoirs of Washington, by his Adopted Son, George Washington Parke Custis, with a Memoir of the Author, by his Daughter, and Illustrative and Explanatory Notes by Benson J. Lossing* (New York: Union Publishing Company, 1859), 224-225.

10. Allen Johnson and Dumas Malone, Editors, *Dictionary of American Biography* (New York: Charles Scribner's Sons, 1931), 3: 9-10. The only full biography of Custis is the one written by his daughter, Mrs. Robert E. Lee, in Custis, *Memoirs of Washington,* 9-72.

11. Custis, *Memoirs of Washington, by his Adopted Son,* 120; see also Mrs. Lee's comments in *ibid.,* 67-68.

12. Custis, *Memoirs of Washington,* 9. Most of the articles date to 1826-1829 and 1840-1843; the last appeared in 1855. Some were first published in the *Alexandria Gazette* and the *American Register and Sporting Magazine.* A number of the articles were reprinted in the Washington, D.C. *United States Gazette* and elsewhere.

13. *Recollections and Private Memoirs of Washington, by G.W. Parke Custis of Arlington* (Washington, D.C.: William H. Moore, 1859); *Memoirs of Washington, by his Adopted Son, George Washington Parke Custis, with a Memoir of the Author, by his Daughter, and Illustrative and Explanatory Notes by Benson J. Lossing* (New York: Union Publishing House, 1859).

14. D.W. Thompson and Mary Lou Schaumann, "Goodbye, Molly Pitcher," *Cumberland County History,* Vol. VI, No. 1 (Summer 1989), 12.

15. See a short discussion of this issue in Thompson and Schaumann, "Goodbye, Molly Pitcher," 12-13.

16. Washington, D.C. *National Intelligencer,* February 23, 1843.This section appears word for word the same in Custis' 1859 books *Recollections and Private Memoirs of Washington,* 29-30, and *Memoirs of Washington,* 286-287.
17. See note 13 above.
18. Letter to the author from James T. Raleigh, January 15, 2003.
19. Benson J. Lossing, *A Pictorial Field-book of the American Revolution* (New York: N.P., 1851), 2:361.
20. Custis, *Memoirs of Washington,* 68.
21. John W. Barber and Henry Howe, *Historical Collections of the State of New Jersey* (New York: S. Tuttle, 1844), 342.
22. Kunitz and Haycraft, *American Authors, 1600-1900,* 52-53, 390.
23. Johnson and Malone, *Dictionary of American Biography,* 2:604.
24. Frederic A. Conningham, *Currier & Ives Prints, An Illustrated Checklist* (New York: Crown Publishers, 1949), 295 nos. 6754, 6755.
25. *Ibid.,* 132 no. 2802.
26. Thompson and Schaumann, "Goodbye, Molly Pitcher," 15.
27. Katharine Schuyler Baxter, *A Godchild of Washington: A Picture of the Past* (New York: F. Tennyson Neely, 1897), 221-224.
28. Broadus Mitchell. *Alexander Hamilton, The Revolutionary Years* (New York: Thomas Y. Crowell, 1970), 197-198, 372; and Baxter, *A Godchild of Washington,* 221, 225.
29. For a full account of the life of Margaret Corbin, see *Margaret Corbin, Heroine of Fort Washington, 16 November 1776* by Edward H. Hall (New York: The American Scene and Preservation Society, 1932). See also Mark M. Boatner III, *Encyclopedia of the American Revolution* (New York: David McKay Company, 1976), 284; and William S. Stryker, *The Battle of Monmouth* (Princeton, N.J.: Princeton University Press, 1927), 190-191. The quotation from her pension is in Hall, *Margaret Corbin,* 15.
30. Hall, *Margaret Corbin,* 16-23.
31. *Ibid.,* 19-22.
32. Benson J. Lossing, *Pictorial Field-Book of the Revolution* (New York: N.P., 1851), 2:164.
33. John B.B. Trussell Jr., *The Pennsylvania Line, Regimental Organization and Operations, 1776-1783* (Harrisburg: Pennsylvania Historical and Museum Commission, 1977), 207-210.
34. Hall, *Margaret Corbin,* 23.

35. Mitchell, *Alexander Hamilton, The Revolutionary Years,* 159 and Broadus Mitchell, "The Battle of Monmouth through Alexander Hamilton's Eyes," *Proceedings of the New Jersey Historical Society,* Vol. 73, No. 4 (October 1955): 251. Mitchell does not make mention in either article about Hamilton telling his wife that General Greene introduced Molly Pitcher to General Washington after the battle.
36. Lossing, *Pictorial Field-Book of the Revolution,* 2:164.
37. *Encyclopedia Americana* (New York, 1953), s.v. Benson J. Lossing.
38. Thompson and Schaumann "Goodbye, Molly Pitcher," 15.
39. Lossing, *Pictorial Field-Book of the Revolution,* II: 361, note 2. Lossing used the text of this note, from the third sentence on ("Molly was a sturdy young camp follower.."), as a footnote on pages 225-226 of Custis' *Recollections of Washington,* which he edited in 1859.
40. Thompson and Schaumann ("Goodbye, Molly Pitcher," 13-14) argue that Lossing's account is based primarily on Custis', since Lossing is known to have visited Custis at Arlington in November 1850, when he took careful notes on Custis' painting of "Captain Molly" at the Battle of Monmouth (see above, Commentary on No. 2F).
41. Hall, *Margaret Corbin,* 31-34.
42. J.T. Headley, *The Illustrated Life of Washington, giving an Account of his Early Adventures and Enterprises, his Magnanimity and Patriotism, his Revolutionary Career, his Presidential Life, and his Final Decease, with Vivid Pen-Paintings of Battles and Incidents, Trials and Triumphs of the Heroes and Soldiers of Revolutionary Times, Together with an Interesting Account of Mount Vernon as it Is, by Benson J. Lossing* (New York: G. & F. Bill, 1859), 329 note.
43. Kunitz and Haycraft, *American Authors,* 353.
44. Headley, *The Illustrated Life of Washington,* 361.
45. James Thacher, *Military Journal of the American Revolution* (Hartford: Hurlbut, Williams & Co., 1862), 138.
46. Thacher, *Military Journal of the American Revolution,* 7, 166; Samuel S. Smith, *A Molly Pitcher Chronology* (Monmouth Beach, NJ: Philip Frenau Press, 1972), 5.

47. James Thacher, *Military Journal during the American Revolutionary War* (Boston: Richardson and Lord, 1823), 165-166; James Thacher, *Military Journal during the American Revolutionary War* (Boston: Cottons and Barnard, 1827), 2nd Edition, 136-137; James Thacher, *Military Journal during the American Revolutionary War* (Hartford: Silas Andrus & Son, 1854), 138-139; and James Thacher, *Military Journal of the American Revolution* (Hartford: Hurlbut, Williams & Co., 1862), 138; see also Smith, *A Molly Pitcher Chronology*, 5.

48. Edward C. Boynton, *History of West Point* (New York: D. Van Nostrand, 1871), 166-167, 318.

49. Boynton, *History of West Point*, title page; and Hall, *Margaret Corbin*, 34.

50. Boynton, *History of West Point*, 166 note, citing Lossing, *Field-Book of the Revolution*, 2:155.

51. Hall, *Margaret Corbin*, 44.

CHAPTER 3

1. *Monmouth Inquirer*, March 16, 1876.

2. *A Memoir of Miss Sarah Smith Stafford, the Patriot and Philanthropist, with Some Statements of her Ancestry* (N.P.: n.p., ca. 1880), 1-9.She donated much of her Revolutionary War collection to the Birchard Library in Fremont, Ohio, *ibid.*, 9.

3. Conversation with John Fabiano, President of the Allentown-Upper Freehold Historical Society.

4. *Monmouth Inquirer*, March 16, 1876.

5. Rev. George Swain, *Historical Discourse in Connection with the Presbyterian Church of Allentown and Vicinity* (N.P.: n.p., ca. 1876), 18-19.

6. F. Dean Storms, *History of Allentown Presbyterian Church, Allentown, N.J. (1720-1970)* (Allenton, N.J.: Allentown Messenger, 1970), 166 note 31.

7. *Ibid.*, 163-166, 183-184.

8. Swain, *Historical Discourse in Connection with the Presbyterian Church of Allentown and Vicinity*, 33 note 38.

9. John O. Raum, *The History of New Jersey* (Philadelphia: John E. Potter and Company, 1877), 2:70-71.

10. John O. Raum, *A History of the City of Trenton* (Trenton: W.T. Nicholson & Co., 1871).

11. C.P. Wing, Letter to the Editor, June 15, 1878, in *The Pennsylvania Magazine of History and Biography* (Philadelphia: Historical Society of Pennsylvania, 1879), 3: 109-110.Wing was a Reverend in Carlisle and wrote a history of Cumberland County. He was deceased by 1905 (Jeremiah Zeamer, "Molly McCauley Monument," *Carlisle Herald,* April 5, 1905).

12. C. Malcolm B. Gilman, *Monmouth, Road to Glory* (Red Bank, New Jersey: Arlington Laboratory for Clinical and Historical Research, 1964), 38.The baptismal records that Gilman cites cannot now be located.

13. William S. Stryker, *The Battle of Monmouth* (Princeton, N.J.: Princeton University Press, 1927), 191.

14. John B. Linn and William H. Egle, *Pennsylvania Archives,* Second Series, 2: 115, 181.The source as cited does not gave the place the marriage bond was recorded.

15. John Landis, *A Short History of Molly Pitcher* (Carlisle: Cornman Printing Company, 1905), 10.

16. Linn and Egle, *Pennsylvania Archives,* Second Series, 9:338.

17. Stryker, *The Battle of Monmouth,* 191.There is also a problem with Stryker's argument, because his John Hays was actually serving in the infantry at Monmouth, not the artillery (see Commentary to No. 3L).

18. Jeremiah Zeamer, "Molly Pitcher Story Analyzed," *Carlisle Volunteer,* February 20, 1907; and Samuel S. Smith, *A Molly Pitcher Chronology* (Monmouth Beach, N.J.: Philip Frenau Press, 1972), 8-13.

19. Smith, *A Molly Pitcher Chronology,* 13.

20. E.M. Woodward, *History of Burlington County, New Jersey* (Philadelphia: Everts & Peck, 1883), 28 note 1.

21. J.A. Murray, article in the Carlisle *American Volunteer,* September 12, 1883.

22. Edwin Salter, letter to Major James Yard, June 22, 1886, *Monmouth County Historical Association Newsletter,* Vol. 2, No. 2 (January 1974): 1.

23. Edwin Salter and George C. Beekman, *Old Times in Old Monmouth, Historical Reminiscences of Old Monmouth County, New Jersey* (Bowie, Md.: Heritage Books, 1999; reprint of 1887 Free-

hold edition), and Edwin Salter, *History of Monmouth and Ocean Counties, New Jersey* (Bayonne, N.J.: E. Gardner and Son, 1890).

24. Salter in *Old Times in Old Monmouth,* 155-156, simply quotes the accounts of Molly given by Barber and Howe (No. 2G) and Lossing (No. 2J above); the latter account contains the same information about "Captain Molly" at Highland Falls that Salter disputes in this letter to Major Yard (No. 3H).

25. Edwin Salter, *A History of Monmouth and Ocean Counties* (Bayonne: E. Gardner & Son, 1890), 220-221.

26. William H. Egle, *Notes and Queries: Historical, Biographical and Genealogical, Relating Chiefly to Interior Pennsylvania* (Baltimore: Genealogical Publishing Company, 1970; Reprint of 1893 Harrisburg edition), Fourth Series, 1: 265-266.

27. William H. Egle, *An Illustrated History of the Commonwealth of Pennsylvania* (Harrisburg: De W.C. Goodrich & Co., 1876).

28. William H. Egle, *Some Pennsylvania Women During the War of the American Revolution* (Harrisburg: Harrisburg Publishing Company, 1898), reprinted as *Pennsylvania Women in the American Revolution* (Cottonport, La.: Polyanthos, 1972), 85-86.

29. William S. Stryker, *The Battle of Monmouth,* 191-192.*Ibid.,* page 192 note 17, shows that Stryker was familiar with Egle's work.

30. Jeremiah Zeamer, "Molly Pitcher Story Analyzed, " *Carlisle Volunteer,* February 20, 1907; and Samuel S. Smith, *A Molly Pitcher Chronology* (Monmouth Beach, N.J.: Philip Frenau Press, 1972).

31. John B. Linn and William H. Engle, *Pennsylvania Archives*, Second Series, 2: 133, 181.

32. *Ibid.,* Second Series, 9:338.

33. Smith, *A Molly Pitcher Chronology,* 10-11; and Zeamer, "Molly Pitcher Story Analyzed."

34. Jeremiah Zeamer, "Molly McCauley Monument," *Carlisle Herald,* April 5, 1905.

35. Frank R. Stockton, *Stories of New Jersey* (New Brunswick: Rutgers University Press, 1961), 186-192.

36. *Ibid.,* iii-vi.

37. Stryker, *The Battle of Monmouth,* 188-192.

38. *Ibid.,* Preface and Introduction.

39. *Ibid.,* 189-190.

40. *Pennsylvania Archives,* Second Series, Vol II: 181. The actual entry does not include the words "a barber from Carlisle."

41. Stryker, *The Battle of Monmouth*, 191, citing *Pennsylvania Archives*, 2nd Series, Vol. X:176 and Vol. X:614.
42. Stryker, *The Battle of Monmouth*, 191-192.
43. *Ibid.*, 191.
44. See also Samuel S. Smith, *A Molly Pitcher Chronology*, 9-10; and Zeamer, "Molly Pitcher Story Analyzed."
45. Smith, *A Molly Pitcher Choronology*, 9, refuting Stryker's account in *The Battle of Monmouth*, 191.
46. Stryker, *The Battle of Monmouth*, 191.
47. Smith, *A Molly Pitcher Chronology*, 11-13.
48. *Ibid.*, 10.

CHAPTER 4

1. Isabella Crater McGeorge, "A New Jersey Heroine of the Revolution," *American Monthly Magazine*, Vol. 17, No. 5 (November 1900), 409-415.
2. C. Malcolm R. Gilman, *Monmouth, Road to Glory* (Red Bank, N.J.: Arlington Laboratory for Clinical and Historical Research, 1964), 38.
3. E.P. Wing, Letter to the Editor, June 15, 1878, in *The Pennsylvania Magazine of History and Biography* (Philadelphia: The Historical Society of Pennsylvania, 1879), 3:109; William H. Egle, *Notes and Queries: Historical, Biographical and Genealogical* (Baltimore: Genealogical Publishing Company, 1970; reprint of 1893 Harrisburg edition), Fourth Series, 1:265; and William S. Stryker, *The Battle of Monmouth* (Princeton: Princeton University Press, 1927), 191.
4. Jeremiah Zeamer, "'Molly Pitcher' Story Analyzed," *Carlisle Volunteer*, February 20, 1907; and Samuel S. Smith, *A Molly Pitcher Chronology* (Monmouth Beach, N.J.: Philip Frenau Press, 1972), 9-13.
5. Smith, *A Molly Pitcher Chronology*, 13.
6. Francis B. Lee, *New Jersey as a Colony and as a State* (New York: The Publishing Society of New Jersey, 1902), 2: 208.
7. Frank R. Symmes, *History of the Old Tennent Church* (Cranbury, N.J.: George W. Burroughs, 1904), 102-103.
8. *Carlisle Herald*, April 5, 1905.

9. John Landis, *A Short History of Molly Pitcher* (Carlisle, Pa.: Cornman Printing Company, 1905).

10. John Landis, "Investigation into American Tradition of Woman Known as 'Molly Pitcher,'" *The Journal of American History,* Vol. 5, No. 1 (1911): 83-95.

11. William S. Stryker, *The Battle of Monmouth* (Princeton: Princeton University Press, 1927), 171.

12. Landis, *A Short History of Molly Pitcher,* 13.

13. *Ibid.,* 14.

14. Zeamer, "'Molly Pitcher' Story Analyzed."

15. John B. Linn and William H. Egle, *Pennsylvania Archives* (Harrisburg: B.F. Meyers, 1876), Second Series, 2: 115, 181.

16. Linn and Egle, *Pennsylvania Archives,* Second Series, 9:338.

17. Martin I.J. Griffin, "Irish Molly Pitcher," *The American Catholic Historical Researches,* New Series, Vol. 5, No. 4 (October 1909), 379-382.

18. "Moll Pitcher," unsigned article in *The Pennsylvania German, A Monthly Magazine,* Vol. XI, No. 2 (February 1910), 122.

19. Landis, "Investigation into American Tradition of Woman Known as 'Molly Pitcher,'" 83.

CHAPTER 5

1. Samuel Craig Cowart, *Address, Battle of Monmouth, and Poem, Patriot Sires of Monmouth, Old Tennent Church, June 24th, 1914* (Hightstown, N.J.: Longstreet House, 1998), 13-14.

2. *History of Monmouth County, New Jersey, 1664-1920* (New York: Lewis Historical Publishing Company, 1922), 1:95.

3. Randolph Keim, "Heroines of the Revolution," *Journal of American History,* Vol. 16 (1922), 31-33.

4. William S. Hornor, *This Old Monmouth of Ours* (Cottonport: Polyanthus, 1974; Reprint of 1932 Freehold edition), 374.

5. Joseph Plumb Martin, *Private Yankee Doodle* (N.P.: Eastern Acorn Press, 2000), 133 n.12.

6. Col. C. Malcolm B. Gilman, M.D., *Monmouth, Road to Glory* (Red Bank, New Jersey: Arlington Laboratory for Clinical and Historical Research, 1964).

7. Gilman, *Monmouth Road to Glory,* Preface, Introduction.

8. *Ibid.*, 37-44. This chapter was published previously under the title "Molly Pitcher – Mary Ludwig, The Huguenot heroine of the American Revolutionary War," in *Proceedings of The National Huguenot Society,* 16 (1959): 97-101.

9. *Ibid.*, 39-40.

10. Lida C. Gedney, *The Church Records of the Presbyterian Church of Lawrenceville, New Jersey and the Bible Records from the Bibles in the Library of the Society* (N.P.: New Jersey Society of the Colonial Dames of America, 1941), 28.

11. Gilman, *Monmouth, Road to Glory,* 40.

12. Linn and Egle, *Pennsylvania Archives,* Second Series, 2: 115, 181.

13. Gilman, *Monmouth, Road to Glory,* 40.

14. *Ibid.*, 41, 43.

15. *Ibid.*, 44.

16. *Ibid.*, 38-39.

17. *Ibid.*, 37.

18. *Ibid.*, 40, 43.

19. Samuel S. Smith, *A Molly Pitcher Chronology* (Monmouth Beach, N.J.: Philip Frenau Press, 1972). Reprinted with the permission of James T. Raleigh. A somewhat revised and more informally written version of this talk was published under the title "The Search for Molly Pitcher" in *Daughters of the American Revolution Magazine,* April 1975, 292-294.

20. Smith, *A Molly Pitcher Chronology,* 3.

21. *Ibid.*, 3-7.

22. It is strange that Smith does not cite Zeamer anywhere in his sources or footnotes.

23. Smith, *A Molly Pitcher Chronology,* 9-10.

24. *Ibid.*, 10.

25. *Ibid.*, 10-11.

26. *Ibid.*, 13.

CHAPTER 6

1. Mollie Somerville, *Women and the American Revolution* (N.P.: National Society, Daughters of the American Revolution, 1974), 6-11, 63.

2. Walter H. Blumenthal, *Women Camp Followers of the Revolution* (New York: Arno Press, 1974), 67-68.
3. John Landis, *A Short History of Molly Pitcher* (Carlisle: Cornman Printing Company, 1905), 24.
4. Mark Mayo Boatner III, *Encyclopedia of the American Revolution*, Bicentennial Edition (New York: David McKay Company, 1974), 710-711.
5. Mark Mayo Boatner III, *The Civil War Dictionary* (New York: David McKay Company, 1959).
6. Boatner, *Encyclopedia of the American Revolution*, 497.
7. John Todd White, "The Truth About Molly Pitcher," in *The American Revolution, Whose Revolution?*, Edited by James Kirby Martin and Karen R. Stubaus (Huntington, N.Y.: Robert E. Krieger Publishing Company, 1977).
8. Elizabeth Evans, "Heroines All: The Plight of Women at War in America," in *Conflict at Monmouth Court House*, Edited by Mary E. Murrin and Richard Waldron (Trenton: New Jersey Historical Commission, 1984), 23-28.
9. *Ibid.*, 23-24.
10. *Ibid.*, 27.
11. *Ibid.*, 28.
12. James Kirby Martin, "Comments," in *Conflict at Monmouth Court House*, Edited by Mary E. Murrin and Richard Waldron (Trenton: New Jersey Historical Commission, 1984), 29-34.
13. *Ibid.*, 31.
14. *Ibid.*, 31.
15. *Ibid.*, 34.
16. Linda Grant de Pauw, "Women in Combat: The Revolutionary War Experience," *Armed Forces and Society*, Vol. 7, No. 2 (Winter 1981), 209-226.
17. *Ibid.*, 214-217.
18. *Ibid.*, 215-216.
19. *Ibid.*, 219
20. Janice E. McKenney, "'Women in Combat': Comment," *Armed Forces and Society*, Vol. 8, No. 4 (Summer 1982), 686-692.
21. *Ibid.*, 690.
22. D.W. Thompson and Merri Lou Schaumann, "Goodbye, Molly Pitcher," *Cumberland County History*, Vol. 6, No. 1 (Summer 1989), 3-26.

23. Biographical information from *ibid.,* 2-3.The statement on the 1976 original date of the original version of this article is from Constance M. McDonald, "Molly Pitcher, Who Was She?", *Field Artillery Magazine,* August 1990.
24. Thompson and Schaumann, "Goodbye, Molly Pitcher," 3-6.
25. *Ibid.,* 6-7.
26. *Ibid.,* 7-10.
27. *Ibid.,* 9.
28. *Ibid.,* 10-16.
29. *Ibid.,* 16-22.
30. *Ibid.,* 30.
31. *Ibid.,* 17.
32. *Ibid.,* 18.
33. *Ibid.,* 20-22.
34. *Ibid.,* 22-23.
35. McDonald, "Molly Pitcher, Who Was She?", *Field Artillery Magazine,* August 1990.
36. Constance M. McDonald, "Molly Pitcher, Who Was She?".
37. Carol Klaver, "An Introduction to the Legend of Molly Pitcher," *Minerva: Quarterly Report on Women and the Military,* Vol. 12, No. 2 (1994): 35-61.
38. Carol Klaver, "Molly Pitcher: Myth and Reality," Rutgers University History Departmental Honors Thesis, 1993 (manuscript copy in the collections of the research library of the Monmouth County Historical Association, Freehold, New Jersey).
39. Klaver, "An Introduction to the Legend of Molly Pitcher," 35.
40. *Ibid.,* 36-37.
41. *Ibid.,* 38.
42. *Ibid.,* 38.
43. *Ibid.,* 39-40.
44. *Ibid.,* 40-41.
45. *Ibid.,* 41-42.
46. *Ibid.,* 42-44.
47. *Ibid.,* 44-45.
48. *Ibid.,* 45-46.
49. *Ibid.,* 46-48.
50. *Ibid.,* 48.
51. *Ibid.,* 48-49.
52. *Ibid.,* 50-52.

53. *Ibid.,* 52-53.
54. Carmela A. Karnoutsas, *New Jersey Women, A History of Their Status, Roles, and Images* (Trenton: New Jersey Historical Commission, 1997), 20-21. Quoted with permission of the New Jersey State Historical Commission, Department of State.
55. Donald F.X. Finn, Letter to the New Jersey Historical Commission, December 5, 1998.Copy given to the author by Mr. Finn.
56. Emily J. Teipe, "Will the Real Molly Pitcher Please Stand Up?," *Prologue: Quarterly of the National Archives and Records Administration,* Vol. 31, No. 2 (1999): 118-126.
57. *Ibid.,* 118.

CHAPTER 7

1. Cumberland County, Pennsylvania, Administrations Book, B-63, No. 193.
2. Orphans' Court Records, Cumberland County Court House, Carlisle, Pennsylvania, Docket No. 3, pp. 37-38. See also Samuel S. Smith, *A Molly Pitcher Chronology* (Monmouth Beach, N.J.: Philip Frenau Press, 1972), 11, and Jeremiah Zeamer, "'Molly Pitcher' Story Analyzed," *Carlisle Volunteer,* February 12, 1907.
3. Orphans' Court Records, Cumberland County Court House, Carlisle, Pennsylvania, Docket No. 3, pp. 37-38; Zeamer, "'Molly Pitcher' Story Analyzed."
4. National Archives, RG 93, as cited in Smith, *A Molly Pitcher Chronology,* 13 n. 49.
5. Smith, *A Molly Pitcher Chronology,* 11.
6. National Archives, RG 15 (BLWt.389-100) as cited in Smith, *A Molly Pitcher Chronology,* 13 n. 50.
7. Smith, *A Molly Pitcher Chronology,* 13; Bounty Land Warrant 389, National Archives.
8. National Archives, RG 15 (BLWt 389-100) as cited in Smith, *A Molly Pitcher Chronology,* 13 n. 11.The grant, which consisted of 200 acres, was sold to Brady for $30, see D.W. Thompson and Merri Lou Schaumann, "Goodbye, Molly Pitcher," *Cumberland County History,* Vol. VI, No. 1 (Summer 1989), 19.

9. National Archives, RG 15 (BLWt. 389-100) as cited in Thompson and Schaumann, "Goodbye, Molly Pitcher," 19 and Smith, *A Molly Pitcher Chronology,* 13 n. 13.

10. *Journal of the Senate of the Commonwealth of Pennsylvania, which commenced at Harrisburg, the fourth day of December, in the year of Our Lord One Thousand Eight Hundred and Twenty-one* (Harrisburg: Charles Mowry, 1821-22), 33: 272.

11. *Ibid.,* 33: 358, 370.

12. *Ibid.,* 33: 371.

13. *Journal of the Thirty-second House of Representatives of the Commonwealth of Pennsylvania* (Harrisburg: John S. Wiestling, 1821-22), 660-661.

14. *Ibid.,* 652.

15. *Journal of the Senate of the Commonwealth of Pennsylvania,* 33: 382.

16. *Ibid.,* 404, 413; *Journal of the Thirty-second House of Representatives of the Commonwealth of Pennsylvania,* 685, 699.

17. Margaret Corbin's pension was form the federal government, but Pennsylvania kept an interest in her well being. See Edward H. Hall, *Margaret Corbin, Heroine of the Battle of Fort Washington, 16 November 1776* (New York: The American Scenic and Historic Preservation Society, 1932), 13-16.

18. *Acts of the General Assembly of the Commonwealth of Pennsylvania* (Harrisburg, 1822), 32.

19. Thompson and Schaumann, "Goodbye, Molly Pitcher," 20.

20. Carlisle *American Volunteer,* September 12, 1883.

21. *Journal of the Thirty-second House of Representatives of the Commonwealth of Pennsylvania,* index p. 6.

22. Carlisle, *American Volunteer,* February 21, 1822.

23. New York, *National Advocate,* March 7, 1822.

24. Hall, *Margaret Corbin,* 22, cites a letter dated September 14, 1782 written by Captain Samuel Shaw, aide-de-camp to General Knox, commandant of the garrison at West Point at the time, in which Shaw states, "There are two resolves of Congress in favor of the above named Mrs. Corbin, she having had a husband and son killed and was herself wounded at Brandywine in 1777."

25. Washington D.C. *National Intelligencer,* March 15, 1822.

26. Philadelphia *Chronicle,* unspecified date in March 1822, as quoted in John Landis, *A Short History of Molly Pitcher* Carlisle: Cornman Printing Company, 1905), 18.
27. Carlisle *American Volunteer,* January 26, 1832.
28. *Carlisle Herald,* January 26, 1832.
29. Carlisle census records for 1800 and 1830; see also Thompson and Schaumann, "Goodbye, Molly Pitcher," 19, 21.
30. Smith, *A Molly Pitcher Chronology,* 11.
31. Landis, *A Short History of Molly Pitcher,* 27.

CHAPTER 8

1. Carlisle *American Volunteer,* March 27, 1856.
2. John B. Landis, *A Short History of Molly Pitcher* (Carlisle: Cornman Publishing Co., 1905), 24.
3. J.A. Murray, "Molly McCauley," in Carlisle *American Volunteer,* September 12, 1883; John B. Landis, *A Short History of Molly Pitcher,* 24; and Agnes Graham as cited in D.W. Thompson and Merri Lou Schaumann, "Goodbye, Molly Pitcher," *Cumberland County History,* Vol. 6, No. 1 (Summer 1898), 6.
4. *Carlisle Herald,* May 18, 1876.
5. Carlisle *American Volunteer,* September 12, 1883.
6. *Ibid.*
7. *Ibid.*
8. *Ibid.*
9. *Ibid.*
10. *Ibid*
11. Polly McClaester's belief that her grandmother was German and had the maiden name Mary Ludwig was also recorded by Agnes Graham, daughter of Carlisle Judge James H. Graham, in 1876; see Thompson and Schaumann, "Goodbye, Molly Pitcher," 16.
12. Carlisle *American Volunteer,* September 12, 1883.
13. Landis, *A Short History of Molly Pitcher,* 26-27.
14. *Ibid.,* 24-25.
15. *Ibid.,* 25-26.
16. *Ibid.,* 33-34.
17. This pitcher is pictured in *ibid.,* 33 and in Thompson and Schaumann, "Goodbye, Molly Pitcher," 8.
18. Trenton N.J. *Sunday Advertiser,* July 23, 1908.

19. Landis, *The Story of Molly Pitcher*, 16.
20. Thompson and Schaumann, "Goodbye Molly Pitcher," 19.
21. William S. Stryker, *The Battle of Monmouth* (Princeton: Princeton University Press, 1927), 192 n. 19.

CHAPTER 9

1. John Landis, *A Short History of Molly Pitcher* (Carlisle: Cornman Publishing Co., 1905), 30-31.
2. Carlisle, Pa. *Valley Sentinel,* July 7, 1876, as cited in Samuel S. Smith, *A Molly Pitcher Chronology* (Monmouth Beach, N.J.: Philip Frenau Press, 1972), 8.Polly Malcaster is Polly McLeaster, granddaughter of Mary Hays McCauley.
3. Edwin Salter to James S. Yard, June 22, 1886, in *Monmouth County Historical Association Newsletter,* Vol. 2, No. 2, January 1974
4. Wesley Miles to unnamed recipient, July 31, 1876, quoted in Edwin Salter to James S. Yard, June 22, 1886, in *Monmouth County Historical Association Newsletter,* Vol. 2, No. 2, January 1974.
5. Carlisle census records, 1830.
6. Carlisle *American Volunteer,* September 23, 1883.
7. Landis, *A Short History of Molly Pitcher*, 21.
8. Carlisle census records, 1830.
9. Carlisle *American Volunteer,* March 25, 1896.
10. Carol Klaver, "An Introduction to the Legend of Molly Pitcher," *Minerva: Quarterly Report on Women and the Military,* Vol. 12, No. 2 (Summer 1964), 49; see also *The Red Bank Register,* February 15, 1963, p. 17 and March 26, 1963, p.1; and *Asbury Park Evening Press,* March 27, 1963, p. 21.
11. John Landis, *A Short History of Molly Pitcher*, 39.
12. *Ibid.,* 37-39.
13. *Ibid.,* 39-58.
14. McDonald, "Molly Pitcher Who Was She," 39.
15. *Ibid.*
16. *History of Monmouth County, New Jersey, 1664–1920* (New York: Lewis Historical Publishing Company, 1922), 1: 97-99.
17. *Harper's Weekly,* 28: 759-760 (November 15, 1884).
18. *Asbury Park Press,* April 1, 1979.

CHAPTER 10

1. Rev. C.P. Wing, Letter to the Editor, June 15, 1878, in *The Pennsylvania Magazine of History and Biography* (Philadelphia: Historical Society of Pennsylvania, 1879), 3:109.

2. William H. Egle, *Notes and Queries: Historical, Biographical and Genealogical, Relating Chiefly to Interior Pennsylvania* (Baltimore: Genealogical Publishing Company, 1970; reprint of 1893 Harrisburg edition), Fourth Series, 1:265.

3. C. Malcolm B. Gilman, *Monmouth, Road to Glory* (Red Bank, N.J.: Arlington Laboratory for Clinical and Historical Research, 1964), 38.

4. Isabella Crater McGeorge, "A New Jersey Heroine of the Revolution," *American Monthly Magazine,* Vol. 17, No. 5 (November, 1900): 28.

5. Lida C. Gedney, *The Church Records of The Presbyterian Church of Lawrenceville, New Jersey, and Bible Records from The Bibles in the Library of the Society* (N.P.: New Jersey Society, Colonial Dames of America, 1941), 28.

6. Researches by the author, January and February 2003.

7. Polly McLeaster as quoted by R.A. Murray in the Carlisle *American Volunteer,* September 12, 1883.

8. C. Malcolm Gilman, *Monmouth, Road to Glory* (Red Bank, N.J.: Arlington Laboratory for Clinical and Historical Research, 1964), 40.

9. William S. Stryker, *The Battle of Monmouth* (Princeton, N.J.: Princeton University Press, 1927), 191; see Commentary to No. 3L above.

10. Linn and Egle, *Pennsylvania Archives,* Second Series, 2:181; Stryker, *The Battle of Monmouth,* 191. We know that William Hays was a barber (see Carlisle Rate Book, 1783, as cited in Samuel S. Smith, *A Molly Pitcher Chronology,* 10). The claim by Stryker and others that John Hays was a barber may be a simple transposition.

11. Linn and Egle, *Pennsylvania Archives,* Second Series, 9:338.

12. The first mention of John Hays as her husband was by C.P. Wing in *The Pennsylvania Magazine of History and Biography,* Vol. 3 (1879): 109, who says that she was married to "John Hays, a barber, a sergeant in a company of artillery."

13. John B. Landis, *A Short History of Molly Pitcher* (Carlisle: Cornman Publishing Co., 1905), 24.
14. J.A. Murray, "Molly McCauley," Carlisle *American Volunteer*, September 12, 1883; Landis, *A Short History of Molly Pitcher*, 24; and Agnes Graham as cited in D.W. Thompson and Merri Lou Schaumann, "Goodbye, Molly Pitcher," *Cumberland County History*, Vol. 6, No. 2 (Summer 1989), 6.
15. Gilman, *Monmouth, Road to Glory*, 38.
16. *Ibid.*
17. Philadelphia Will Book O-357.
18. Philadelphia Orphans Court Book 9-106.
19. Philadelphia Orphans Court Book 12-387.
20. Ella Marie Kramer Bender, "Information on Surname Ludwig" in packet entitled "A DAR Lineage on 'Molly Pitcher,'" deposited by the Cumberland County Chapter, DAR at the United States Army Military History Institute, Carlisle.
21. *Monmouth Inquirer*, March 16, 1876.
22. Rev. George Swain, *Historical Discourse in Connection with the Presbyterian Church of Allentown and Vicinity* (N.P.: n.p., ca. 1876), 18-19.
23. Donald F.X. Finn, Letter to New Jersey Historical Association, December 5, 1998.
24. Swain, *Historical Discourse,*, 33 note 8.
25. Allentown *Messenger-Press*, May 25, 2000 and *Princeton Packet Online*, May 28, 2000. The chief proponents of this theory are Ann Garrison and John Fabiano of Allentown.
26. R.A. Murray, "Molly McCauley," Carlisle *American Volunteer*, September 12, 1883.
27. Landis, *A Short History of Molly Pitcher,"* 24. See also Thompson and Schaumann, "Goodbye, Molly Pitcher," 16. However, other sources say that she really did not attend any specific church.
27. Most notably, Wesley Miles in Carlisle *American Volunteer*, September 12, 1883.

CHAPTER 11

1. See, for example, Walter H. Blumenthal's chapter on "British Camp Women on the Ration" in his book *Women Camp Followers of the American Revolution* (New York: Arno Press, 1974), 15-54.
2. *Ibid.*, 18-19.
3. *Ibid.*, 22.
4. See Blumenthal's chapter on "American Camp Women Under Washington," *ibid.*, 57-92.
5. *Ibid.*, 79.
6. John U. Rees, "...the multitude of women: An Examination of the Numbers of Female Camp Followers with the Continental Army," Part 1, *Brigade Dispatch (Journal of the Brigade of the American Revolution)*, Vol. 23, No. 4 (Autumn 1992): 5-17; Part 2, in *ibid.*, Vol. 24, No. 1 (Winter 1993): 6-16; Part 3, in *ibid.*, Vol. 24, No. 2 (Spring 1993), 2-6. Also "...the number of rations used to the women in camp: New Material Concerning Female Followers with the Continental Regiments," Part 1, *Brigade Dispatch (Journal of the Brigade of the American Revolution)*, Vol. 28, No. 1 (Spring 1998): 2-10; Part 2, *ibid.*, Vol. 28, No. 2 (Summer 1998): 2-14.
7. Rees, "...the multitude of women: An Examination of the Numbers of Female Camp Followers with the Continental Army," Part 1: 7.
8. Rees, "...the number of rations issued to the women in camp," Part 2: 5-6.
9. Rees, "...the multitude of women," Part 3: 2.
10. Blumenthal, *Women Camp Followers of the American Revolution*, 81-82.
11. Linda Grant De Pauw, "Women in Combat: The Revolutionary War Experience," *Armed Forces and Society*, Vol. 7, No. 2 (Winter 1981), 213.
12. *Ibid.*, 213.
13. *Ibid.*, 214.
14. Janice E. McKenney, "'Women in Combat': Comment," *Armed Forces and Society*, Vol. 8, No. 4 (Summer 1982): 686.
15. *Ibid.*, 686-692.
16. *Ibid.*, 688-689.

17. The pun on "Molly Bucket" is by this author, not Ms. McKenney.
18. McKenney, "'Women in Combat': Comment," 57-58.1.
19. As quoted in Rees, "...the multitude of women," Part 1: 5.
20. See McKenney, "'Women in Combat:' Comment," 686.
21. De Pauw, "Women in Combat: The Revolutionary Experience," 209.
22. Enlistment figures drawn from *The World Almanac and Book of Facts* (World Almanac Books, 2001), 209. De Pauw, "Women in Combat: The Revolutionary Experience," 218, estimates at least 400 women posed as soldiers during the Civil War; this number is also presented by Deanne Blanton and Lauren M. Cook, *They Fought Like Demons: Women Soldiers in the American Civil War* (Baton Rouge: Louisiana State University Press, 2002), 6-7. Math done by the author.
23. For a full account of the life of Margaret Corbin, see *Margaret Corbin, Heroine of Fort Washington, 16 November 1776*, by Edward H. Hall (New York: The American Scene and Preservation Society, 1932). See also Mark M. Boatner III, *Encyclopedia of the American Revolution* (New York: David McKay Company, 1976), 184; and William S. Stryker, *The Battle of Monmouth* (Princeton, N.J.: Princeton University Press, 1927), 190-191. The quotation from her pension is in Hall, *Margaret Corbin*, 15.
24. De Pauw, "Women in Combat: The Revolutionary Experience," 218.
25. John Landis, *A Short History of Molly Pitcher"* (Carlisle, Pa.: Cornman Printing Company, 1905), 24-25.
26. De Pauw, "Women in Combat: The Revolutionary Experience," 218.
27. Boatner, *Encyclopedia of the American Revolution*, 968.
28. Boatner, *ibid.*, 968-969. See also Emily J. Teipe, "Will the Real Molly Pitcher Please Stand Up?", *Prologue: Quarterly of the National Archives and Records Administration*, Vol. 31, No. 2 (1999): 121-122.
29. Pension File of William Norton, No. W4556, National Archives.
30. John C. Dunn, Editor, *The Nagle Journal: A Diary of the Life of Jacob Nagle, Sailor, from the year 1775 to 1841* (New York: Weidenfield and Nicolson, 1988), 6-7.
31. File labeled "The Potts' of Middlesex County, New Jersey," Monmouth County Historical Association Library, Freehold.

CHAPTER 12

1. William Hays' service record, National Archives, Washington, D.C.
2. For a survey of this company, see John B.B. Trussell Jr., *The Pennsylvania Line, Regimental Organization and Operations, 1776-1783* (Harrisburg: Pennsylvania Historical and Museum Commission, 1977), 199.
3. Thomas L. Montgomery, *Pennsylvania Archives*, (Harrisburg: Harrisburg Publishing Company, 1906), Fifth Series, 3: 995.
4. *Ibid.*, 3:1019.
5. Samuel S. Smith, *A Molly Pitcher Chronology* (Monmouth Beach, N.J.: Philip Frenau Press, 1972),12. Quotation from Wayne Manuscripts, Historical Society of Pennsylvania, Philadelphia, as cited by Smith, *A Molly Pitcher Chronology,* 12.
6. Smith, *A Molly Pitcher Chronology,* 12, citing Wayne Manuscripts, Historical Society of Pennsylvania, Philadelphia.
7. Smith, *A Molly Pitcher Chronology,* 12 and John B.B. Trussell Jr., *The Pennsylvania Line,* 210.
8. As cited in Smith, *A Molly Pitcher Chronology,* 10-11.
9. As cited in Smith, *A Molly Pitcher Chronology,* 11.
10. Benjamin M. Nead, "A Sketch of General Thomas Proctor, with Some Account of the First Pennsylvania Artillery in the Revolution," *The Pennsylvania Magazine of History and Biography* (Philadelphia: Historical Society of Pennsylvania, 1880): 4: 454..
11. *Ibid.*, 454-455; Trussell, *The Pennsylvania Line,* 189-193.
12. *Ibid.*, 203-204.
13. John Linn and William H. Egle, *Pennsylvania Archives* (Harrisburg: B.F. Meyers, 1876), Second Series, 11:176.
14. William S. Stryker, *The Battle of Monmouth* (Princeton, N.J.: Princeton University Press, 1927), 191-192; see also Trussell, *The Pennsylvania Line,* 201.
15. Trussell, *The Pennsylvania Line,* 193.
16. *Ibid.*, 205-207.
17. *Ibid.*, 209.
18. *Ibid.*, 209-210.
19. *Ibid.*, 194; Heitman, *Historical Register of Officers of the Continental Army* (Washington, D.C.: Rare Book Shop Publishing Company, 1914), 453-454.
20. Trussell, *The Pennsylvania Line,* 200.

21. *Ibid.,* 201.
22. *Ibid.,* 199.
23. Smith, *A Molly Pitcher Chronology,* 12.
24. Revolutionary War Rolls, 1775-1783, National Archives, Micro-copy 246, reel 120. Missing names can be filled in from an abridged version published in *Pennsylvania Archives,* Fifth Series, 3:980. I am indebted to Dr. Garry Wheeler Stone for supplying his edited transcription of this report.
25. Trussell, *The Pennsylvania Line,* 196, 198; Francis B. Heitman, *Historical Record of Officers of the Continental Army,* 453.
26. Trussell, *The Pennsylvania Line,* 198; Heitman, *Historical Records of the Officers of the Continental Army,* 453.
27. William S. Stryker, *The Battle of Monmouth* (Princeton, N.J.: Princeton University press, 1927), 74.
28. Benedict Arnold to George Washington, June 22, 1778, Washington Transcripts, Alderman Library, University of Virginia.
29. Charles H. Lesser, *The Sinews of Independence: Monthly Strength Reports of the Continental Army* (Chicago: University of Chicago Press, 1976), 68-69.
30. *Ibid.,* 72-74.
31. *Ibid.,* 75-138.
32. *Pennsylvania Archives,* Fifth Series, 3: 959 ff.
33. *Ibid.,* Fifth Series, 3: 961.
34. Wright includes "Philadelphia-Monmouth" among the list of engagements in which "elements of this regiment served," see Robert K. Wright Jr., *The Continental Army* (Washington, D.C,: Center of Military History, United States Army, 1983), 341.
35. Excerpt from pension Record, Jonathan Ford Morris; widow Margaret S.; W135, National Archives.
36. Heitman, *Historical Record of Officers of the Continental Army,* 402-403.
37. Neville B. Craig, *Sketch of the Life and Services of Isaac Craig, Major in the Fourth (usually called Proctor's) Regiment of Artillery, During the Revolutionary War* (Pittsburgh: J.S. Davison, 1854).
38. Craig, *Ibid.*; Trussell, *The Pennsylvania Line,* 197; Heitman, *Historical Register of Officers of the Continental Army,* 197; *Pennsylvania Archives,* Fifth Series, 3:161.

39. DAR application of Mrs. Della Miller Heiner, No. 20925, National Society of the Daughters of the American Revolution, Vol. 21, p. 326.
40. I am grateful to Richard Walling, President of the Friends of Monmouth Battlefield, for suggesting this interpretation and assisting with the evidence for it.
41. *Pennsylvania Archives,* Fifth Series, 3:961.
42. Trussell, *The Pennsylvania Line,* 199.
43. Robert W. Gibbes, *Documentary History of the American Revolution* (New York: D. Appleton and Co., 1853), 2:256.
44. *Ibid.,* 2: 248, 255-256.
45. *Ibid.,* 2: 258-259.

CHAPTER 13

1. Robert W. Gibbes, *History of the American Revolution* (New York: D. Appleton and Company, 1857), 2:256.
2. Garry Wheeler Stone, "Who Was Molly Pitcher?" (Privately printed, ca. 1999), 2. For a detailed account of the afternoon's fighting in the Sutphin farm, see Garry Wheeler Stone, Daniel M. Sivilich and Mark Edward Lender, "A Deadly Minuet: The Advance of the New England 'Picked Men' against the Royal Highlanders at the Battle of Monmouth, 28 June 1778," *The Brigade Dispatch (Journal of the Brigade of the American Revolution),* Vol. 26, No. 2 (Summer 1996), 2-18.
3. Joseph Plumb Martin, *Private Yankee Doodle* (N.P.: Eastern Acorn Press, 1998), 132.
4. Garry Wheeler Stone, "Battle of Monmouth Battle Maps" (Unpublished manuscript, 1999); William S. Stryker, *The Battle of Monmouth* (Princeton, N.J.: Princeton University Press, 1927), 208; Samuel S. Smith, *The Battle of Monmouth* (Monmouth Beach, N.J.: Philip Frenau Press, 1964), 21.
5. Joseph Plumb Martin, *Private Yankee Doodle,* 128.
6. Stone, "Battle of Monmouth Battle Maps;" Smith, *The Battle of Monmouth,* 22-23.
7. Of course, Clendenin also could have learned after the battle about "Captain Molly" bringing water to the thirsty troops. However, such a camp story would not have made as much of an impression on him—an impression worth repeating to his wife

later—as it would have made if he had witnessed her bringing water himself.

8. This is marked as location "1" in Garry Wheeler Stone, "Who Was Molly Pitcher?" (Privately printed, ca. 1999), 2-3.
9. *New York Herald Tribune,* April 23, 1937.
10. *Freehold Transcript,* November 9, 1943.
11. *Freehold Transcript,* February 26, 1937.
12. *Freehold Transcript,* August 30, 1956; William D. Perrine, *Molly Pitcher in Monmouth County, New Jersey, 1778 to 1960* (Freehold: Privately printed, ca. 1960), 4.
13. *Asbury Park Sunday Press,* April 18, 1943.
14. *New York Herald Tribune,* April 23, 1937.
15. Stone, "Battle of Monmouth Battle Maps."
16. *Freehold Transcript,* March 26, 1937.
17. *Freehold Transcript,* June 9, 1937; see also *Asbury Park Evening Press,* March 8, 1937.
18. Stone, "Battle of Monmouth Battle Maps."
19. This is marked as location "2" in Stone, "Who Was Molly Pitcher?", 2-3.
20. *Asbury Park Press,* April 17, 1977.
21. *Asbury Park Sunday Press,* April 18, 1943.
22. Stone, "Battle of Monmouth Battle Maps."
23. Stone, "Who Was Molly Pitcher?", 2; William S. Stryker, *The Battle of Monmouth* (Princeton, N.J.: Princeton University Press,1927), 192, n. 15.
24. Freehold *News Transcript,* February 28, 2001, under the heading "75 Years Ago."
25. *Freehold Transcript,* undated article from the late 1800s, Monmouth County Historical Association Library and Archives, Freehold, NJ.
26. *Freehold Transcript,* September 17, 1948.
27. *Asbury Evening Park Press,* March 8, 1937.
28. This is marked as location "3" in Stone, "Who Was Molly Pitcher?", 2-3.
29. Stone, "Battle of Monmouth Battle Maps."
29. This is marked as location "4" in Stone, "Who Was Molly Pitcher?", 2-3.
31. *Asbury Evening Park Press,* June 28, 1968.
32. Stone, "Battle of Monmouth Battle Maps."

33. This is marked location "5" in Stone, "Who Was Molly Pitcher?", 2-3.
34. Samuel S. Smith, "The Search for Molly Pitcher," *Daughters of the American Revolution Magazine,* Vol. 109, No. 4 (April 1975): 294.
35. Stone, "Who Was Molly Pitcher?", 2-3.See also Stone, Sivilich and Lender, "A Deadly Minuet," 2-18.
36. This is marked location "6" in Stone, "Who Was Molly Pitcher?", 2-3.
37. This water site is favored by John Fabiano, President of the Allentown-Upper Freehold Historical Society, who believes that Molly Pitcher was born as Mary Hanna, and that she may have served on Comb's Hill through a connection with Lt. Col. David Rhea.
38. This is marked location "7" in Stone, "Who Was Molly Pitcher?", 2-3.
39. Stone, "Who Was Molly Pitcher?", 2-3.
40. Frank R. Symmes, *History of the Old Tennent Church* (Cranbury, N.J.: George W. Burroughs, 1904), 103.
41. Joseph Plumb Martin, *Private Yankee Doodle* (N.P.: Eastern Acorn Press, 1998), 130-131.
42. Stone, "Who Was Molly Pitcher?", 4; Stone, Sivilich and Lender, "A Deadly Minuet," 12-15.

Molly Pitcher Tobacco Card. Collection of the author.

BIBLIOGRAPHY

Acts of the General Assembly of the Commonwealth of Pennsylvania. Harrisburg, 1822.

The American Volunteer (Carlisle, Pennsylvania), 1832, 1856, 1896.

Asbury Park Evening Press, 1937, 1963, 1968.

Asbury Park Press (N.J.), 1943, 1977, 1978 1979.

Barber, John W. and Henry Howe. *Historical Recollections of the State of New Jersey.* New York: S. Tuttle, 1844.

Baxter, Katharine Schuyler. *A Godchild of Washington: A Picture of the Past.* New York: F. Thompson Neely, 1897.

Bender, Ella Marie Kramer. "A DAR Lineage on 'Molly Pitcher.'" Packet deposited by the Cumberland County Chapter, DAR at the United State Army Military History Institute, Carlisle, Pennsylvania.

Blanton, DeAnne and Lauren M. Cook. *They Fought Like Demons: Women Soldiers in the American Civil War.* Baton Rouge: Louisiana State University Press, 2002.

Blumenthal, Walter Hart. *Women Camp Followers of the American Revolution.* New York: Arno Press, 1974.

Boatner, Mark M, III. *Encyclopedia of the American Revolution.* New York: David McKay Company, 1976.

Boynton, Edward C. *History of West Point.* New York: D. Van Nostrand, 1871.

Buckingam, J.T. and E. "Moll Pitcher, A Poem." *The New-England Magazine,* Vol. 2, Issue 5 (May 1832): 441-442.

Carlisle Herald, 1832, 1876, 1905.

Cometti, Elizabeth. "McCauley, Mary Ludwig Hays." In Edward T. James, Editor. *Notable American Women, 1607-1950, A Biographical Dictionary.* Cambridge, Mass.: Harvard University Press, 1971. 2:448-449.

Conningham, Frederic C. *Currier & Ives, An Illustrated Check List.* New York: Crown Publishers, 1949.

Cowart, Samuel Craig. *Address, Battle of Monmouth, and Poem, Patriot Sires of Monmouth, Old Tennent Church, 1914.* Edited by David G. Martin. Hightstown, N.J.: Longstreet House, 1998.

Craig, Neville B. *Sketch of the Life and Services of Isaac Craig, Major in the Fourth (usually called Proctor's) Regiment of Artillery, During the Revolutionary War.* Pittsburgh: J.S. Davison, 1854.

Cumberland County, Pennsylvania, Administrations Book, B-63, No. 193.

Currier, Thomas Franklin. *A Bibliography of John Greenleaf Whittier.* Cambridge, Mass.: Harvard University Press, 1937.

Custis, George Washington Parke. *Memoirs of Washington, by his adopted Son, George Washington Parke Custis, with a Memoir of the Author, by his Daughter; and Illustrative and Explanatory Notes, by Benson J. Lossing.* New York: Union Publishing House, 1859.

-----. *Recollections and Private Memoirs of Washington, by G.W. Parke Custis, of Arlington.* Washington, D.C.: William H. Moore, 1859.

De Pauw, Linda Grant. "Women in Combat: The Revolutionary War Experience." *Armed Forces and Society,* Vol. 7, No. 2 (Winter 1981): 209-226.

Dunn, John C., Editor. *The Nagle Journal: A Diary of the Life of Jacob Nagle, Sailor, from 1775 to 1841.* New York: Weidenfield and Nicolson, 1988.

Egle, William H. *An Illustrated History of the Commonwealth of Pennsylvania.* Harrisburg: De W.C. Goodrich & Co., 1876.

-----. *Pennsylvania Women in the American Revolution.* Cottonport, La.: Polyanthos, 1972.

-----. *Some Pennsylvania Women During the War of the American Revolution.* Harrisburg: Harrisburg Publishing Company, 1898.

-----. "Two Heroines of the Revolution." In *Notes and Queries: Historical, Biographical and Genealogical, Relating Chiefly to Inte-*

rior Pennsylvania. Baltimore: Genealogical Publishing Company, 1970. Reprint of 1893 Harrisburg edition. Fourth Series, 1: 264-266.

Evans, Elizabeth. "Heroines All: The Plight of Women at War in America, 1776-1778." In Mary R. Murrin and Richard Waldron, Editors. *Conflict at Monmouth Court House* (Trenton: New Jersey Historical Commission, 1984), 23-28.

Finn, Donald F.X. Letter to the New Jersey Historical Commission, RE: *New Jersey Women, A History,* by Carmela Karnoutsas, December 5, 1998. Copy given by the author by Mr. Finn.

Freehold Transcript, 1937, 1943, 1948, 1956.

Gedney, Lida C. *The Church Records of the Presbyterian Church of Lawrenceville, New Jersey and the Bible Records from the Bibles in the Library of the Society.* N.P.: New Jersey Society of the Colonial Dames of America, 1941.

Gibbes, Robert W., Editor. *Documentary History of the American Revolution, consisting of letters and papers relating to the contest for liberty, chiefly in South Carolina, from originals in the possession of the editor, and other sources.* New York: D. Appleton and Co., 1853-1857. 3 Volumes.

Gilman, C. Malcolm B. "Molly Pitcher – Mary Ludwig, The Huguenot Heroine of the American Revolutionary War." *Proceedings of the National Huguenot Society* 16 (1959): 97-101.

-----. *Monmouth, Road to Glory.* Red Bank, N.J.: Arlington Laboratory for Clinical and Historical Research, 1964.

Griffin, Martin I.J. "Irish Molly Pitcher." *The American Catholic Historical Researches.* New Series, Vol. V, No. 4 (October 1909), 379-382.

Hall, Edward H. *Margaret Corbin, Heroine of Fort Washington, 16 November 1776.* New York: The American Scenic and Historic Society, 1932.

Harper's Weekly, 1884.

Headley, J.T. *The Illustrated Life of Washington, Giving an Account of his Early Adventures and Enterprises, his Magnanimity and Patriotism, his Revolutionary Career, his Presidential Life, and his Final Decease, with Vivid Pen-Paintings of Battles and Incidents, Trials and Triumphs of the Heroes and Soldiers of Revolutionary Times, Together with an Interesting Account of Mount Vernon as it Is, by Benson J. Lossing.* New York: G. & F., Bill, 1859.

Heitman, Francis B. *Historical Register of Officers of the Continental Army during the War of the Revolution.* Washington, D.C.: Rare Book Publishing Company, 1914.

History of Monmouth County, New Jersey, 1664-1920. New York: Lewis Historical Publishing Company, 1922.

Hornor, William S. *This Old Monmouth of Ours.* Cottonport: Polyanthos, 1974. Reprint of 1932 Freehold edition.

James, Edward T., Editor. *Notable American Women, 1607-1950, A Biographical Dictionary.* Cambridge, Mass.: Harvard University Press, 1971. Three Volumes.

Johnson, Allen and Dumas Malone, Editors. *Dictionary of American Biography.* New York: Charles Scribner's Sons, 1931.

Journal of the Senate of the Commonwealth of Pennsylvania, which commenced at Harrisburg, the fourth day of December, in the year of Our Lord, One Thousand Eight Hundred and Twenty-one. Harrisburg: Charles Mowry, 1821-22.

Journal of the Thirty-second House of Representatives of the Commonwealth of Pennsylvania. Harrisburg: John S. Wiestling, 1821-22.

Karnoutsas, Carmela A. *New Jersey Women, A History of their Status, Roles and Images.* Trenton, N.J.: New Jersey Historical Commission, 1997.

Keim, Randolph. "Heroines of the Revolution, Mary Ludwig Hays, the Heroine of 'Monmouth,' and Margaret Cochran Corbin, the Heroine of Fort Washington." *Journal of American History,* Vol. 16 (1922), 31-35.

Klaver, Carol. "An Introduction to the Legend of Molly Pitcher." *Minerva: Quarterly Report on Women and the Military,* Vol. 12, No. 2 (1994), 35-61.

-----. "Molly Pitcher: Myth and Reality." Rutgers University, History Departmental Honors Thesis, 1993.

Kunitz, Stanley J. and Howard Haycraft, Editors. *American Authors, 1600-1900: A Biographical Dictionary of American Literature.* New York: H.W. Wilson Company, 1938.

Landis, John A. "Investigation into American Woman Known as 'Molly Pitcher.'" *The Journal of American History,* Vol. 5, No. 1 (1911): 83-95.

-----. *A Short History of Molly Pitcher.* Carlisle, Pa.: Cornman Printing Company, 1905.

Lee, Francis Bazley. *New Jersey as a Colony and as a State, One of the Original Thirteen.* New York: The Publishing Society of New Jersey, 1902. 2 Vols.

Lewis, Alonzo and James R. Newhall. *History of Lynn, Essex County, Mass., 1619-1893.* Lynn, Mass.: George C. Herbert, 1890. Two volumes.

Linn, John B. and William H. Egle. *Pennsylvania Archives.* Harrisburg: B.F. Meyers, 1876. Second Series, Vol. 2, "Marriages of Persons for whom Marriage Licenses were issued in the Province of Pennsylvania Previous to 1790."

-----. *Pennsylvania Archives.* Harrisburg: Lane & Hart, 1880. Second Series, Vol. 9: 285-440. "Marriage Records of St. Michael's and Zion Church, Philadelphia, 1745-1800."

Lossing, Benson J. *A Pictorial Field-book of the American Revolution.* Three volumes. New York: N.P., 1851.

Martin, David G. *The Philadelphia Campaign.* Conshohocken, Pa.: Combined Books, 1993.

-----. *The Story of Molly Pitcher.* 2nd Edition. Hightstown, N.J.: Longstreet House, 2000.

Martin, James Kirby. "Comments." In Mary R. Murrin and Richard Waldron, Editors. *Conflict at Monmouth Court House* (Trenton: New Jersey Historical Commission, 1984), 29-34.

----- and Karen R. Stubaus, *The American Revolution, Whose Revolution?* Huntington, N.Y.: Robert E. Krieger Publishing Co., 1977.

Martin, Joseph Plumb. *Private Yankee Doodle, Being a Narrative of Some of the Adventures, Dangers and Sufferings of a Revolutionary Soldier.* Edited by George F. Scheer. N.P.: Eastern National, 2000.

McDonald, Constance A. "Molly Pitcher, Who Was She?" *Field Artillery,* August 1990.

McGeorge, Isabella Crater. "A New Jersey Heroine of the Revolution." *American Monthly Magazine,* Vol. 17, No. 5 (November 1900): 409-415.

McKenney, Janice E. "'Women in Combat': Comment." *Armed Forces and Society,* Vol. 8, No. 4 (Summer 1982): 686-692.

A Memoir of Miss Sarah Smith Stafford, The Patriot and Philanthropist, with Some Statements of her Ancestry. N.P.: n.p., ca. 1880.

Mitchell, Broadus. *Alexander Hamilton, The Revolutionary Years.* New York: Thomas Y. Crowell, 1970.

-----. "The Battle of Monmouth through Alexander Hamilton's Eyes." *Proceedings of the New Jersey Historical Society,* Vol. 73, No. 4 (October 1955): 239-257.

"Moll Pitcher." Unsigned article in *The Pennsylvania-German, A Monthly Magazine,* Vol. XI, No. 2 (February 1910), 122.

Monmouth Inquirer, March 16, 1876.

Montgomery, Thomas L. *Pennsylvania Archives* (Harrisburg: Harrisburg Publishing Company, 1906). Fifth Series, Vol. 3.

Murray, J.A. Article "Molly McCauley," Carlisle *American Volunteer,* September 12, 1883.

Murrin, Mary R. and Richard Waldron, Editors. *Conflict at Monmouth Court House.* Trenton: New Jersey Historical Commission, 1984.

National Advocate (New York City), March 7, 1822.

National Archives. Pension Records of John and Rebecca Clendenin (W 3223).

The National Intelligencer (Washington, D.C.), 1822, 1840.

Nead, Benjamin M. "A Sketch of General Thomas Procter, with Some Account of the First Pennsylvania Artillery in the Revolution." *The Pennsylvania Magazine of History and Biography* (Philadelphia: Historical Society of Pennsylvania), 4: 454-470.

New-Jersey State Gazette, December 1, 1837.

New York Herald Tribune, 1937.

News Transcript (Freehold, N.J.), 2001.

Orphans' Court Records, Cumberland County, Carlisle, Pennsylvania, 1788.

Pennsylvania Archives. Edited by John B. Linn and William H. Engle. Second Series. Harrisburg: B.F. Meyers, 1876.

Perrine, William D. *Molly Pitcher in Monmouth County, New Jersey, 1778-1960.* Freehold: Privately printed, ca. 1960.

Pickard, Samuel T. *Life and Letters of John Greenleaf Whittier.* Boston: Riverside Press, 1894.

Raleigh, James T. Correspondence with the author.

Raum, John O. *The History of New Jersey, from its Earliest Settlement to the Present Time, Including a Brief Historical Account of the First Discoveries and Settlement of the Country.* Philadelphia: John E. Potter and Company, 1877.

Red Bank Register (N.J.), 1963.

Rees, John U. "...the multitude of women": An Examination of the Numbers of Female Camp Followers with the American Army," Part 1. *Brigade Dispatch (Journal of the Brigade of the American Revolution),* Vol. 23, No. 4 (Autumn 1992): 5-17.

----- "...the multitude of women": An Examination of the Numbers of Female Camp Followers with the American Army." Part 2. *Bri-*

gade Dispatch (Journal of the Brigade of the American Revolution), Vol. 24, No. 1 (Winter 1993): 6-16.

-----. "…the multitude of women": An Examination of the Numbers of Female Camp Followers with the American Army," Part 3. *Brigade Dispatch (Journal of the Brigade of the American Revolution)*, Vol. 24, No. 2 (Spring 1993): 2-6.

----- "…the number of rations issued to the women in camp": New Material Concerning Female Followers with the Continental Regiments," Part 1. *Brigade Dispatch (Journal of the Brigade of the American Revolution)*, Vol. 28, No. 1 (Spring 1998): 2-10.

-----. "…the number of rations issued to the women in camp": New Material Concerning Female Followers with the Continental Regiments," Part 2. *Brigade Dispatch (Journal of the Brigade of the American Revolution)*, Vol. 28, No. 2 (Summer 1998): 2-14.

Rhodehamel, John. Editor. *The American Revolution: Writings from the War of Independence*. New York: Literary Classics of the United States, Inc., 2001.

Salter, Edwin. *A History of Monmouth and Ocean Counties, New Jersey, Embracing a Genealogical Record of Earliest Settlers in Monmouth and Ocean Counties and their Descendants; The Indians: Their Language, Manners and Customs; Important Historical Events, The Revolutionary War, Battle of Monmouth, The War of the Rebellion; Names of Officers and Men of Monmouth and Ocean Counties Engaged in It, etc.* Bayonne, N.J.: E. Gardner and Son, 1890.

-----. Letter to Major James S. Yard, June 22, 1888. *Monmouth County Historical Association Newsletter*, Vol. 2, No. 2 (January 1974): 1.

----- and George C. Beekman. *Old Times in Old Monmouth, Historical Reminiscences of Old Monmouth County, New Jersey, Being a series of historical sketches relating to Old Monmouth County (now Monmouth and Ocean)*. Bowie, Md.: Heritage Books, 1999. Reprint of 1887 Freehold edition

Saretzky, Gary D. "Searching for Molly Pitcher: An Exhibition, Monmouth County Library, Manalapan, October 2001." Exhibition leaflet, Monmouth County Archives, 2001.

Smith, Samuel S. *The Battle of Monmouth*. Monmouth Beach, N.J.: Philip Frenau Press, 1964.

-----. *A Molly Pitcher Chronology*. Monmouth Beach, NJ: Philip Frenau Press, 1972.

-----. "The Search for Molly Pitcher." *Daughters of the American Revolution Magazine*, Vol. 109, No. 4 (April 1975): 292-294.

Somerville, Mollie. *Women and the American Revolution*. N.P.: National Society, Daughters of the American Revolution, 1974.

Stockton, Frank R. *Stories of New Jersey*. New Brunswick, N.J.: Rutgers University Press, 1961. Reprint of 1896 edition.

Stone, Garry Wheeler. "Battle of Monmouth Battle Maps." Unpublished study, 1999.

-----. "Who Was Molly Pitcher?" Privately printed, ca. 1999.

-----, Daniel M. Sivilich and Mark E. Lender. "A Deadly Minuet: The Advance of the New England 'Picked Men' against the Royal Highlanders at the Battle of Monmouth, 28 June 1778. *The Brigade Dispatch (Journal of the Brigade of the American Revolution)*, Vol. 26, No. 2 (Summer 1996): 2-18.

Storms, F. Dean. *History of Allentown Presbyterian Church, Allentown, N.J. (1720-1970)*. Allentown, N.J.: Allentown Messenger, 1970.

Stryker, William S. *The Battle of Monmouth*. Edited by William S. Myers. Princeton: Princeton University Press, 1927.

Sunday Advertiser (Trenton, N.J.), 1908.

Swain, Rev. George. *Historical Discourse in Connection with the Presbyterian Church of Allentown and Vicinity*. N.P.: n.p., ca. 1876.

Teipe, Emily J. "Will the Real Molly Pitcher Please Stand Up?" *Prologue: Quarterly of the National Archives and Records Administration*, Vol. 31, No. 2 (1999): 118-126.

Thacher, James. *Military Journal during the American Revolutionary War from 1775 to 1783, describing interesting events and transactions of this period, with numerous historical facts and anec-*

dotes, to which is added an appendix containing biographical sketches of several officers. Boston: Richardson and Lord, 1823.

-----. *Military Journal during the American Revolutionary War from 1775 to 1783, describing interesting events and transactions of this period, with numerous historical facts and anecdotes, to which is added an appendix containing biographical sketches of several officers.* 2nd Edition, revised and corrected. Boston: Cottons and Barnard, 1827.

-----. *Military Journal during the American Revolutionary War from 1775 to 1783, describing interesting events and transactions of this period, with numerous historical facts and anecdotes, to which is added an appendix containing biographical sketches of several officers.* Hartford: Silas Andrus & Son, 1854.

-----. *Military Journal of the American Revolution from the commencement to the disbanding of the American Army, comprising a detailed account of the principal events of the battles of the Revolution, with their exact dates, showing the wise policies and generalship of the Immortal Washington, and a Biographical Sketch of the Most Prominent Generals.* Hartford: Hurlbut, Williams & Co., 1862.

Thomas, Emory M. *Robert E. Lee, A Biography.* New York: W.W. Norton and Company, 1995.

Thompson, D.W. and Mary Lou Schaumann. "Goodbye, Molly Pitcher." *Cumberland County History,* Vol. VI, No. 1 (Summer 1989), 3-26.

Trussell, John B.B. *The Pennsylvania Line, Regimental Organization and Operations, 1776-1783.* Harrisburg: Pennsylvania Historical and Museum Commission, 1977.

Valley Sentinel (Carlisle, Pa.), 1876.

Wade, David R. "Molly Pitcher Rediscovered." *Military History,* Vol. 15, No. 2 (June, 1998): 50.

White, John Todd. "The Truth about Molly Pitcher." In *The American Revolution, Whose Revolution?,* edited by James Kirby Martin and Karen R. Stubaus. Huntington, N.Y.: Robert E. Krieger Publishing Company, 1977.

Wing, C.P. Letter to the Editor, June 15, 1878. *The Pennsylvania Magazine of History and Biography.* Philadelphia: Historical Society of Pennsylvania, 1879. 3: 109-110.

Woodward, E.M. *History of Burlington County, New Jersey, with Biographical Sketches of Many of the Pioneers and Prominent Men.* Philadelphia: Everts & Peck, 1883.

Wright, Robert K. Jr. *The Continental Army.* Washington, D.C.: Center of Military History, United States Army, 1983.

Zeamer, Jeremiah. "Molly McCauley Monument." *Carlisle Herald,* April 5, 1905.

----. "'Molly Pitcher' Story Analyzed." *Carlisle Volunteer.*

"Moll Pitcher, The Heroine of Monmouth," after Currier and Ives (see No. 2H).

INDEX OF SOURCES

**Old Tennent Church, Monmouth Battlefield. Photograph by the
author.**

ABOUT THE AUTHOR

Dr. David Martin was born in Michigan and now resides in New Jersey. He received his B.A. from the University of Michigan and his M.A. and Ph.D. from Princeton University. He is the author of more than twenty books on military history, including *The Philadelphia Campaign, Jackson's Valley Campaign, Confederate Monuments at Gettysburg, The Fluvanna Artillery,* and the award-winning *Gettysburg, July 1.* He is a member of the Sons of the American Revolution (SAR), and is a past commander of the New Jersey Department, Sons of Union Veterans of the Civil War (SUVCW) as well as a trustee of the Friends of Monmouth Battlefield. Presently he teaches Latin at The Peddie School in Hightstown, New Jersey. This book combines his passion for American history with his training as a Classicist in source criticism.

NEW JERSEY CIVIL WAR REGIMENTS SERIES

Give it to Them, Jersey Blues!, A History of the 7th Regiment, New Jersey Veteran Volunteers in the Civil War, by John Hayward. An all-new history with 356 pages, roster, and photographs of over 70 unit members. Published 1998. $35.00

History of the Eleventh New Jersey Volunteers, by Thomas Marbaker. Reprint of the 1898 edition with a new introduction by John Kuhl. 490 pages, over 90 illustrations, 10 maps, roster and index. Published 1990. $32.00.

To Gettysburg and Beyond: The Twelfth New Jersey Volunteer Infantry, II Corps, Army of the Potomac, 1862-1865, by Edward G. Longacre. An all-new history with 467 pages, roster, index, 15 maps, and over 90 illustrations, including 53 portraits of unit members. Published 1988. $36.00.

Reminiscences of the Thirteenth New Jersey in the Civil War, by Samuel Toombs. Reprint of the scarce 1878 edition with a new introduction, index, and eight maps. The only full history of this unit from the Twelfth and Twentieth Corps which fought in both the eastern and western theaters. 300 pages. Published 1994. $25.00.

The Monocacy Regiment: A Commemorative History of the 14th New Jersey Infantry in the Civil War, edited by Dr. David Martin. Out of print, but a new edition is in preparation. Write us for availability and price.

Three Rousing Cheers: A History of the Fifteenth New Jersey from Flemington to Appomattox, by Joseph G. Bilby. Revised and expanded edition of our 1993 edition, which quickly sold out. 453 pages, 20 maps, over 140 illustrations, including portraits of over 90 unit members. Published 2001. $42.00.

Jersey Cavaliers: A History of the First New Jersey Volunteer Cavalry, by Edward G. Longacre. An all-new history by the award-winning author of *The Cavalry at Gettysburg.* 423 pages, roster, 15 maps, over 90 illustrations, including 50 individual portraits. Published 1992. $35.00.

Order from Longstreet House, PO Box 730, Hightstown, New Jersey 08520. Shipping $4.00 per order. New Jersey residents kindly include sales tax. Library and dealer discounts available. Phone us at 1-888-448-1501. Our website address is: longstreethouse.com.

NEW JERSEY CIVIL WAR REGIMENTS SERIES

Remember You are Jerseymen: A Military History of New Jersey's Troops in the Civil War, by Joseph G. Bilby and William C. Goble. Contains chapters on every regiment and battery, plus quarterly ordnance reports and much more. 753 pages, 17 maps, over 100 illustrations, fully indexed. Published 1998. $48.00.

Fifty Years Ago: A Brief History of the 29th New Jersey Volunteers, by T.C. Morford. Reset text of very rare 1012 edition. Introduction, roster and index by Dr. David G. Martin. 54 page booklet. Published 1990. $8.00.

Hexamer's First New Jersey Battery in the Civil War, edited by Dr. David G. Martin. 36 page booklet. Published 1992. $6.00.

History of Battery B, First New Jersey Artillery, by Michael Hanifen. Reprint of the 1905 edition. One of the scarcest of all New Jersey regimentals. The only monograph on any of the state's five batteries in the war. 200 pages, roster, 44 illustrations, and new indices. Published 1991. $25.00.

New Jersey Troops in the Gettysburg Campaign, by Samuel Toombs. Reprint of 1888 edition, with new introduction and index by Dr. David G. Martin. 440 pages. Published 1988. $30.00.

Final Report of the New Jersey Gettysburg Battlefield Monument Commission. Reprint of the scarce 1891 government report. Gives excellent background on the erection of the monuments and their dedication ceremonies. Published 1997. $20.00.

Forgotten Warriors: New Jersey's African American Soldiers in the Civil War, by Joseph G. Bilby. Out of print, but a new edition is in preparation. Contact use for availability and price.

Cavalryman in Blue: Colonel John Wood Kester of the 1st New Jersey Cavalry in the Civil War, by Donald E. Kester. 200 pages. Published 1997. $25.00.

Order from Longstreet House, PO Box 730, Hightstown, New Jersey 08520. Shipping $4.00 per order. New Jersey Residents kindly include sales tax. Library and dealer discounts available. Phone us at 1-888-448-1501. Our website address is: longstreethouse.com.

OTHER BOOKS BY LONGSTREET HOUSE

History of the First Regiment Delaware Volunteers, by Alexander Seville. Enhanced reprint of 1884 edition. 163 pages, index. Hard bound. Published 1998. $20.00.

My Sons were Faithful and They Fought: The Irish Brigade at Antietam, An Anthology, edited by Joseph Bilby and Steve O'Neill. Collection of essays by several noted authors. Royalties will go to support the new Irish brigade monument dedicated in September 1997 at Antietam. 140 pages, 30 illustrations, 5 maps. Softbound, oversize, attractive color covers. Published July 1997. $18.00.

The Civil War Diaries of Col. Theodore B. Gates, Twentieth New York State Militia, edited by Seward Osborne. This regiment from Ulster County served in the First Corps at Antietam and Gettysburg and then in the Army of the Potomac's Provost Guard. 197 pages, 35 illustrations, 11 maps, index. Hard bound. Published 1992. $25.00.

The Plymouth Pilgrims: A History of the Eighty-Fifth New York Infantry in the Civil War, by Wayne Mahood. Revised edition of our 1989 book, which quickly sold out. The regiment fought in North Carolina and was captured almost intact at Plymouth and then sent to Andersonville Prison. 367 pages, expanded roster, 15 maps, over 100 illustrations. Hard bound. Published 1992. $30.00.

Charlie Mosher's Civil War: From Fair Oaks to Anderson vale with the Plymouth Pilgrims (85th N.Y. Inf.), edited by Wayne Mahood. Gives new insights into the war on the North Carolina coast, plus a very moving account of prison life at Andersonville and Florence. 350 pages, 30 illustrations, indices. Hard bound. Published June 1994. $30.00.

Written in Blood: A History of the 126th New York Infantry in the Civil War, by Wayne Mahood. An all-new annotated history, with roster. Great content on Gettysburg and 1864 Virginia Campaigns. 548 pages, 20 maps, 63 illustrations including portraits of 23 unit members. Published 1997. $40.00.

The Saga of the Mountain Legion (156th N.Y. Vols.) of "The Modest Hero Who Saved Our Flag", by Seward Osborne. The first study of this unit from Ulster County. 40 page booklet, 10 illustrations. Published 1994. $6.00.

Enlisted for the War: The Struggles of the Gallant 24th Regiment South Carolina Volunteers, 1861-1865, by Eugene Jones. An all-new annotated history with full descriptive roster. 528 pages, 17 maps, 40 illustrations including portraits of 20 unit members. Published 1997. $40.00.

Order from Longstreet House, PO Box 730, Hightstown, New Jersey 08520. Shipping $4.00 per order. New Jersey residents kindly include sales tax. Library and dealer discounts available. Phone us at 1-888-448-1501. Our website address is: longstreethouse.com.

The Friends of Monmouth Battlefield, Inc.

The Friends of Monmouth Battlefield, Inc., is a non-profit organization of volunteers dedicated to the enhancement of Monmouth Battlefield State Park and National Landmark. Members assist in education and research at the Park, its historic sites and lands, and raise funds for special projects to benefit visitors to this historic landmark.

Founded in 1990, the Friends have undertaken numerous projects to preserve and enhance the Park. The group works in the spirit of public/private cooperation; the administration of the State Park is assisted by the Friends in many ways.

The Visitor Center exhibits have been augmented by artifacts uncovered under the direction of the Friends and the State Historic Preservation Office; the historic Craig House is interpreted by Friends; park lands are in-part maintained by the organization; and special events are sponsored and cosponsored by the Friends.

For membership information, contact:

Friends of Monmouth Battlefield, Inc.
P.O. Box 122
Tennent, NJ 07763-0122